MY ESTONIA

2

JUSTIN PETRONE

My Estonia

BERRY JUNKIES, NORDIC ELVES
AND REAL ESTATE FEVER

PART 2

PETRONE PRINT

Copyright: Justin Petrone and Petrone Print, 2011

Editor: Epp Petrone
Cover design: Anna Lauk
Cover photo: Remo Savisaar
Map: Kudrun Vungi
Photo gallery: Justin Petrone, Raivo Hool
Layout: Aive Maasalu
Printed in: OÜ Greif

ISBN 978–9985–9996–7–7 (set)
ISBN 978–9949–9076–5–6 (part 2)

PETRONE PRINT

www.petroneprint.ee

CONTENTS

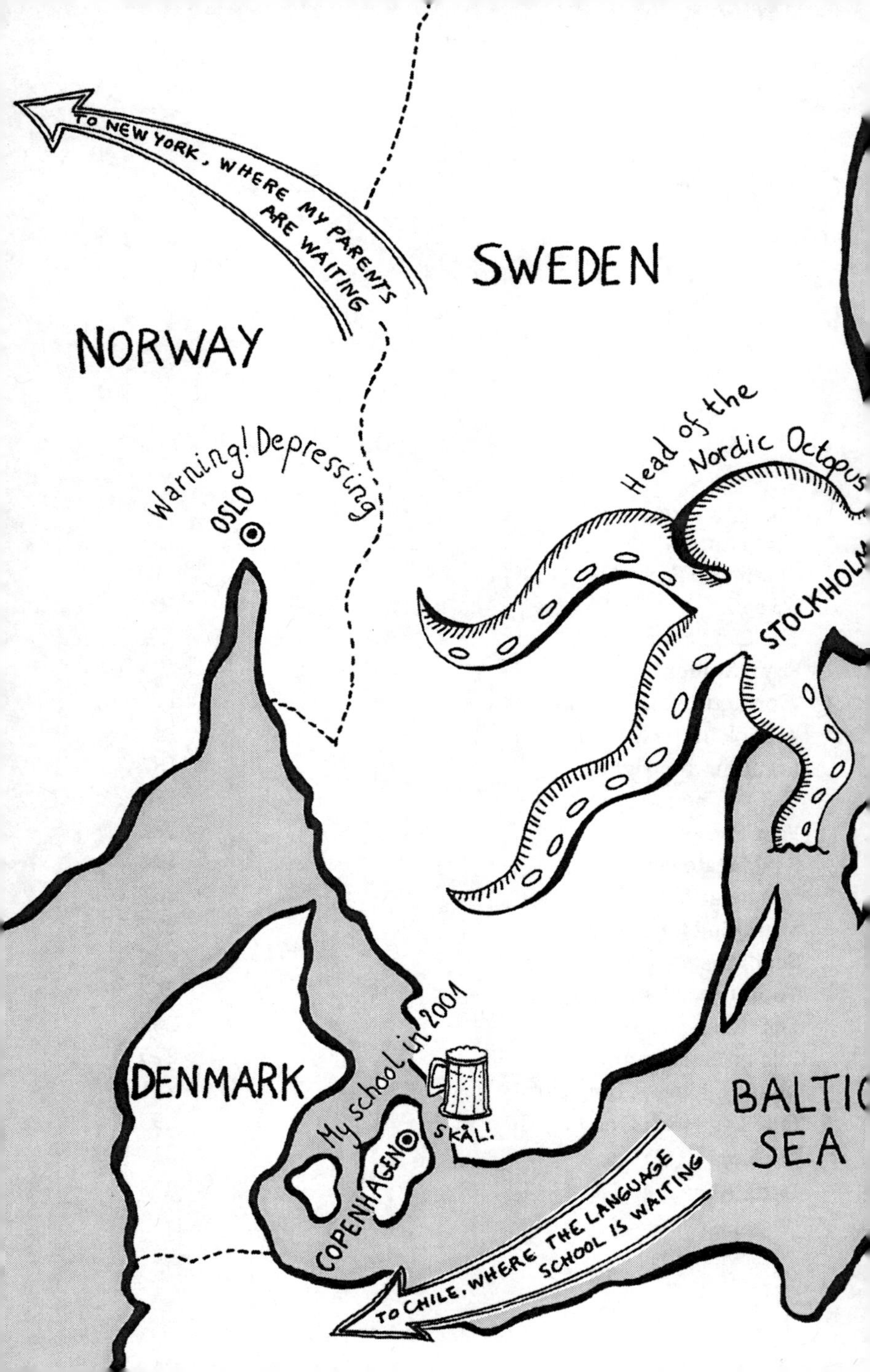
TO NEW YORK, WHERE MY PARENTS ARE WAITING
SWEDEN
NORWAY
Warning! Depressing
OSLO
Head of the Nordic Octopus
STOCKHOLM
DENMARK
My school in 2001
COPENHAGEN
SKÅL!
BALTIC SEA
TO CHILE, WHERE THE LANGUAGE SCHOOL IS WAITING

FINLAND
TURKU
Leena Saari's sauna
HELSINKI
The most romantic place
TALLINN
ST.PETERSBURG
NOAROOTSI
My home in 2003-2004
HIIUMAA
ESTONIA
TARTU
Is Russia our friend?
vikings
SAAREMAA
MULGIMAA
RUSSIA
dark genes
RIGA
Home of Tims
LATVIA
LITHUANIA
VILNIUS
TO INDIA, WHERE Epp's GURU IS WAITING

PROLOGUE

"... And the worst part of the book was that he kept asking me what I wanted in life. 'What do you want? What do you really want?' And I was like, 'What if I don't know what I want?'"

"You mean you don't want anything? You just take life as it is? Go with whatever is before you?"

I stood in front of the Olümpia Hotel with my good acquaintance Vello Vikerkaar. It was a brisk December day at the end of the year 2009, and the snow flurried down from the gray skies. I watched the snow bounce off the towering hotel and felt pangs of nostalgia, but only just for a moment. Then I was distracted again by the very big question at hand: What do you really want?

The talk during the ride into Tallinn that morning from Vikerkaar's home in Nõmme had been about that question; as Vello turned the wheel to his jeep, we veered from one philosophical conundrum to the next. Estonia's most controversial columnist wouldn't let up. And now, all was laid bare.

"You have no wants, no goals, and no desires? You seek to achieve nothing?" Vikerkaar raised his bushy gray eyebrow and I knew the old guy had me.

"Alright, I have goals, but they are more like emotional goals. It's not like I want a particular job or car."

"But some people here really want certain cars. For them, a car is like a moving advertisement that they've finally made some money. It's like they say, first the car."

"And then the house," I sighed.

"So you have certain ways you want to feel, and to feel that way you have to think about how to get there. Not to knock cars though. When I was 25, I definitely wanted certain cars."

I tried to think if I had ever wanted a car. I couldn't remember. "You know after our daughter was born I thought I knew what I wanted, where I wanted to go. But I never thought I could really control everything."

Vello stared back at me but didn't say anything. I suspected that, in some way, he pitied me. Then my pocket began to vibrate. I picked up my phone.

"Justin, are you coming? We're waiting for you."

"I'm right in front of the Olümpia. I'll be there soon."

"Great. We were beginning to worry. See you." I glanced at the clock on the phone. 10.06 am. I was six minutes late.

"Who was that?" asked Vello.

"Merle Liivak, the editor of *Anne ja Stiil* magazine."

"I remember her. She was a host on the Estonian 'Dancing with the Stars'."

"You watched 'Dancing with the Stars'?"

"Oh yeah," Vikerkaar snorted. "My wife Liina loves that show. And I remember Merle. She's pretty, right?" He said it with indifference, as if he had said "she's religious, right?" or "she's got leprosy, right?"

"You could say that," I nodded. "But I have to go," I held out my hand. "It's always fun."

I left Vello at the Olümpia and walked past the new cylindrical headquarters of Nordea Bank. Years ago, when I first moved to this town, the mouth to Maakri Street in downtown Tallinn was dotted with crooked wooden buildings and abandoned lots. I used to walk it all the time to go visit Epp when she worked at a magazine called *Anne*. But now there was no more *Anne*. Well, there was, but it had been combined with another magazine called *Stiil* to form *Anne ja Stiil**. And the magazine's office was no longer on the sixth floor of the publishing house. It was now on the eighth.

I opened the glass door to the publishing house and the heat hit me, but what struck me more were the lingering hints of the past. Where there once had been a nail salon that saturated the air with fumes, there now stood the lone desk of the Russian-language magazine *Jana*. Where there once sat a perky, redheaded security guard named Irina, there now was a cranky, bald one whose name tag said 'Peeter.' And, other than the flashbacks, all I could think about as I rode the elevator up to the eighth floor was Estonian motivational speaker Peep Vain and his thought-provoking questions.

---

* "Talent and Style". (In Estonian)

Peep Vain (yes, that's his real name) is well-known in Estonia for encouraging businessmen and athletes to do even better than their best. Tall and thin, his light hair shorn nearly to the scalp, Vain struts across the stage of his esteem-building conferences, summoning the inner courage of attendees who enter losers and leave doing jumping jacks. Vain had caught my attention and his ideas intrigued me. I had seen Vain compete on the Estonian version of "Dancing with the Stars", watched a documentary about the man's self-help summits, and spent the previous week digesting the important questions in his best-selling self-help book, *The Most Important Question.*

"What do you want, Justin?" Vain ambushed me again as I stepped into the elevator and took the ride up. "Look inside yourself. Tell me."

Was this really what I wanted? Seven years after I had taken photos of designers and actresses and writers for *Anne*, I was now back in the same building getting my own picture taken for the column I had agreed to write for *Anne ja Stiil*. It had all happened by accident, naturally. Someone had suggested me as a new columnist, the magazine liked the idea, and within a few seconds I said yes, not even knowing exactly what I had signed up to do, let alone weighing if it was a job I truly desired. Somehow it had happened that I had become a best-selling author in Estonia. For months, I had donned make up to give early morning interviews on TV, entertained magazine photo shoots in my home, and even was chased down by a journalist eager to learn my pasta recipes.

But I was a little anxious about the impending photo shoot, probably because of a *Stiil* cover I had once seen, one that

11

featured an up-and-coming actor who had been done up with mascara, lipstick, and pink fluffy wings, like an emasculated angel. I even remembered the name of this *enfant terrible*: Juhan Ulfsak. I wasn't sure if the angel wings were his idea or not, and I didn't know what the stylists had in store for me, but I was determined that morning to not wind up looking like him.

The interior of the publishing house was just as I remembered it, but I remembered the soul of the place more, that buzzing of media egomaniacs, of painfully stylish men and women stabbing each other in the back to make it to the most coveted position of all: editor-in-chief. When you were editor-in-chief, you could get first dibs on new creams and lotions. You could take off to opulent spas and bill it to the company. Maybe write an article about it, if you felt like.

And the women here knew what they wanted. They wanted to run the show. Everybody wanted to be editor-in-chief in the publishing house, so you had to look down when you walked, just to make sure you didn't trip over anybody's purposefully outstretched stiletto heel.

I arrived at the office at the end of the hall, and plunged right into the small crowd of colorful magazine people. The room was long and brightly lit. The air smelled of cosmetics and plastic furniture. I reached out first to shake Merle the editor's hand. Standing there dressed in a dark tunic with her angular cropped hair, like a ghost from the '20s, Merle was just as Vello had described her. Pretty.

"Good to see you again," I said.

"Yes," she glittered, pushing her raven-dark bangs away from her eyes and moving closer, "I believe we've met before. How do you like your new job as a columnist?"

I ignored the question and told Merle I was working on some great pieces on alcoholism, infidelity, pornography – everything Estonian women wanted to read about. I decided not to say how I actually felt about sharing these ideas.

As I spoke, I noticed Merle's apple-red lips part, framing a luminous smile. "Those ideas are perfect!" she clasped her hands together in delight. "Our readers will love them."

Merle then introduced me to the two men standing behind her: the Stylist and the Photographer. The Stylist was long, wiry, a specimen of urbanity whose perfectly arranged shirt, jeans, sneakers all looked fresh out of the bag; The Photographer was stocky and square, dressed in a modest sweater and jeans. I looked at them. They looked at me. We both knew that I was now in their hands.

"So, um, what will I be wearing, guys?"

"Here," the lanky Stylist displayed an innocuous black sweater. "Let's start with this and then we'll try the other shirts."

I glanced down at the wardrobe that had been selected for me. Besides the sweater, there was a gray button down and a white shirt with a herring-bone pattern.

"What's the matter?" the Stylist ran his hands through his perfectly coiffed brown hair and then scratched at his goatee.

"I was worried you were going to make me look like somebody."

"Like who?"

"Like that actor... Juhan Ulfsak."

"Ulfsak?" the Stylist folded his arms. "What about him?"

"There was a *Stiil* cover a few years back. They dressed him up in angel wings."

"Oh, right, the angel wings," the Stylist clicked his tongue and turned to the Photographer with a grin. "They should be arriving any minute now."

"*What?*"

"Calm down," said the Photographer. "No angel wings," he leaned down to adjust his tripod, "at least not this time."

◗ ◗ ◗

I put on the sweater and sat on a chair while the Stylist and Photographer discussed the appropriate lighting. It had been seven years since I was last up here in the publishing house. Seven years is all it took to go from a person involved in the assembly of a magazine to a character inside its covers, from the content provider to the content itself. I never had the ambition to be here this morning getting my photo taken in a strange pullover. Or had I? Maybe I had been secretly lusting after moments like these all along. So many things happened in life. Sometimes it was hard to remember what you had wished for.

"Turn your head a little to the left, now a little to the right," the Photographer said in his deep voice, the camera flashing four times. "Now, cross your arms."

"Like this?" I crossed them.

"Try to relax more. You should look like you are saying, 'Hi, I'm Justin, and I really want you to read my new column.'"

"Ok."

"That's it! Don't move." The camera flashed three more times. "Super!"

To the others, it looked like I came alone. But Peep was there the whole time, buzzing in the air like a mosquito, a question mark on his forehead. And no matter how many times he asked me what I wanted, I just couldn't answer. I didn't trust Peep because I didn't trust myself. People like him tried to inspire us to an almost religious quest for personal achievement. And here I was, a writer, a columnist, a husband and father, but, at my core, an individual who apparently could not answer the most important questions.

"Ok, last photo," the photographer made a funny face and I cracked up.

"There you go!" the camera flashed one, two, three, four more times. "Super!"

"Those flashes are kind of bugging me," I blinked.

"Don't worry, it should only take about four days for the flashes to wear off," the Stylist quipped.

"*What?*"

"My God," the Stylist said to the Photographer. "He may be the most gullible one we've had yet."

In the elevator, Peep began whispering in my ear again. But this time his voice was smooth and relaxed, like the disc jockey of a jazz station. It was as if we were in an Old Town café having a chat. Peep wasn't the enemy. He was a motivational speaker. He just wanted to help.

15

"Is this what you really wanted, Justin?" Peep asked one last time.

"Of course it is, Peep," I conceded as the floors clicked by. "I'm here, aren't I? It has to be."

"Good," he crossed his legs and smiled. "Then I never, ever, want to hear you complain."

December 2010, Viljandi, Estonia

P.S. Some names have been changed in the following story to protect the individuals' privacy. While most of the following really happened, this book must be considered a work of fiction.

HIIU
HUMOR

I toyed with my wedding ring and stared at the tape on the airplane wing. It was August 6, 2003, and I had been married for exactly two months.

I thought the flight from Tallinn to Kärdla would last, at the most, 30 seconds, but we were still up in the air, gliding above the thick, dark forests of western Estonia, bouncing in the wind. I rolled the fat metal band around my finger and realized it had probably been days since I last noticed its slight weight. I had taken the ring off a few times in the two months since it came to reside there, just to see if my hands felt any more at ease, but, no, they actually felt naked without the ring, so I put it back. My finger had come to expect the ring to be there, and there it would stay.

"What are you thinking about?" Epp asked me.

"The tape on the wing."

"Let me see." She leaned over, her face illuminated by the August sunshine. "Oh," her eyes widened as she peered through the small window at the tape, the plastic and glue that held part of the aircraft together. "Wow." She settled back into her seat and seemed a little troubled. "Anne Helene was in a plane crash, you know."

"Anne Helene?"

"The designer we're going to interview."

"Oh, right."

"And she was flying this same route."

"She was?"

I looked at the small plane's sole flight attendant, seated outside the cabin door, an expression of utter boredom on her face, and wondered why she signed up for this job of all jobs, to fly everyday on an old plane with tape on the wings back and forth to Hiiumaa.

Epp often asked what I was thinking, as if my mind only processed one thought at a time. I usually picked one to answer her, the one that was easiest to describe, but there had been at least half a dozen thoughts crowding in there, mixing and sloshing together. Physically, the two of us were up in the sky. But emotionally, metaphysically, I was at sea, lapped by the tides, knocked around, but strangely, as a whole, unstirred. I used to worry about so many things, but I had come to put my faith in the ocean of life. Everything would turn out alright. I would not sink, and I would not founder. No matter what happened, I told myself, I would stay afloat, seaworthy, treading water to the horizon.

Assuming our plane landed in one piece.

The flight attendant walked the aisle, collecting the wrappers from the one piece of candy that had been distributed to each passenger. I handed her ours, and she returned to her seat, fastening its safety belt as we prepared for descent to Hiiumaa.

Just days before, I was in New York. I went to pick my older brother up at the train station. It was a humid, rainy summer day, and the ride back to our parents' home seemed like the ideal moment for a brother to brother chat. Eight years older than me, my brother was single, again, and, according to him, "loving every minute of it." I meantime was a young newlywed and, in most people's minds, in need of some mentoring.

"So," he buckled his seatbelt. "How are you doing with this whole thing?" He whispered the question.

"I'm fine with it."

"Are you sure?" he looked more deeply into my eyes. "Because, you know, it's a lot of responsibility."

"Yep," I turned my eyes back to the road.

"Dude, you're 23 and you're going to have a kid!"

"What? People my age have kids."

"People your age *had* kids. Like in the forties."

"Look, I'm fine with it, ok?"

"Ok," he looked out the window. "If you say you're fine."

"I am. I'm fine."

And I was. I was convincing myself more and more of it each day. When my brother talked about children, he spoke of expenses: diapers, high chairs, doctor's visits. But what gave me faith these days is the thought of Salvatore, my great grandfather. I had never seen a photo of him and I had never heard a good word about him either. According to family lore, Salvatore Petrone was an immigrant bootlegger who disciplined his kids with a belt. But he was tough. And he had eight kids.

Eight. Epp and I were waiting on just one child. Just one and I had been dreaming about it for weeks.

The baby was not due until January, but Epp had been giving birth in my dreams on an almost nightly basis. Sometimes it was a boy, sometimes a girl, but, whatever it was, the child was coming, and what put me at ease was this image of Salvatore, leaning over my shoulder, the stink of homemade wine on his breath, telling me, "Relax, kid, have a drink. I mean, it's just one kid!" This mythological Salvatore was usually friendly, but if I ever had a second thought about anything, he got angry, gritted his teeth, and growled at me from the shadows. "Pull it together," he'd snap, and I could see the sepia-toned outline of his bushy moustache and fedora cap, a pipe suspended from his lips, like an extra from *Casablanca*. "Be a man!" he would grunt. And I listened to him. To whom else could I listen?

Epp dozed as we descended, the magazine rolled in her hands. Her brows were furrowed, as if she was concentrating on the plot twist of a book she had yet to write. Of all the places I could have been at that moment, I was there with her, and I had chosen to be there with her. It was my choice to be with her on a plane to Hiiumaa, checked in under the Estonian phonetic spelling of our name: *Petroon*. And even if it gave others pause, I was satisfied with my situation.

From the sky, Hiiumaa looked to me like a diamond or a star. I could see dark forests and patches of farms and open fields, thin lines of roads connecting the tiny hamlets where the islanders, called *hiidlased*, lived. And all of it was surrounded by water, dark blue seas salted with breaking white-tipped waves.

I wanted to go to Hiiumaa because it seemed far away. I had seen photos of the island's wild beauty before, images of windswept beaches and commanding lighthouses. I had read that, in winter, people could even travel across the ice to get to the island. It seemed solitary and peaceful. I wanted to be there.

At the airport we caught a cab to Kärdla, the island's capital. The cab driver kept mostly to himself, other than to grunt from time to time as he turned the wheel. When he heard us speaking English, he turned his head and looked at us with a set of steely eyes, a slight grin on his lips.

"First time in Hiiumaa?" he asked in English.

"Yes," I answered.

"Well, you should know that there have been three great naval powers in history." I noticed that the driver's left eye was a little lazy when he said it, and I couldn't tell if he was looking at Epp or at me.

"Which ones?"

"Guess."

"I don't know. The English, the Dutch, and the Spanish?"

"Wrong! Hiiumaa, Saaremaa, and then England."

"Shut up!"

"I'm serious," the driver said, turning his lazy eye in my direction. Then he grunted again and returned his gaze to the road.

"Is he joking?" I slunk down in the seat and whispered to Epp.

"I think so," she answered in a hushed tone. "But you can never tell with these Hiiu people."

We rolled down past doll-like houses and sunlit gardens into Kärdla, a village by the sea framed by an apothecary, a handicrafts shop, and one supermarket. At the supermarket, we stopped to get a snack. In a nearby park we found shelter under an old oak for a picnic.

We were supposed to prepare for the interview with Anne Helene, but we weren't talking about her. Instead, we spoke of Airi, the closest *hiidlane* we knew, the one with whom Epp went backpacking in India two years before on a search for the meaning of life. I had met Airi only a few times. The first time I met her at the publishing house, her hair was purple. The second time I met her at our apartment, it was orange.

"I met Airi one night a few years ago. She came over with a friend," Epp lazed on her back in the shade of the Kärdla oak. "I said, 'I'm Epp.' She said, 'I'm Airi.' Then Airi looked around and put her hands on her hips," Epp sat up to imitate her. "'Well,' Airi said, 'what are we doing standing around here? Let's go to the store! Buy some something to eat or something!' I fell in love with her at this moment, and that's just how people from Hiiumaa are. They're jolly good fellows who are not afraid of things. They take you as an old friend."

On Epp's lips her name was pure magic. Whenever Airi surfaced, Epp was whisked back in time to some ancient temple in the jungles of India; places where they had gone searching for something. "That time with Airi." Such tales trembled with possibility. Airi was a constant of some kind, a parallel, and

I began to wonder what it was like for our influential Airi to grow up on Hiiumaa.

"I bet *hiidlased* eat a lot of fish," I said, staring up at the oak branches.

"Mmmhmm," Epp nodded dreamily. "And, you know, Airi has a sister, Triin. They are like twins. One year apart."

Airi and Triin. *Hiidlased.* I could see them growing up together on this island like twin Pippi Longstockings, nurtured only by their wandering sea captain father, Efraim with his wild beard and seafaring earring.

"Her father's nothing like that," Epp rolled her eyes. "His name is Rein. He's an engineer."

"Oh," I was a little disappointed.

"But people from Hiiumaa are different," Epp said. "Airi writes fairy tales, she even won an award for one. The other big island, Saaremaa, is for, like, hardworking people. *Saarlased* are very principled, concrete. But *hiidlased*? They believe in fairies. Airi says that Hiiumaa is full of elves and fairies."

It sounded so exotic, but I also knew what it meant to be from an island. I was from Long Island, after all, born in the same hospital where my father was born and his father before him and where my great grandfather, the Italian immigrant bootlegger Salvatore, died. This special hospital was just a quick walk from the sea, so the salt had been in my lungs since I could breathe on my own and I'd always been among the horseshoe crabs and starfish and mussels and seaweed, the stench of low tide as familiar to me as the smell of my own shorts.

I remembered how my mother would take me to the seafood store when I was young. The clerk would put a live lobster down on the floor and the two of them would chuckle as the lobster sprinted towards the wailing youth, its alien legs tapping at the tiles. Later, of course, we boiled the lobster alive and ate him with melted butter, so I had my revenge, but I knew the sea well and was acquainted with its creatures.

I also knew what growing up on an island did to you. There was no easy way off. As a boy I thought about how, if the Soviets decided to strike New York City, we would be stuck on that island, nowhere to go, nothing to do except boil in the sea. As teenagers we would sit in parking lots at the beach and plot our escape, maybe across the sound to Connecticut or even beyond to California. A lot of us did manage to escape the island. Some of those who stayed behind went mad. Maybe this was the source of the aquatic tension within me.

"Wait, what time is it?" Epp asked as we lazed beneath the trees.

I checked my mobile. "12.25."

"We have to go!" Epp stood up suddenly, dusting off her shorts. "It's time to meet her."

◊ ◊ ◊

Anne Helene was a Norwegian designer who had a workshop in Kärdla. Epp was there to write a story about her for *Anne.* I would take the photos.

I liked being a photographer because I got to look at people, to really look at them because, unless the person was asleep, you couldn't really look at them. As *Anne* was a magazine for women, most of the people I photographed were women and if I had looked at Anne Helene in a cafe the way I viewed her through the lens that day, she would have probably gotten up and moved. She would have thought I was crazy. Instead, I had a Norwegian woman standing on a swing with the white caps of the Gulf of Tareste glimmering behind her and the wind tossing her long locks of red hair all over and she was smiling down at me, like she actually liked me. And I kept looking. One might think that a man like me enjoyed this photo shoot too much, that there was nothing more exciting than seeing a woman get pounded by the spray of the surf. But I liked looking at Anne Helene because she was a person and I thought people were interesting. "People always want to look at other people," Epp had once said. Take a photo of a temple in India and it is static. But put Epp and Airi in front of it, colorful as peacocks, road-weary circles under their eyes, henna on their hands, and suddenly the image is vibrant, people fall in love with it, like I did.

I stole a few long looks at Epp there on the beach, too, but to look at her, to photograph her, was different. Epp was immediate, accessible with her thick dirty blonde hair pulled back into a ponytail, her fertile figure restrained by a red tank top, her blue eyes, which always looked like they were smarting with secrets, staring back at me.

With Anne Helene, though, I felt nothing. There was a wall between us, a closed gate through which I could not pass. I stared at her pretty face, her red curls whipped about by the cool winds, but I couldn't connect with her. Maybe it was because she was a Norwegian, just another aloof northern person it would

25

take eons to get to know. I remembered seeing a poster for a Norwegian comic in Oslo two years before, a billboard of a so-called "entertainer" with sad, droopy, alcoholic Scandinavian eyes. And I couldn't figure it out. He was a comic, but he wasn't even smiling. Such manifestations of northerliness could never be explained, I decided. They could only be accepted or ignored.

So even with a camera in my hand, with *carte blanche* to look at Anne Helene any way I pleased, I couldn't get through to her. And yet, despite her northern aloofness, I still tried to relate to her because even if Norwegians were the obtuse people who gave the world *The Scream**, they were still Westerners and I was a Westerner and together we were one.

I hated the term 'Westerner.' I hated the very idea of the West. I hated the thought of any imaginary curtains descending between Estonia and me, cutting me from Epp, cleaving me from my own unborn child, carving us up because I had Reagan and she had Gorbachev or we had Volvos and they had Ladas.

Besides, I thought that Estonia, of all countries, was actually a part of the West, a stealth West, accidentally submerged by Stalinism, disconnected by historical aberration, a sort of diplomatic "oops!" at some post-war conference. Estonia wasn't meant to be part of the USSR. No. It was like Lennart Meri had said in his speeches, the ones I had read in old articles in the Baltic Times office in Tallinn. "Estonia isn't former Soviet Union," the former president had said. "It's former Swedish

---

* A depressing, world famous painting by Norwegian artist Edvard Munch.

26

Empire." I loved it. It sounded like Estonia was encrusted in gold and emeralds and diamonds, its squares dominated by regal stone lions and ejaculating fountains and string quartets. And it made sense to me. Just look at those windmills and Lutheran churches, those gingerbread houses and artesian wells. Just look at Hiiumaa. This wasn't some backward, shit-ridden, fermenting post-Soviet toilet. This was Estonia.

And this whimsical island was among the westernmost parts of Estonia. If any place was former Swedish empire, this was it. If there was any part of Estonia where Anne Helene and I could walk as Westerners, it was in Kärdla. Indeed, the island seemed mostly unspoiled by the Soviet years. There were old rusty watch stations, sure, but they were childlike, like the crow's nests of forgotten shipwrecks. Even the Soviet apartment blocks, usually jarring in the Estonian towns with their white-brick ugliness, were tucked into wooded lots crossed with dark, deep-running streams, their banks peppered with yellow flowers. I was grateful for this because if there was one thing I wanted to do to Tallinn, it was bulldoze every revolting Communist-era building and hand the property over to Finnish developers, gratis. I wasn't a destructive person, really. I just wanted Estonia to look like it was supposed to look.

At lunch it was Epp and me, Anne Helene and Maret, the manager of Anne Helene's design shop. I sensed a little tension in the air. Anne Helene wanted to talk about her work. Epp wanted to know more about the plane crash. "I think it's my angle," she had confided in me. "Estonian women will want to read about a designer who's survived a plane crash."

But Anne Helene was reluctant to relive the accident. "I was hit on the head. I was bleeding," said Anne Helene. "I am lucky when you think about it," she looked out the window at the sea. "And I've never flown that route again. I always take the ferry now."

"But what happened before you crashed," Epp ventured, "when you were in the air?"

"It was confusing," Anne Helene frowned.

"I was once on a bad flight," Maret suddenly cut her off, her fingers fluttering with inspiration. The islander Maret had been quiet all this time, sharing nothing except for a peculiar grin. Now she sat up, her gray, birdlike eyes moistening behind her spectacles. "It was so bumpy. We were frightened. And all the time, we were looking at the one man on the plane and wondering why he wasn't helping. 'You are the man!' we cried, 'can't you save us?' And he did nothing, can you believe that?" she folded her arms and sat back. "The man did nothing!"

Anne Helene looked across the table at me. She made eye contact. I looked back at her. And for the first time all day, I thought we connected. There was a glimmer in her eyes, a quiet understanding passed between us. We said nothing but we shared the same thought: feminism had not yet reached Estonia.

That's not say that Estonian womanhood was still stuck in a 19th century bodice of *kinder, küche, und kirche**. Some

---

* Children, kitchen, and church (In German)

Estonian women had gone on to illustrious careers in politics and business with their form-enhancing power suits, their hair just right, and their make-up just so, but, still, Maret's comment made me think: What if there had been no man on her flight that night? Who would have been there to save them? And what gave some Estonian ladies the idea that just because there was a man aboard, he knew how to land an airplane in a storm?

You are the man. Save us.

I couldn't stop thinking about it. I imagined Anne Helene clucking to herself at that moment that a "Norwegian woman would never say such a thing." And maybe she was right. I was alarmed, though. If any airplane I was on hit turbulence over this country, I now understood it was my gender-specific duty to get behind the wheel and fly the womenfolk to safety.

"Did you hear her? 'You are the man, save us.' Like, just because I'm a man, I know how to fly a plane? Hasn't she ever heard of Amelia Earhart?"

"Don't let it into your heart, Justin. Just pedal, and save your energy! We need to get to the other side of this island before it's too late."

"Aren't you tired?"

"No," Epp beamed from her bike. "The magazines say that women who are four months pregnant have lots of energy. And I am four months pregnant!"

Epp and I had rented a pair of bicycles in Kärdla and set out for Käina on the southern coast of the island. I didn't know how long the journey would take, but it seemed we had been on the road for a long time.

"I thought women didn't need men anymore," I pedaled on and screamed at her while she rode strongly ahead of me. "It's like they say on that bumper sticker: a woman without a man is like a fish without a bicycle."

"Estonian women aren't that interested in that stuff," Epp yelled back, as if the category excluded her. "The Finns say Estonians need more feminism, the Estonians say that the Finnish feminists are ugly. The Estonian women say they have always worked. They think they don't need feminism."

Estonia didn't need to import every fad that had passed through the West, it seemed. They would take our good things and ignore our psychodramas. Yes to *The Bold and the Beautiful*, no to political correctness. Yes to online shopping, no to feminism. They'd have the EU and NATO, thanks, but don't expect them to stop saying *neeger* or believing that all technical issues could be resolved by consulting the nearest male.

It was this last belief that baffled me. All foreign men in Estonia eventually came to understand that there were certain things they were expected to do and not to do. Men were never to offer to make dinner or do the dishes. But when it came to plumbing, electronics, or furniture assembly, it was up to the man to use his God-given divining rod to figure it all out. Epp had been sympathetic. She didn't push me to fix the plumbing. She called a plumber instead. Still, there had been a few times when she would pore over a task and say blankly, "My father would know how to do it." That's all it took to get me down on my knees to revive a broken chair or fix the connection on our

TV. We both knew that I was mostly useless. If I did manage to fix something, Epp would applaud. "You're my hero," she'd say. If I fixed something as treacherous as a clogged toilet, I might even get a kiss.

"I think Airi's parents live around here," Epp said, her voice echoing through the forest as we rolled along. "The trees look familiar."

The last time I had seen Airi had been at our apartment in Tallinn. She came to visit after Epp and I married in June. Airi and Epp had spent their time together looking at old photos of India and reflecting on their magical wanderings, that is, when Airi wasn't responding to urgent text messages from her boyfriend Tõnu.

"Why does he keep messaging you?" I asked.

"He says he's hungry," said Airi. "He wants me to come home."

"But if he's hungry, why doesn't he make himself something to eat?"

Airi stared at me. "Tõnu? Make food?"

"What? He doesn't know how to cook?"

"But Justin," Airi shook her head, "Tõnu is an Estonian man."

Poor Tõnu. If Airi hadn't gone home that night he might have starved to death in their kitchen.

"One time Airi and I wrote an article together about looking for fairies in Hiiumaa," Epp yelled as she pedaled in front of me. "We met some people who said that the fairies had picked up a ship and dropped it in the forest. And they even showed us the shipwreck or something like it!"

"Whoa."

"And I was looking at them, wondering, were they kidding or were they really being serious? I couldn't tell."

"So, there's a shipwreck in the woods?" I peered into the trees.

"Then, when we went back to the mainland, Airi's mother called and said that I had left a pair of pink slippers at their house. And I said, 'What pink slippers? I don't have any pink slippers.' And she said that someone had left them there. I mean, was she joking or did they really find some pink slippers?"

"Whose pink slippers were they?"

"I don't know! They have some weird sense of humor here, or perhaps the weird things really happen? The editor-in-chief read our article about the fairies and heard about the slippers and said, 'Epp, you must be going crazy.'"

Through the woods, I spied a distant home here and there. This was how the Estonians lived, away from one another. Estonians never met to mend fences, as there were no fences. There was just distance. If luck had it, they wouldn't meet at all.

It was different from what I had left behind, of hot summer nights spent pub crawling, riding around in the subway trains, tethered to the flashing electronic eyes of emptiness, the deafening thrum of humanity in perpetual motion. This was where I had been a few days before. New York, a giant city, a metropolis, arrested by masses, unable to move freely, unable to think clearly, chafed and displaced in an urban contusion where one had to yell obscenities to merely be heard.

But I wasn't there. I was on a bike on Hiiumaa and my nerves still felt raw. A few days out of New York and they were still tingling, craving more noise, craving more light. Things seemed too quiet here, a bit too serene, the only dissonance coming from the mosquitoes and the shiny black Mercedes and BMWs that roared past us at astounding speeds, their windows tinted, each containing a male driver in sunglasses: quiet, self absorbed, reckless, Estonian.

"Holy shit these drivers are crazy," I cried out after another bullet-like BMW shot by. "People don't drive like that in New York. Why is everyone here in such a goddamn hurry?!"

"Oh, look, an anthill!" Epp swerved off the road into the forest. "Let's go have a look."

It wasn't really an anthill. Knee-high, sandy and round with a dark opening at the top, like a pregnant woman's belly button, this was like an apartment complex for ants. "There are even more of them over there," Epp motioned deeper into the forest.

I saw them, thick mounds, the apartment blocks of the Hiiu ants. It was new to me, different. I watched the line of ants trickle down into the long black entrance of the extraterrestrial-looking heap.

"We're a long way from New York," I said under my breath.

Even Tallinn seemed distant out here in the forests. And who cared about Tallinn? Who cared about its unscrupulous businessmen or vain politicians or death-cheating drunks? Who cared about its ugly old buildings or shiny new shopping centers? Who needed Tallinn? At that moment, to me, Hiiumaa was Estonia.

I'd be lying if I told you they weren't intimidating. They were large, fat, brown, hairy, ugly, smelly, and spread along the bay, some sitting, others standing, a few swaying down the road fresh grass dropping from their jaws. There were definitely more Scottish Highland Cattle than people on Käina Bay that day and they were looking at us like we were idiots. What kind of people would cycle across an island until their legs felt like butter and still head out for an evening ride after checking into their B&B?

It was evening and what struck me, as I dipped my hand into the dark waters of the bay at sunset and rinsed my face, was the raw sadness of it all, the vast emptiness. It had stalked me all my life and here it was again on Käina Bay. All day long I had cycled under the bluest of blue skies, almost close enough to touch. But now as the sun was about to retire, the island was swept by the same lingering melancholia that fills the air of all northern lands; that tinge of bitterness, like a raw berry that has just burst in your mouth. But I had come back here; I had come back to the sad north. I could only conclude that I liked its taste.

We arrived at our B&B when it was still light out. The B&B owner didn't come to the door, but her neighbor did, a bucket of berries in her hand, trying to steal a few clients while her competitor was at the shop. The neighbor was blonde going on white with old blue eyes and calloused, grimy fingers, dripping with worm guts and berry seeds. She drifted into the yard in her knee-high rain boots, trying to seduce us.

"What are you paying her?" she asked with a sly smile, and I noticed she toyed with a small knife as she spoke.

"How much do you want for a night?" Epp was interested.

"Oh, nothing," she shook her head and laughed. "You can stay for free. I could use the company."

Suddenly, an old car rattled and coughed up the driveway, and the neighbor stepped back into the shadows of her yard, her berry bucket swinging from her arm.

"See you," Epp waved to her.

The neighbor nodded and winked. Then she disappeared behind her house. The B&B owner emerged from her car, round and clad in a blue dress with a lion's mane of dyed black curly hair that bobbed in the evening light.

"Just give me a minute," the owner said, ducking inside her house to deposit an armful of groceries. She reemerged with a set of keys a second later. "Let me show you to your room."

Ours was located in a separate barn, with its own door to the yard. It was cluttered with old furniture and flies, but I didn't mind. Instead I sat on the edge of one the beds and undid my sandals, running my fingers along the raised patches of sore skin.

"Almost 30 kilometers," I sighed. "And we have to ride back tomorrow."

Epp didn't respond. She was too busy sniffing the air. "Do you smell it? This place really stinks! It's moldy here!"

"It is?" I took a few whiffs of the air. To me the room smelled as bad as anything else.

"You mean you can't smell it?"

"I'm too tired to smell anything."

"Maybe it's the pregnancy. I read it makes you more sensitive to smells."

"Maybe we should try the neighbors'?" I offered. "She said it's free."

"Of course it's not free, Justin. It was just Hiiu humor."

"Hiiu humor?"

"It's like they say. If you believe a quarter of what a *hiidlane* says, then you have been deceived by half."

I did the math in my head. The neighboring B&B was definitely not free.

"Will you go talk to the owner?" Epp asked.

"Who? Me?" I looked up.

"Justin, you're the man in this family. You need to take the initiative sometimes too."

"Oh, right. But, you know, my Estonian's not so good."

"Fine then, I'll go talk to her."

Moments later we were ushered into the B&B owner's home.

"I have another room for you down the hall," she apologized. "It used to be my son's room."

The interior of the B&B was disappointing. I thought that Hiiumaa was separated by the mainland by more than just water. I expected something with a nautical theme, paintings of ships on the walls, canopies of fishing nets, a complimentary cup of clam chowder, for that added maritime effect. I thought it would be like any B&B in any New England seaside village, the ones I had known as a kid growing up. I would stay there in the moonlight, awake late into the night, listening to the beautifully freckled Irish girls who worked locally as they gathered together in the yard to play guitars and sing sea shanties.

The Käina B&B was nothing like that. It was dark and musty with the sad blue wallpaper and glossy dark Soviet-style bookshelves you found in many Estonian homes. The walls too were plastered with the same black and white photos of the same gang of bored-looking Estonian guys with identical moustaches; no smiles, no body language, not even any Hiiu humor. You could find such photos in any house in this country. You might even be able to switch photos between homes and feel secure that the residents wouldn't notice the difference for a few weeks.

"Those are my sons," the owner pointed at the men.

"Do they live around here?" I asked her.

"Not anymore," she frowned. "Here's your room."

Our new room may have been cluttered with baskets of old magazines and dusty furniture, but I didn't care. I just needed to lie down. I sat down on the edge of the bed and once again undid my sandals.

"It's not pretty," Epp shrugged after the owner left. "But at least it doesn't stink."

🌢 🌢 🌢

The other guests at the B&B were a German couple. He had a moustache and an expensive timepiece. She had bangs and looked very tidy. For breakfast they ate granola and flipped through guidebooks.

"What will it be today, Ulrika? Maybe start with the Rudolf Tobias museum?" he asked.

"Who's Rudolf Tobias?"

"It says here that he was a composer."

Germans. Why did they come to Hiiumaa of all places? Was it to bask in their former glory?

Maybe. Later, in the graveyard of a chapel, on an island called Kassari across the bay from Käina, I stooped down to rub my hands in the grooves of the old stones and crosses. Some merely said *Puhka rahus** but the older ones were inscribed in the language of the German tourists. Were these Hiiu people German? No. But in the 19th century, life was recorded in German, the language of the manor owners. Estonians were born, married, and buried in German. Many had German names and many still do. But, despite this overwhelming Germanization, the Estonians had never become Germans. The stubborn islanders had always remained who they were.

The Kassari chapel was crooked and white, like an old woman. And in the graveyard of the chapel, as we stopped to take a rest, I knelt down to read off the names of the old stones. Georg. Elsa. Karl. Minna. All these people were bones. Anyone that could remember anyone that remembered them was dead. But one name caught my eye. It looked a little different. Alive. It didn't seem especially German or Estonian. Instead, there was something grander there. It could be the name of an Italian film star or a Brazilian singer.

Marta.

It was like a hot spark. There was energy in that name, adrenaline. Is this how you recognize the right name for your kid? I didn't know, but it felt right.

---

* Rest in peace (In Estonian)

"I had a great aunt named Marta," Epp crouched down beside me.

"Do you remember her at all? What was she like?"

"She died a long time ago," Epp wrinkled her brow. "But I remember she had a cool doll sitting on top of her cabinet."

"What do you think?"

"You mean for us?" Epp said and paused to think for a moment. "Well, it does sound international," Epp said. "And it's a family name."

"Little does our Marta know," I reached out and touched the stone one more time, "but she's going to be named after some dead chick from Hiiumaa."

"Let's do it," Epp agreed. "It's the name if it's a girl!"

On the way back from the Kassari chapel we stopped to take a break in an old fashioned *villavabrik* – a wool factory. We laid our bikes against a stone wall in the deserted parking lot, but there were no cars parked there and there was no one around, no evidence of life other than the odd home in the distance here and there with its dark wooden walls and thick thatched straw roof looking cozy and ancient, like a movie set for *The Lord of the Rings*.

"So, when we get back to Tallinn," Epp began to speak as we walked to the factory door.

"Shh!"

"What?"

"Do you hear that?" I whispered.

"No."

"Just listen."

And we stood there, both silent, listening. We heard nothing. Not a sound. No cars. No radios. No construction. And then, in the distance, a sheep let out a gentle cry.

"It's so quiet here," I whispered looked out into the fields of flax beyond the stone wall.

"Tere!" a voice boomed from the steps of the factory. I turned to see a man with brown hair, gray on the sides, a cowlick in the back, and a middle-aged paunch. He was dressed in blue overalls, as if he had just come from milking a cow.

"Tere," Epp answered him. "Is your store open?"

"It is, come in."

The store was tidy and adorned with caps and sweaters and booties embroidered with colorful folk patterns made in subtle blues and reds, greens and golds, zigzagging and crisscrossing like diamonds, snowflakes, tree branches, insects, and thunderbolts. The air in the room was thick with the smell of pungent wool. Epp found a locally made shawl to bring home with us. As we paid, I chatted with the owner.

"Are you from around here?" I asked.

"Born and raised," he said. "And I've been running this shop since the Russian time ended." And as he shifted his glance to me, I noticed his left eye was a little lazy. Again, an islander was looking in my direction, but not at me.

"The *Russian* times, eh, so you've been running this shop since 1917?" I winked to the owner.

"Ok, ok since the *Soviet* time ended," he said with a peculiar grin, as if he was incredibly amused by something, but not by me.

"So, is it true what they say about Hiiu humor?" I asked him. "Does it really exist?"

"Of course it exists," the owner answered with that odd grin still on his lips. "An Estonian from the mainland will stop in here and ask, 'Where does this road lead?' And I'll tell him every time, 'The road doesn't lead you anywhere, you have to follow it yourself.' Now that's Hiiu humor!"

Epp laughed when he said it, but I didn't, and I didn't get anything about this country, its wacky humor, its pervasive silence, its sexual mores, but I had definitely married into it. And all this, I looked around at the woolen folk costumes hanging on the wall, had seemingly been my choice.

"I know a joke too," Epp volunteered. "Why shouldn't a Hiiu guy tell a joke to a mainlander on Wednesday?"

"Because they start to laugh in the church on Sunday!" the factory owner deadpanned.

"Ha!" Epp chuckled.

"Yeah, that's a good one!" the owner wiped a tear from his eye and handed the bag to me. "You know, I could go on telling jokes like that all day."

"Was that joke supposed to be funny?" I whispered and held the door for Epp as we exited the shop a moment later.

"Don't worry, Justin," she touched my arm on the way out. "You will probably get it later."

OUT IN
THE FOREST

Vane, Karin, Rait, Nele...

Epp's cousin Helina introduced us, but I couldn't tell one from the other. The quartet lived in a summer cottage in Lilli on the Latvian border. After returning from Hiiumaa, we turned south: for meeting these new relatives, we had to drive down a long forest road, and when we arrived there wasn't much around, a house here, a house there, and everywhere the thick, looming trees.

Golden-haired Karin, also Epp's cousin, was the mother. Bearded Vane was the father. Of the two teenage children, I was told skinny Rait was the son and petit Nele was the daughter. Or at least that's what I thought, because after five minutes I couldn't remember if the mother was Vane and the daughter Karin, or if the daughter was Rait and the mother was Nele. Estonian names were all the same. "Which one is that?" I would whisper in Epp's ear. She would tell me, but I would forget.

To make matters more confusing, the relatives all looked the same. Cousin Helina had blonde hair and blue eyes. Her son Ken had blond hair and blue eyes. Vane, Karin, Rait, and Nele? You get the picture. The only one who really stood out in the big family photo we took in the yard was that tall, dark, foreign guy Epp had married. The family was babysitting Paula, Karin's angelic three-year-old niece, and little Paula refused to even stand near me. "I think she's afraid of you," Helina told me as we gathered for the photo. "She's never seen someone so dark."

Dark? How was this possible? In America, I was your average white guy. In Estonia, I frightened small children. I had always been aware of the language barrier in Estonia, but I was unprepared for the color barrier. The Estonians even had a word for people like me – *tõmmu* – the same adjective they used to describe a dark beer or a smoked sausage or a chocolate candy. *Tõmmu*. It was an appellation with a touch of Latin allure. Once while trying on shirts at a department store in Tallinn, the gray-headed clerk had looked me up and down, licked her lips and said: *Oi kui ilus tõmmu poiss!**

In New York, there were people who looked like me everywhere. I had never thought of myself as unusual, or even particularly Mediterranean. In Estonia, I was a coffee-flavored ice cream scoop in a sundae of vanilla. I pitied anyone who was chocolate. If someone like me could scare Estonian children, I imagined that the sight of an actual black person might cause trams to collide or construction workers to slip from the tops of Tallinn's unfinished skyscrapers.

And I knew that even if I mastered the Estonian language, ate *sült* every night, and taped a blue-black-and-white flag

---

* Oh, what a beautiful brown boy (In Estonian)

43

to my window, my looks would always betray my origin. But it wasn't just looks or language that kept me apart. There were other ways to sort out who was an Estonian and who was not.

        ♦ ♦ ♦

I met Helina at a train station on Long Island, New York, the month before. She arrived with her teenage sister Maarja and two rolling suitcases. It struck me immediately how different they were from the other disembarking train passengers. They were both blonde and thin and quiet, polite and tidy. No shirt was wrinkled and no hair was out of place. I played one of my favorite bossa nova songs in the car. By the end of it, my soul swirled with emotion. But the sisters were unmoved. Epp's cousins didn't speak, they murmured.

Helina and Maarja didn't come to New York to attend our wedding blessing. They just happened to be visiting their brother Ivo who lived in Queens. But it was good that they were there because the event needed Estonian reinforcements. It had been strange to sit at that table with Epp and Helina and Maarja, surrounded by people who had known me since birth. The guests' faces were familiar to me but I felt as if they had no idea exactly who this Justin Petrone character was, let alone his strange wife with her odd name and curious accent, the girl with the red star on her school uniform in the childhood photos we had on display. Justin the college graduate met some girl in Finland and moved to some place called Estonia? They got married and are expecting a baby?

Had the guests been privy to my innermost thoughts the year or two before I met Epp the whole affair would have made sense. It would seem like the fulfillment of some desperate inner fantasy, the kind of life preserver that keeps lonely people afloat at 3 am. Who knows from where such desires spring? They manifest themselves over time. Like the currents of the sea at night, you can feel them pulling you in your dreams, even if you don't notice you're moving.

There was a bar in Copenhagen I used to frequent when I studied there for a semester, an Irish bar, located deep in the old city. On a night in December 2001 the place was packed with partygoers, the interior illuminated by Christmas lights that reflected off the window glass. As I ordered myself a drink that evening, two old men came in with their wives. One looked just like Paul Newman, the other a bit like Clint Eastwood. And the old-timers made their way to the bar. The bartender served them and, as they waited, I saw them laugh and tell jokes to their wives in Swedish. Then, when the ladies excused themselves, the men switched to English, and not just any old English.

"Hey, where are you guys from?" I asked.

"New York," Paul Newman smiled and lifted the beer to his lips. "Good Old New York."

"Where in?"

"You know New York?"

"Yeah."

"Rockville Centre."

"I'm from Long Island," I blurted out.

"Hey Clint," Paul summoned his friend.

"What?" he grunted and leaned in.

45

"This kid here's from Long Island."

"No kidding," Clint Eastwood croaked. "I'm from Brooklyn. *Skål**."

Our mugs clinked.

"But are you on vacation or something?" I asked.

"Vacation?" Paul raised an eyebrow. "Eh, not exactly. We live right across the strait," he glanced out the window.

"We've been there for, wait," Clint looked at the ceiling and rubbed his forehead. "32 years."

"How do two guys from New York wind up here?"

Paul put his elbows on the bar and leaned in. "We were encouraged to relocate by one Lyndon Baines Johnson."

"He wanted to send us to the Republic of South Vietnam," said Clint, "but we got sidetracked along the way."

"Are you happy about that?"

"With what?" Clint grunted.

"That you got sidetracked?"

"Am I happy about it?" Paul stepped back for a moment as if insulted. "Best goddamn decision I ever made!"

"And we only have Lyndon Baines Johnson to thank for it," Clint shook his head and looked at the ceiling again. "*Skål*."

Our mugs clinked.

"Now, if you'll excuse us," Paul said as he wrapped an arm around his blonde wife as she returned, "we've got to get going."

That night in Denmark, I finished my beer a bit more hopeful than I had been when I ordered it. Like a lot of young men, I had indulged in expatriate dreams. To me it had even

---

* Cheers (In Swedish)

seemed like the path of least resistance. Getting through college was tedious, dull, but nothing could compete with the idea of a shitty little apartment in some foreign land with a journal in my hand. I called this the Hemingway fantasy. It had followed me to a lot of places already. The Pacific Northwest. Mexico. Iceland. Denmark. But the draft dodgers made it seem more real. They had come from the same place as I had and jumped ship in Scandinavia. They even said three decades later it was the best goddamn decision they had ever made. I believed them.

Two hours later I was in her arms. She had looked at me first and I invited myself to her table. A massage therapist with light brown hair and sparkling blue northern eyes, like all northern European women, she managed to look both beautiful and a little miserable at the same time, even when she smiled, even when she showed me her ID to help me pronounce her name. I didn't want to show her mine when I noticed she was 13 years older than me.

"You really sure you want to see?" I asked.

She sipped her wine and held out her palm in the candlelight.

I deposited my driver's license in it.

"1979?" she put down her glass. "I'm not sure if we can be friends," she squinted at me.

"Come on!" I told her. "You were born in the sixties. I was born in the seventies. We're practically the same age."

"Uh huh," she leaned in closer. But she didn't make me leave. Instead she helped explain the muscular layout of my forearms and back. "I get paid good money to do this, you know," she said later as she rubbed my shoulders. "I studied in school."

There were precious few fellow students in my study abroad program with whom I connected. The American girls thought I was weird. I thought they were vain. But stick me in a bar in Copenhagen, and I would inevitably wind up in the arms of some 35-year-old Danish massage therapist. When I left her later my body was still shaking, either from the cold or from being so close to her. As I walked home alone through Copenhagen that night, I began to suspect that if you really lusted after something in your heart, it might come to you.

What had happened between me and the Estonian must have been the manifestation of some inner fantasy then. I was sure of it. But what I was dealing with at the wedding blessing that day with Epp and Helina and Maarja, or at the summer cottage in Lilli with cousins Vane, Karin, Rait, Nele, and Paula, is what came after the fulfillment of the fantasy. Up to that point, most of my dreams had ended abruptly with me running off to Europe with some foreign babe. I had never really thought about what came next.

💧 💧 💧

What came next, in my case, were cloudberries. They were honey-sweet constellations of orange-colored berries suspended above the forest floor. I had never tasted cloudberries before I came to Estonia, but they had made their way past my lips via the abundant rich yogurts they sold at stores, quickly becoming a personal favorite.

In the forest, Epp's teenage brother Aap spotted the cloudberries first and when he did he summoned the others with whooping sound, wind-milling his arms to point out their location. Within seconds they descended upon the bushes like hungry flies, popping as many cloudberries into their mouths as possible. Epp had paused to pee behind a nearby bush but when Aap signaled that the cloudberries had been sighted, she yanked up her trousers and ran across the trail, diving head first into the bushes, hoping to get a taste before her siblings and cousins picked the place clean.

I took pictures of them and, honestly, I didn't understand what all the fuss was about. I thought cloudberries were delicious but, they were just berries, right? To Epp and her family, it wasn't so. Berries meant more to them than they did to me. This had been their childhood. Long walks in the woods, nude lake swimming, scrumptious berry picking. It reminded me of photos I had seen in Mart Laar's history book *The War in the Woods*. It was the summer of 1941. The Germans were approaching. And the Estonian partisans prepared for battle by taking to the woods and picking berries. It was unbelievable but there they were in the old black and white pictures, rifles on one shoulder and hats full of fresh berries in their arms. Though war was in the air and violence burned on the horizon, some of the partisans were even smiling, posing for the camera with their day's take of cloudberries. For Estonians, berries were like nature's Prozac. Even during wartime, a fresh cloudberry could be counted on to bring a smile to any Estonian's face.

Helina led our berry brigade into the forest. It included Epp and me, Epp's brother Aap, her sister Eva and Eva's young daughter Simona, and Ken, Helina's 9-year-old son. The rest of the family remained at their cottage, preparing for a summer barbeque. The forest was green below, blue above. But what mosaics could be made from simple green and blue. The sky seemed eternal, the slight wisps of clouds suspended in place as if they had been painted there. You could look into the forests and never see out. Here were stark birches, their thin torsos etched in black and white, there were thick pines, spindling towards the sun like staircases. When I was a kid my friends and I would disappear for hours into woods like these. When we played hide and go seek, I would climb to the top of the tallest pine, only coming down when the game was long over, covered in sap and sweat. "Where were you?" my friends would ask, but I never revealed my secret hiding place.

I had heard that the forest changed the way you thought, too. My college roommate – an artist from the mountains of West Virginia – told me that your brain began to operate at some kind of different, more intuitive frequency as soon as you had spent 10 good minutes surrounded by trees. Some thought processes slowed down, others sped up, he said. It was a different kind of existence here in the woods, a new rhythm. I felt it now, here with the Estonians. And it had been so long since I had been in a forest. Why was that?

Gathering fruit was actually just a perk of our expedition. Our real destination was the other side of the Estonian-Latvian border. I was told that you could cross the border, take your photo, and cross back to the other side, all without getting shot at by Latvian border police. This excited me; it even seemed subversive. Resourceful Helina knew the way, the secret path through the underbrush to Latvia.

I had actually only met Helina a few times, but she already seemed like family to me, probably because she had been to the inner sanctum of my parents' home on Long Island. She had been given the tour of the establishment by my mother, complete with being shown Cousin Vito's black and white Communion photo from 1946. I also knew of Helina from the old photos in our apartment in Tallinn and I possessed intimate knowledge of the sometimes unwise hairstyles she had chosen in the past.

One series of photos were of Epp and her first boyfriend, a Catalan named Octavi. It was 1992 and Epp's hair in the photo was wild, irrepressible, with mountains of brown sloping down in every direction. Helina's meantime was like an explosion of scrambled eggs, an electric perm amplified by the moisture of summer. And between them was Octavi, Epp's pen friend from Barcelona who had come to visit his girl.

Most of the men in Epp's life had vanished without a trace, but there were some lingering hints of former courters. I referred to them as my "predecessors," as if living with her was some kind of government appointment. One chap had even left behind a whole wedding photo album. Octavi, for his part, had bequeathed an English-Catalan dictionary that sat on the bookshelf in our apartment. As I looked at him in the photos, with his jet black hair and Mediterranean tan, I realized that I hadn't been the first coffee-colored ice cream scoop in the Estonian sundae. There had been others, my predecessors, and Helina had seen them all.

"How are your parents?" Helina asked me as we left the wooden planks of the trail and headed off into the woods. The ground was soft and mossy. I walked with care.

"They're fine," I told her. "They both said to say hello. They are going to come and visit Estonia in winter."

51

"Winter? They should come in summer," she wrinkled her nose.

"But the baby isn't coming in summer."

"But they can come again."

Would they come again? More than once to Estonia?

Mom and Dad were not like Epp and me. They couldn't live out of one bag for weeks at a time. Any trip would have to be planned with meticulous attention to detail in advance. They would require a comfortable hotel room with the right sized beds, a buffet breakfast, and access to CNN Headline News.

"Epp said that you were pregnant with Ken in the summer," I decided to change the subject.

"Oh, yeah, I remember sitting in my parents' basement trying to stay cool," Helina wrinkled her nose again. "That was a hot summer, 1994."

Helina and her first child Ken were 20 years apart, as were Helina and her mother Randi, and Epp and her mother Aime. Two decades was typically how long it took Estonians to reproduce. It was a common tale in Estonia and, despite our more advanced ages – Epp was 29, I was still 23 – our own story wasn't so different. If our child were to show up on its due date, it would have taken us 16 whole months since we first set eyes on each other to deliver a new individual to planet Earth.

Helina and I were interrupted by the cries of birds that sat at the tops of the trees above. We were getting closer to the mystical Latvian border and the woods were getting thicker and darker. There was preciously little blue sky visible now, everything was just dark and green.

"Hey Justin, is it really true that Arnold Schwarzenegger is going to be the next governor of California?" Helina's young son Ken tugged at my shirt in the forest.

I looked down at Ken and was reminded of his mother. He had her blond hair and healthy smile. He also reminded me of the main character in an Estonian children's book I had seen: *Little Jussike's Seven Friends*.

In the book, a young, blond school boy named Jussike wants to go to Sundayland, but to get there he must pass through Mondayland, Tuesdayland, Wednesdayland. And what does young Jussike do in such far-flung locales? He is put to work, naturally. In Mondayland, he gathers hay. In Tuesdayland, Jussike lays bricks. In Friday land, he does the laundry. And so Jussike works his way towards Sundayland, a do-good smile on his face the whole way.

The Estonians had a word for such honest, hardworking children: *tubli*. For a boy like Jussike, work was fun, something you did with a wholesome grin on your face. Maybe if you worked especially hard, you might be rewarded with some yummy treats. And Ken reminded me of Jussike. He was a *tubli poiss*, a good boy, studious and pleasant, a little more *tubli* than the rest. Ken was gracious and interested in the world. Nine years old, he already spoke enough English to ask about Californian politics.

"Schwarzenegger could be the next governor, Ken," I said. "But there are other candidates. I mean, if I could choose, I would vote for Gallagher."

"Gallagher?" Ken was intrigued. "Who's he?"

53

"Gallagher's a comedian, Ken. He has wild brown hair and he carries around this giant hammer called the Sledge-o-matic, and at the ends of his shows he smashes watermelons, and everyone in the front row gets soaked in watermelon guts! It's awesome."

"And he wants to be governor?"

"Uh huh. But he's not the only one. Gary Coleman is running too."

"Who's Gary Coleman?" Helina asked.

"Who's Gary Coleman? We'll he's," I rubbed my face. How could I explain to these Estonians who Gary Coleman was? They had probably never seen Coleman's famous eighties TV show *Diff'rent Strokes*, let alone heard his special catch phrase, "Whatyoutalkinbout, Willis?" They knew nothing of how the small-of-stature child star had once sued his parents or been arrested after he punched a woman who asked for his autograph.

"He's just another actor," I said, unsatisfied with my explanation.

"The only time I ever felt that you were really American was that time they showed the preview for *Terminator 3* in the movie theater," said Epp, who now walked alongside us, her thick lips stained with freshly picked lingonberries. "That movie looked so stupid, but everybody in the theater cheered. You were cheering too. And I was like, 'Ok, he really is one of them.'"

"Of course it's stupid, but," I paused. "That's the beauty of it."

"I didn't cheer."

"You don't get it. It's like I told you, Americans arrived from all over the world, speaking different languages. When they went to the theater, entertainers had to get down to the lowest common denominator to amuse them, like smashing watermelons. Americans like stupid things."

Helina, Epp, and little Ken all stared at me.

"Oh, nevermind!"

In my previous American life, my friends and I could go on and on talking about Arnold Schwarzenegger and Gary Coleman. But here in Estonia, such talk was meaningless. Estonians were more interested in berries than idiotic theatrics. They ate watermelons. They didn't destroy them on stage with a hammer. And who was I to be talking about The Terminator in the woods? The Estonian-Latvian border was a sacred place. It was pure, free from the dumb chaos of the cities, an organic wonder salve for cynicism. I felt hopelessly out of place. I knew a lot about comedians and actors, but I couldn't tell you whether or not that mushroom in your hands was poisonous.

And I was perhaps the only person on that day in all of Estonia who was excited about going to Latvia.

"It's so cute how he wants to go there," Helina told Epp. "I mean, it's just Latvia."

"But it's exotic for him," Epp answered. "Could you imagine that I took you on a hike somewhere in America and then led you into a forest and on the other side of the forest was Canada?" Epp said.

"Hmm," Helina wrinkled her nose. "Maybe you are right."

The forest gave way to a clearing, and there before my eyes was the Estonian-Latvian border. No trees stood for 30 yards or more between the two countries. The border had been almost shaved into the land, stretching on in either direction for as far as I could see; a narrow, rolling, grassy corridor between the evergreens.

The boundary between these neighbors had once been in dispute, I had read. The nascent Estonian and Latvian governments were deadlocked. Finally, in 1920, the British stepped in and resolved the matter, truncating in the process the city of Valga, leaving two thirds of the town on the Estonian side and the other third in Latvia. The Estonians thought they deserved more but, allegedly, the British colonel who settled the dispute had a Latvian girlfriend.

                ◖ ◐ ◖

"Are you sure we can cross?" I asked Helina. "I don't have my passport."

"No, they don't mind," Helina said, walking with confidence across the clearing. "There are always people in here picking berries and mushrooms."

We moved towards a small knoll, on top of which stood a striped pole that looked like the Latvians had lifted it from a barbershop. Above it, I saw a plain sign in black and white: *Latvijas Republika*. Latvia was a *Republika*, I noticed, not a *Vabariik*. By just traversing a small clearing, we had entered a whole new Indo-European language zone, one that stretched all the way to the frontiers of Europe.

"What kind of language do they speak in Latvia?" I motioned to the sign.

"Latvian," Helina said plainly.

"I know they speak Latvian, but what is it like? Like Russian or Polish?"

"It's a Baltic language."

"No, I know that Latvia is a Baltic country. But I mean what kind of language is it? Is it a Slavic language?"

"You mean you don't know this?" For the first time I sensed impatience in Helina's voice.

"Know what?"

I knew the shape of Latvia and that its capital was Riga. I could recognize in any photograph the image of President Vaira Vīķe-Freiberga, its iron lady president with the iron haircut. I knew that the Latvian language was locked in some kind of struggle with Russian for dominance on the streets of Riga. But the actual language? To me it looked like all the other Eastern European tongues on the back of the Estonian cereal box.

There had been two girls from Riga in my study program in Copenhagen, Natasha and Olesia, both of whom were infamous for wearing tight dresses and high-heeled shoes. Everyone called them "the Latvians," and when a story went around that mentioned "the Latvians," it usually meant that some kind of wild party had taken place. But to me, it was hard to distinguish the Latvian Olesia from the Russian Olesia who had been in our foreign correspondents' program in Helsinki. Eastern Europe seemed like a patchwork of interrelated tongues and peoples and outrageous fashion statements, a region where borders in some cases had been drawn up late at night by British colonels with the help of their local girlfriends.

For years, I had watched the news, trying to detangle the ethnic and religious rivalries in the former Yugoslavia. One

57

news report said that if you ordered coffee with a Bosnian accent in Belgrade, you could quickly find yourself at the wrong end of a knife.

"Come on, Helina, all the languages in Eastern Europe are the same," I sighed. "In one country it's *dobrý den** 'and in the other it is *dober dan***."

"Not in Latvia," she wrinkled her nose again. "In Latvia, it's *labdien.*"

"And in Lithuania, it is *labas dienas*," Epp said and smiled.

Now I really felt like a stupid American.

"They are Baltic languages," Helina said. "Not Scandinavian, not Slavic, not Finno-Ugric. There used to be more of them, but Latvian and Lithuanian are really the only ones left."

"Hmm," I scratched my neck. "And what do you think of these Latvians?"

"We think they have six toes," Helina flashed a toothy smile.

"We don't have a lot of jokes about Latvians but they have jokes about us," Epp said. "I remember the Latvian journalist in our foreign correspondents' program told me all these jokes about Estonians, about how slow and clumsy we are. And then she asked me for Estonian jokes about Latvians, but I didn't know any. And she was a bit mad. The Latvians are a bit jealous of us, I think. It's like Estonians used to be jealous of Finns, so we had lots of jokes about them. But now we feel more secure. We don't joke about Finns so much," Epp said. "We make jokes about ourselves."

---

* Good day (In Czech)
** Good day (In Slovenian)

♦ ♦ ♦

Nele, Karin, Rait, Vane. I couldn't tell one from the other, but they all were polite to me. Later, when we returned from our forest sojourn, the family gave us a tour of their summer cottage, including the chance to see the writing desk of my wife's great grandfather Peeter Lenk, a first cousin of the famous Estonian writer Anton Hansen Tammsaare, author of the great book series *Tõde ja Õigus**.

The old schoolmaster Peeter Lenk was a sort of family legend, an embodiment of all that was good in the Estonians: educated and hardworking and respectable. His desk was ancient and dark, made of sturdy wood. It sat in a corner on the second floor. No one wrote on it anymore. It was now just an heirloom, a 19th century curiosity.

"This is his desk," Vane said. Or was it Nele? I couldn't remember.

The Estonians looked down on it, and Epp touched its glossy surface. Lenk was the forefather of everyone in that room at that moment, cousins who shared common roots, roots that joined everyone, except for me.

---

* *Truth and Justice*, a five-part classic of Estonian literature published between 1926 and 1933 that all high school students are obligated to read.

ONE
LIFE

"So, you came back?"
"What? Not everyone comes back?"

"No," Heli shook her head and looked up at me from her desk for a moment. "Most freelancers like you come and go."

The Baltic Times office on Pärnu Road was warm and bright that morning, so sunny that it was hard to believe that I had sat in this very same space in the depths of winter, surrounded by nothing but dust and darkness.

But here it was: same old desks, same old bookshelves. Heli Munk, the office manager, and Ivan Spengler, the paper's main Estonian reporter, had already spent many seasons in this space together. They shared its air, shared its light. They were like one entity, one organism protected by an exoskeleton of plaster and tile and fluorescent lighting.

They were different though. Heli was an Estonian Estonian, thin and angular, as if assembled from triangles and rectangles and squares and trapezoids, her shoulder-length blond hair framing deeply set blue eyes that had seen too much weather.

Ivan was different, a Russian Estonian, dark and diminutive with features so boyish it still surprised me that we were the same age. Sometimes his mother or his wife or his t.A.T.u-obsessed little sister Ekaterina would call him on his mobile phone, and when they did Ivan would slink down in his chair and whisper a symphony of *dah, net,* and *harasho** until they left him alone again to write his articles about Estonian politics and EU accession.

Ivan knew me better than Heli – he did take a photo of Epp and me on our wedding day in June – but I couldn't really say either knew me well. And even after spending months together with these two people in the same small space, I knew almost nothing about them. What did Heli do in her spare time? Where did she live? Was she married? Did she have children? She didn't tell me, and I didn't particularly feel like announcing to her that I was a 23-year-old expectant father.

Why would I tell her anyway? Most people in New York were unnerved that I was on the verge of fatherhood. They told me I was "too young," as given such knowledge I could somehow rearrange the situation. One friend even told me that I should "get a vasectomy or it might happen again." Being in New York had been like running through a gauntlet of condemnation. I had broken the rules, defaced social mores. I had been raised to be one person, but had wound up as someone else. I was a failure.

---

* 'Yes', 'no', and 'alright' (In Russian)

So it was a relief to be in Estonia. Here, nobody cared if you became a father when you were 23. I could keep my personal details to myself. It wouldn't be too hard, I reckoned, because up here in this northern European newspaper office, the principle of "I don't touch you, you don't touch me" was in full effect. We were all atomized in Estonia, separated by time and space and distance. The anonymity suited me fine.

"How are you, Heli?" I held out my hand to the office manager. She raised a platinum eyebrow at the strange object, and then lifted hers and waved politely in return. "Alright," she nodded, quickly returning her hand to the keyboard.

"And you Ivan?" I strode across the office. "What's up, man?"

Ivan slowly swiveled around in his office chair and sipped on his coffee, enjoying the comical sight of me, as if I were a polar bear at the Tallinn zoo.

"I'm fine," he answered in an unenthusiastic deadpan. "I got the travel piece you wrote about Hiiumaa," he said, swiveling back to his desk. "But I don't understand something. You said the place was 'elvish.'"

"Because it is," I said, plopping into a chair beside his desk. "Why?"

"Because it looks like the set for *The Lord of the Rings.*"

"I see," he placed his coffee cup down and sighed, either because he was unconvinced or simply didn't care. "Would you be interested in writing something else for us?"

"Yes." And I always said yes when offered a new writing assignment.

"Good," Ivan nodded and held the day's newspaper. "Eesti Telefon is being rebranded as Elion," he tapped at the front page. "They spent – heh – eight million kroons just to come up with that name."

"Elion? Is that supposed to mean something?"

"Who knows?" Ivan tossed the paper back onto his cluttered desk. "But we should write a story about it." He pulled out his mobile. "Write this number down," he showed it to me. "It's for Piret Mürk. She's Eesti Telefon's, pardon me, Elion's PR person."

I scribbled the digits down on a post-it note. A minute later I was back in my old chair by the window, setting up an appointment. Piret said she wanted to meet in half an hour, which gave me plenty of time to do the interview before I was supposed to meet Epp at the hospital.

"I should be able to turn this story around quick," I told Ivan as I left the office. "Piret wants to meet today."

"Ok, but do you know where their new office is?" he asked.

I remembered the place. One year before, on my first night in Tallinn, Epp and I walked past the very spot. Then it was just a hole in the ground, a sandy construction site I could almost feel the warm summer air on my neck from that night. I could see Epp standing beside me in her red corduroy jacket. I found the image soothing.

"It's a new building," said Ivan. "I mean, it's huge, but all you have to do is go in and ask at the desk for her."

"I'll manage."

"And there's one other thing," said Ivan.

"What?"

"One should be very careful around Piret Mürk," Ivan stared at me.

"Why?"

"Because her last name means 'poison.'"

"And then he said, 'You should be very careful around Piret Mürk. Her last name means 'poison'!'"

"Ha!"

I met Epp at the entrance to the huddle of gray Soviet-era structures that made up Tallinn Central Hospital. We still had a few minutes until our appointment, and we walked leisurely into the complex towards one of its buildings.

"Ivan's not so bad," Epp said. "He just has an Estonian sense of humor."

"But I thought Ivan was Russian."

"But Estonian Russians are different from Russian Russians," Epp said. "I know one Estonian Russian guy who went to St. Petersburg. He was lost and asked directions from an old lady on a tram. Then some other old lady overheard the question and started to argue with the first old lady about the best way to get there. And then a man nearby started to argue with the two old ladies, and was like, 'You babushkas don't know what you're talking about, the best way to get there is this way!' Soon everyone on the tram was yelling at each other about the right way to get where this poor Estonian Russian guy was going. And he just couldn't say anything. He had never seen people argue like that on a tram before. The way he told me this, it was, I swear, pure Estonian!"

"I guess things are different there. Ivan definitely doesn't seem like the kind of guy who would fold his arms and do one of those Cossack dances."

"But, anyway, how did your interview go? How was the poisonous PR girl, Piret Mürk?"

"She was kind of normal, I mean, for someone with that name. Piret gave me a free notebook, too," I pulled the small white book from my bag. "It says *Värsked ideed*. Fresh ideas. I can write down song lyrics in it."

"Or book ideas."

"Uh huh. That's what I like about being a journalist. You don't get paid much, but everyone gives you free notebooks, t-shirts, yogurt."

"Who gave you free yogurt?"

"The Estonian Dairy Association. Remember the day I brought home all that vanilla pudding?"

"You should go to more of their meetings," Epp smiled. "Well, we are getting something else for free – a trip to Saaremaa! I have to go interview a designer and an artist. We agreed to meet the day after tomorrow."

"Saaremaa? But how will we get there? By plane again?" I thought of the Hiiu plane with the tape on its wings.

"No, let's go by bus," Epp said. "There's a direct route from Tallinn to Kuressaare."

We finally arrived at a tall concrete slab of a building. The monument to maternity was surrounded by uncut tufts of weeds, grass, and mottled sidewalks that probably hadn't been renovated since the concrete was poured in the seventies. This is where our child would be born in January. I could see us, here, trudging through the gusts of snow and ice from our apartment on Kentmanni Street like stoic pilgrims, over the broken sidewalks, then up the five flights of stairs.

"What do you think," Epp asked. "Boy or girl?"

When you are a child your own birth seems significant, profound; even divine. Your parents frame photos of you as a newborn. Maybe they hang them on the wall or position them atop their bedroom nightstands. My mother kept "baby books" for my brother and me, jotting down the dates we got our first teeth, when we first sat up, laughed, and uttered our first words. Not only were there written mementos, but physical ones as well. My brother's baby shoes still sat on a shelf in our parents' house alongside mine. Inscribed on them were our birthdates, birthdates that in 2003 already seemed distant and irrelevant.

My parents once quizzed each other about the gender of their pending baby, just like us. Dad never gave up hope for a son. Mom, and everyone else, thought I would be a girl. But when the doctor finally pulled my slimy green carcass from my mother's ravaged womb on a wet and foggy November night, an arch of piss shot triumphantly across the room, my very own personal rainbow of masculinity: it was a boy, me. And here I was, almost 24 years later, standing in the entrance to the maternity building of a hospital in a city 4,000 miles from my point of origin, preparing to reenact the event.

"Who told you that story, about how you peed when you were born?" Epp asked as we waited in the hospital corridor.

"My Dad," I grinned. "He always tells that story."

"See," her eyes narrowed to tiny Finno-Ugric slits. "Where you were born, fathers were allowed in hospital rooms. But even when my younger brother was born in the late eighties, my father couldn't go in. We had to look at Mom and Aap through a window."

"Why?"

"That's just how it was in Soviet times. And they didn't have cell phones in those days. I don't even know how she knew we were there," she played with her hands. "I think it worked like this – the father would show up with a gift, and they would bring up the package to the mother, and that's how she'd know that her family was there, and she would come to the window and show us the baby. I remember how we drove to Viljandi and she showed us Aap from the third-floor window. I mean, I understood that we could bring in viruses so we couldn't go in, but it was so alienating. It was like that during the entire whole Soviet time, pregnant women were taken away from their families for five days and then given back."

I searched for something to say, but all I could do was think of Epp's mother holding Aap up to the window 15 years before. I could see her face through the window, framed by those big glasses she wore in the old photos. The image in my mind was blurred and the tone had faded from it, like an old Polaroid.

"What about when you were born," I winked. "Do you remember anything?"

"No," Epp shook her head. "But I remember walking through the Old Town of Viljandi with mother and she showed me the white house where I was born."

"Viljandi? But your passport says Tallinn."

"It always used to confuse me when I was small. Both of my parents were registered in Tallinn, so I was officially registered as being born there. But I was born in Viljandi. Even today when I fill out paper work, I have to write that I was born in Tallinn, though it's not true! But that white house in Viljandi isn't a hospital anymore. It's a hotel. When we had our little honeymoon in Viljandi, I thought we could stay there. For some reason, I changed my mind. Let it be my birth place, not anything else."

"Was it more natural in those days, to give birth?"

"No, from what I have heard, It was like some kind of hardcore technological event," Epp said. "Mom lost a lot of blood and she wasn't in good shape. And then she picked up some kind of nasty bacteria at the hospital. The other women had it too. Inflammation of the breast, mastitis. So after we got home, she had to be hospitalized again. I spent my first days like that: Papa had to drive back and forth to the hospital, bringing me released breast milk. I wasn't with my mother."

"Papa? Were your parents living with your grandparents?"

"They were only 20 years old. They were students. Father was studying in Tallinn and so was mother. They lived in the backroom at my grandparents' house."

"But your grandparents only have three rooms!"

"They were in the backroom, my uncles Vello and Toivo – who were schoolboys then – shared the middle room, and

Mamma and Papa lived in the front room." Epp paused for a moment, thinking. "How old were your parents when you were born? They were older, right?"

"32."

"And they had a house?"

"A big one, near the beach. They bought it the year before I was born and renovated it."

"See. Soon my parents had two more kids in a row and we moved away, to a two-room apartment. It was so tiny. I was small back then and it even seemed small to me. And it was father, mother, me, my sister Eva, and my brother Priit, all in that little place. Sometimes Aunt Kuste would come and watch us, too, and stay overnight, I cannot imagine, how did they manage to find space for her! Do you remember I told you about Kuste?"

"She was the one who lost her fiancé in the War of Independence?" A grainy image of the little old bachelorette Kuste from the old photos, hunched over with a scarf on her head came to mind.

"Think of us all in that little apartment! My poor mother. Her life was not easy."

"But you are going to give birth here, in a hospital" we looked around at the ward; its familiar sights of clinical, off-white walls; of nurses traveling back and forth with clipboards, the gurgling sounds of old phones echoing down the hall. "Are you worried you might get sick after that? Like she did?"

"Things should be different than they were back then," Epp looked up. "It should be a more natural birth. And you can help me. They allow fathers in the hospital now."

Squirt! The nurse shot a handful of clear silicon jelly onto Epp's belly and then maneuvered a plastic imager above her abdomen, running it back and forth until the ultrasound machine began to pop to a steady beat – pop pop pop pop pop.

I looked to the screen of the nurse's machine for any trace of our baby, but all I saw in the black and white soup was spiraling globs, shapes without meaning, splashing back and forth without any form or direction.

"It's quite active," the old nurse smiled to us, and Epp lifted her head up from the hospital bed so that she could see the show. Then I realized what I was looking at. Our child was doing somersaults in the womb, rolling and splashing like a kid at the beach. First you'd see its shoulders, and then you'd see its feet, moving up and down and around and around like a chalk drawing doing calisthenics.

I glanced at the equipment: beige with big black buttons, everything on it was written in German; not Estonian. How old was it? It looked sturdy but discolored, like it had been in use for a long time, but if it was good enough for the rest of Tallinn, wasn't it good enough for us?

"It has a strong heartbeat too," the old nurse said. "160 beats per minute."

"But can you tell if it's a boy or a girl?" Epp asked, lifting her head up again before resting it on a pillow.

"I've been trying to figure that out, but this baby keeps moving," said the nurse, adjusting the imager. "No, I just can't get a good look. It could be a girl, but I can't be sure. One thing is for sure: it has longer legs than average."

Long legs! Our child had long legs. It had two arms and a head too. Day after day, the old Estonian nurse sat here, using her aged surveillance tools to image oceans of uteruses, reading back two-tone images of the unborn to expectant fathers and mothers like us. That was her life. These images were common, nothing special. To me, though, the ultrasound was like an earthquake. Our child was active, alive and growing. It had long legs. It was in there and would get bigger. Eventually, it would want to come out. By that time, I had to be ready.

"Why are they rebranding Eesti Telefon again?" Epp said as we crossed the street and headed back to our apartment.

"Piret Mürk said they had something like six different brands and they wanted to consolidate them under one 'brand umbrella', whatever that means," I answered. The sky was now gray, and a light rain had begun to fall on the city.

"It's too bad we forgot our umbrella."

"Piret also said that she likes the new name because Elion is a more feminine brand. Did you know there are masculine brands and feminine brands? Piret told me so. She said Elion is more delicate and feminine, but Selver? Selver is masculine, can you imagine?"

"Justin, do you really want to do this for the rest of your life?" Epp sighed.

"What?"

71

"Write about feminine brands and masculine brands?"

"Not really," I shrugged. "But that's what they asked me to write about. That's my job."

"Yeah. But why did you even become one, a journalist?"

"Because what else was I going to study? Sociology? Astronomy? For what? They said I was a good writer and it was kind of easy for me. I remember my roommate crying because he didn't know what he wanted to do."

"Crying?"

"Oh yeah. He wanted to do theater, to be a musician, and he was a good musician, but he was also good at computer science. I told him to get a degree in computer science, it paid more. He said it wasn't his passion. But that's how American universities sell themselves. 'Follow your dreams, fulfill your passion,' as if people actually dream about statistics or geography. 'What passion?' I told him. 'Your passion can change in a week.' And that's why I became a journalist. It takes other people a whole day to do what I can do in two hours. I figured, why not get paid for it?"

"But even if you do get paid for it, where does it get you? You give your energy, your life, to brand umbrellas and new ferry terminals," Epp went on. "I have been writing for years and think of all the articles I have written. Some of them were good, really good, but most? It's just a waste of energy. We are wasting our energy, we are wasting our lives. We should be putting our energy into things that matter, like writing books."

I mumbled "Yeah," in response, but what I really thought was "Damn you." Damn you, Epp, for shattering my comfortable, innocent, mindless world of brand genders and ferry terminals.

Damn you, Epp, for bringing up the big picture. And what was the big picture anyway? That we were all going to die? We had to use our time wisely? How lovely.

"A person is only given one life, one," Epp continued her rant. We were standing near our apartment building, and it was raining even harder. "And this one opportunity can end at any moment. I've seen it. It can all just …"

"Evaporate?"

"Yes!" her voice was strained. "And we have to remind each other of this, every day."

"You're right," I sighed. And she was, but what to do with such information?

"Think of my mother," Epp eyed me passionately as I opened the building's front door. "Think of how she died. Did she know she'd only have 41 years?"

I looked back at her and said nothing.

THE OLD
SAILOR

The bus ride to Saaremaa was uninspiring and uneventful.

Estonia to me seemed like one big nature preserve, there were forests of birch and pine and nothing else, the monotonous green punctured only by villages with poetic names and views of fields and harbors, hamlets with stone walls and manor houses and church spires. But only the imaginative could find such villages endearing, because between the quaint yellow and red wooden homes and school houses lay poverty, unpainted facades, broken windows, and buildings marred by decay and ruin, collapsing into each other like old drunks.

"What happened to this place?" I asked Epp. "How come there are so many buildings that are ruined? How could a whole village be left to rot?"

"The young moved away to the cities and then only the old people were left in the villages," she gazed from the bus window. "Then the old people died."

While the cities of Tallinn and Tartu and Pärnu glistened with new shopping centers and hotels and boutiques and spas and salons, the villages of Estonia's west coast combusted, the young moving away, the old people dying out. All that was left were the old drunks collapsing into each other, staggering along, walking the streets, back and forth, from daybreak to dusk, until the day when they too died, a childless obituary, a stony face in the back of a newspaper, a skeleton in the spare bedroom.

That was the story of the mainland. I looked to the islands for hope, a chance, a faith that the water had made them different, that the sea had spared them Estonia's fate. I hoped that out there on Muhumaa and Saaremaa was another reality, a more positive one, distant from the sorrows of mainland Estonia. And when we finally boarded the ferry at Virtsu bound for Muhu, things began to look up. The sun broke through the oppressive gray clouds. The vessel was full of voyagers, some foreign, some local, all pleased to get away, away from Estonia, away to Saaremaa. I was content too.

"This is an island of principled people," Epp said as our bus cleared the causeway between Muhumaa and Saaremaa.

"I don't understand."

"I used to work with an editor from Saaremaa. If he didn't want to do something, he always used to say, 'It's against my principles.'" "It's against my principles." It was and is a common expression in Estonia. Sometimes, it seemed to me that an Estonian would do anything, push any button, insult any monarch, kick any sick dog, so long as it met the measure of

75

his cherished principles. Most Estonians did not coach their actions in lust or desire. It was always a matter of principle, as if life was a document, a set of rules, operating guidelines for all behaviors. I had even known an Estonian passport forger who told me he did it not as much for the money as for the fact that he had no personal respect for British law. He may have been a criminal you see, but he was an Estonian, and that meant he still had his principles!

Saaremaa stole away through the windows, familiar birches standing like gangly teenagers, long, sprawling meadows spreading out like a dream-less sleep. The island did seem more peaceful than the mainland, maybe because I wanted it to feel that way. Estonia was behind us and Saaremaa felt safe, a haven, a retreat, a ship moored off the coast. I could have been anywhere really by that point. But Saaremaa? Why Saaremaa? Why not? It felt good to be away though. Away was the way I liked to feel.

We rolled into Kuressaare and disembarked at its bunker-like brick bus station. From there we entered the heart of the city, its old town. Kuressaare sparkled that day in the sunlight, and, no matter where you were, whether in some dingy apartment house or pristine forest, the sun always made Estonia look a little better. The storefronts along the main street were restored and attractive. There was money here, money for new spas and gourmet restaurants and cafes. Kuressaare was one of the few winners, its boutiques and art galleries painted in cozy oranges and disarming pinks, the old wood-cut doors popping out in even more extravagant colors, bold colors, blues and yellows and reds, and then the dark, towering churches glaring down, tall, sober, bathed in the soft sunlight. The people of Saaremaa moved along the sidewalks of their capital, and the norther-liness of the place touched me, the blonde ponytails of the girls, the square silence of the men, everything tidy, everything tucked in, everything in its place, because that's how Estonians liked things. In fact, it was their favorite question. *Kas kõik on korras?** They needed to know.

"I don't see any principled people yet," I said as we walked through the city's center. Unlike lazy Kärdla on Hiiumaa, Saaremaa's Kuressaare was alive with people, each one headed in a specific direction.

"Well, what did you expect? It's not that obvious!" Epp answered. "But my friend Airi told me that they are just like that. She's from Hiiumaa. She knows these things. *Saarlased* don't have the letter 'õ,' they only have 'ö.' And Airi has a friend who refuses to use the letter 'õ.' He speaks to all his friends in Tallinn with a Saare accent, on purpose."

"I don't understand."

"Like he doesn't say *õlu***, he says *ölu*. When he sings the national anthem, it's not, *Mu isamaa, mu õnn ja rõõm****, it's, *Mu isamaa, mu önn ja rööm*."

"Oh."

"And not only that. Airi said he wrote his entire master's thesis at the University of Tartu in the Saare dialect. He just refuses to use 'õ' anywhere. He said it's against his principles."

"*Saarlased* sound like a bunch of weirdos."

"Heh. You could be a *saarlane*."

---

* Is everything in order? (In Estonian)
** Beer (In Estonian)
*** My Fatherland, My Happiness and Joy. (In Estonian)

"Not with the way I look."

"Vice versa. I think there are two places you could be from in Estonia, Saaremaa or Setomaa," Epp studied my face. "Setomaa because it was – as the story goes – raided by the Mongols, Saaremaa because of the pirates."

"Pirates?"

"Of course, Spanish, Portuguese. This is an island, remember."

And I could see them when she said it. The swarthy Iberian scallywags arrived just after dusk, mooring in the harbor, and then rowing past the castle's ancient walls in the light of the full moon to the mouth of the city. Then, when the night fell, the debauchery began, the whole bloody scene illuminated by fiery torchlight, the murder and the mayhem, the flash of the cutlass, the beauty of burning buildings, and everywhere sound, the wild screams of lust and pain, the motion and the fury, the hot sweat of violence and violation.

"I don't think it was like that at all," Epp shook her head. "I just think they went to the pub and were all singing romantic songs with guitars and mandolins, and the Saare girls fell in love with these handsome guys."

"And then a few years later the fields of Saaremaa farms were filled with little brunettes?"

"Sure," she nodded. "Something like that."

Estonian supermarkets are all the same. The old drunks sitting on the bench outside, the amateurishly arranged shelves of preserved foods, the vast alcohol section, the bored-looking check out girls, and then the music, and what music it is. A trip to an Estonian supermarket is journey back to the fabled nineteen eighties. That's how it was that day in Kuressaare in 2003 and that's probably how it is now. First I heard Starship, singing, "We Built This City," followed by Crowded House and their sad, glistening guitars, pleading with me, "Don't Dream It's Over." And then, for the finale, Boy George and his Culture Club, serenading the shoppers of Kuressaare:

"Do you really want to hurt me? Do you really want to make me cry?"

I was there in this supermarket at the end of the world, because I was hungry, but what to eat? I headed to the bakery to find something to alleviate my raw hunger, that nagging, gnawing sickness of emptiness. I had been hungry all day and I couldn't sate my appetite. I had read that sometimes men's bodies mirrored their pregnant partner's, so if Epp got thirsty, I could get thirsty too, or if Epp felt like cleaning, I might suddenly reach for a broom, and if she was hungry, well, here I was. And the bakery was always the best bet for a quick bite to eat in Estonia. Here nothing needed to be unpeeled or defrosted or fried, it was just stick it in a bag and go; here all was soft and sweet and laden with rich *kohupiim.*

What the heck was *kohupiim*? English dictionaries defined the sweet soft cheese as "quark," a distant relative of the Italian ricotta. In Estonia, the white stuff was a staple of bakers, all of whom managed to sneak a little into every treat.

"What will it be today, boss?" I asked myself. "Something with *kohupiim*?"

What other options did I really have? Frozen peas? Canned soup? No, it would be *kohupiim*, again, and I decided to go for something simple, the familiar *kohupiimakorbid*, round pastries filled with the white stuff. I usually picked two or three up on my way to the office in Tallinn. The ladies behind the counter would sit in the corner reading their newspapers until I signaled that I wasn't going away by loudly clearing my throat. Then one of the Tallinn ladies would slowly stand to take my order. These *kohupiimakorbid* were dependable: they would hit my appetite before I could find myself a table at a local restaurant and get something real to eat, a beer too maybe. Epp's interview with the artist could go on for a long time and I had time to kill. From the bakery I wandered over to the alcohol section. It wasn't too early to start drinking, not at all. It was already 5 pm and the Kuressaare shoppers were out, stocking up for a long weekend of Gin Long Drinks and blackcurrant vodka and premium beers.

Two of the shoppers were tall, muscular, blonde guys, your standard-issue Estonians. Between them though stood a different person, one with a darker complexion; this shopper was swarthier, *tõmmu*, with long black hair tied back in a pony-tail. I watched him load a six pack into a shopping cart and realized that he could have been me if I hadn't been standing there opposite him. I suspected he was a foreigner, an Italian or Portuguese friend of this Estonian gang. It wasn't inconceivable. Maybe they had met abroad. Maybe he was just working here for the summer. And as he turned around to load a six pack into their shopping cart, I was shattered: he was speaking Estonian and he looked just like me.

It was true about the pirates.

And the image hit me again, the stealthy rowboats, oars wrapped in cloth to muffle their sound, and then, under the lantern light, the attack, the screams, the sweat, the bloodlust, and the chaos. The pirates that night came for the three things, the three things all men secretly want: sex, food and entertainment. Whenever I jested with my good friend Eamon back in New York about his drinking and womanizing, he would protest: "I can't help it, man! I do it because I'm bored." And so it was for the pirates, and Kuressaare was ripe for the plucking. Food, entertainment, *sex*? I glanced back at the bored-looking blonde cashiers. Yeah, this was the place alright. It was almost too perfect.

This *tõmmu* beer buyer was unquestionably the son of pirates, the spawn of sin, nothing like the romantic, idyllic Estonian, all blonde and pure and good, covered in peach fuzz, the rapture of pagan mythology. But I forgot to get a price for my *korbid* so I left pirate boy and the Saare booze brothers behind and returned to the bakery to weigh my bag on the scale. And that's when I saw her, a gorgeous specimen of Estonianness, so Estonian she might as well have been Miss Estonia. She was about half my height and I saw she had opted for the *kohupiimakorbid*, too. Good choice. And with that flaxen hair, those sky blue eyes, she was the ethno-national ideal, the kind of girl they put on postcards in Tallinn or advertisements for Estonian Air: blue, black, and white in the flesh.

Miss Estonia wasn't wearing the national colors that day. She had on tight red pants and a tight pink top displaying two glittery, eye-popping words: *Great sex*. "Oh really?" I thought. It wasn't hard to find an Estonian girl with such a provocative

81

shirt. I had seen a girl in a Tallinn department store with jeans that said, "Yummy" on the ass. Sometimes I wondered if these fashionable young ladies even understood what the English words on their clothes meant.

I glimpsed her stringy top once more, as she weighed her deliciously thick *korbid*, each one laden with warm, rich *kohu-piim*. The treats were so greasy that the paper bag was already coming apart. And then her phone rang, and Miss Estonia bent over to pull the phone from her purse in the shopping cart, digging around. And when Miss Estonia finally located the plastic rectangle, its cry loud and urgent, like a newborn babe, she tugged the sleek futuristic box from the bag and answered it.

In Russian.

I had never seen a cup of coffee so big, and when the Old Sailor lifted it to his lips that night, when I realized he really was going to drink it, all of it, a whole bowl of coffee before he went to sleep, I understood: he was an addict.

Not that it troubled Epp. She had been a coffee addict too, like most Estonians. She had struggled to switch to milder tea instead, but I noticed she had a cup at the art show that afternoon, and perhaps succumbed to another one when she did her interview with the artist, another woman named Epp. I dutifully snapped photos of this other Epp in the gallery. After I photographed the artist, the two Epps had taken off for an interview. I in the meantime consumed a bag of greasy *kohupiimakorbid*, and then downed a few beers at a dimly lit café with a windmill motif.

I sat inside the bar, looking at black and white photos of old mills on the wall, all the time listening to Estonian sea shanties, each accordion-driven number a repeat of the other, the melodies rising and crashing like the waves of the sea, each one about the same character, a sailor, a *meremees*. Oh *meremees* this, and oh *meremees* that. For nearly an hour all I heard was, *Meremees, meremees, meremees*. The singers never shut up. If I had a gun, I might have shot the café's stereo. The sailor music, the discordant, monotonous grind of the accordions, it made me ill, queasy, seasick, especially after I downed a plate of greasy *küüslauguleivad*, each toasted, crispy brown finger of rye bread smothered in butter and garlic, and then dipped by my hungry hands in sour cream.

What would happen to you if you ate Estonian food every day? Would your heart just explode? Or could your body somehow adapt? After all, Estonian men were still living deep into their sixties and Estonian women even beyond. Generous helpings of *kohupiim* were apparently not immediately fatal.

After the interview, Epp and I met up at the city center and then went to check in at our B&B. It was located down a winding lane of homes, east of the center. The houses here were mostly well kept, the streets quiet. The smell of drying fish was in the air.

It was there we met the Old Sailor. He was a jolly man, neither tall nor short, but with a bushy brown mustache, thick dark eyebrows, and piercing blue eyes, eyes that glistened even in the Soviet navy portrait that hung on the wall of the guesthouse. Beside this photo was another, a picture of his son, Young Sailor, this time with an American flag behind his white sailor's cap.

83

One sailor had served the Soviets; the other now served the Americans. "He lives in Florida," the sailor explained.

With his family grown and gone, the Old Sailor had transformed his big home into a guesthouse for travelers. The building was spacious, modern and square with futuristic, circular windows, like the portholes of a spaceship. The Old Sailor lived in a smaller house in the back of the property and when we strolled up his driveway he was handling an old fishing pole. He told us that, if we wanted, he could take us out that night on his fishing boat. "You two should come out with me," the Old Sailor said in his thick, smoky voice, a half-smoked cigarette dangling from his fingers. And after that, he annouced proudly, "We can eat what we catch."

Later, I found myself standing beside my driven, active, pregnant spouse as she dug passionately through the Old Sailor's garden looking for fish bait. The Old Sailor helped at first too, between him and Epp, the two frenetic diggers easily filled up the bottom of a bucket with worms. Then he took a rest, lit up another cigarette, and explained that he needed to run a few errands and would be back around nightfall, which was quickly approaching. He climbed into his old car in the driveway and sped away towards town.

"I was a little child when I already learned how to dig in our yard, we grew most of our food ourselves and needed to take good care of our yard, and sometimes we would dig up worms for fishing, too," Epp said as she continued her frantic search for bait.

"Don't you think that's enough?" I said, plopping a fat, dirty worm into the bottom of a small tin bucket.

"Ha, that's only like 20!" Epp turned and looked in the bucket. "We'll need more than that if we're going to catch anything good. And I want to catch eels. Mmm. So delicious," she licked her lips.

I meantime eyed the 20 pink worms, each covered in dirt and excrement, writhing on top of the other. I still didn't feel well. Maybe it was the *kohupiimakorpid* or the *küüslauguleivad* or the sea shanties. Or maybe it was just the fact that worms were kind of gross.

"Twenty is more than enough," I said. "What, do you want to catch 20 fish?"

"Don't be such a girl, Justin!" Epp scolded me, as she pulled another ugly worm from the ground and tossed it in the bucket.

"If I am a girl, then what are you?"

"An Estonian girl," Epp answered, digging all the time. "Now come on, help me."

I could almost taste the night as I dug, I could see us sitting on the edge of the boat on the sea, nothing but shadows, the silhouettes of Epp's lion's mane of hair and the Old Sailor's cap, the two of them bantering back and forth like old friends in Estonian, a language of which I still understood so little. I could see the green moon glowing above, the water rocking us gently, and then to the worms, fumbling with their dark soft shapes in the twilight, their guts dripping from the hooks.

We can eat what we catch.

By the time the Old Sailor returned, another brown cigarette hanging from his lower lip, we had filled half the tin bucket with writhing, slimy, fish bait. It was now dark, and our host seemed less jolly than before, his face bore a sullen pallor.

"Listen, I'm sorry," he grumbled to us. "But my wife, she gets off soon from work at the hospital. It's her sister's friend's cousin's birthday or something. I've already gone out fishing three nights this week. If I don't go with her to the birthday party..." He took another drag from his smoke.

"What?" Epp threw her shovel to the ground and stood up. "Are you serious? You said we could eat what we caught!"

"We would have gone earlier, but she works late nights at the hospital, you see. She gets off in an hour."

"Maybe we can go out a little later then," Epp approached him. "When you get back? I was really looking forward to this."

"I'm really sorry," the Old Sailor apologized again, touching his chest with one hand, taking another drag of his cigarette with the other. "I wanted to go too, but my wife."

"It's ok," I stood up, dusting off my pants. "I totally understand."

"You do?" Epp looked at me, a disappointed hand on her hip.

"Well, it's like he said," I shrugged. "His wife works at the hospital."

"Hmm," Epp frowned again. "Well, what are we going to do with all these worms?"

"I don't know. Put them back?"

When the Old Sailor heard me try to speak Estonian he began to chuckle. "I like you kids, you're good kids," he said. "You two should come inside and talk with me for a while before I go."

The inside of the Old Sailor's little wooden bungalow was like something out of an old Japanese movie. Every wall was wooden, and even though the house was small, there was space between everything: a sole screen of paper and bamboo separated the living area from the Old Sailor's sleeping quarters, a bathtub sat naked beside a sink, and an old television silently broadcast a black and white soccer game from a distant shelf. The sailor watched it as he put a pot of water and a tea kettle to boil on the stove.

"Coffee?" he grunted in his muddy voice.

"Sure," Epp said as the Old Sailor cut open a plastic bag, dumping its contents into the pot.

"You like prawns?" he asked me, displaying the bag and its images of the pink sea creatures.

"Ok."

"Good, because we are going to eat tonight. You hungry?"

"Always."

"That's what I like to hear!" he grunted again, the cigarette hanging from his lip.

"I like him," Epp whispered to me as we waited for both the prawns and the coffee to be ready. "He seems really friendly."

"It's done!" the Old Sailor said, straining the pot and then sprinkling dill and spoonfuls of butter on top, stirring it a few times, then setting it out on a small, plain, brown table.

"And the coffee," he poured himself a bowl of black liquid, and then topped it off with cream from a container. He offered a smaller cup to Epp.

"You are definitely not Estonian, right?" the Old Sailor asked, pulling his chair up the table and plucking a buttery prawn from the pot. The air smelled like dill and cigarette smoke and the thick smell of wood, of which nearly everything around us was made. I ran my hands on the smooth wooden table. It calmed me.

"He's from New York," Epp answered.

"Ah, a Yankee. But you don't look like an American," he gestured with his brown cigarette at my dark hair. "You look like you're Portuguese or something."

"Italian," I said.

"Ah, an Italian Yankee. Yes. Please, please, help yourself," he pushed the prawns towards me. I picked one up and slipped it between my lips, savoring the taste of flesh and butter and salt and dill.

"But tell me, Yankee, what do you like about Estonia?"

"Well, it's pretty and peaceful," I looked around the dimly lit room, searching for answers in Estonian. "Way more relaxing than New York."

"Uh huh," he grunted and exhaled smoke.

"I like Saaremaa too."

"You've been here before?"

"No, but I like Saaremaa beer, Saaremaa vodka."

"I would like that stuff too if it was actually made here," he puffed his smoke. "I hate to tell you this, but anything you buy with the name Saaremaa on it in Estonia is probably made somewhere else."

"Oh no! I thought I was drinking a little Saaremaa every time I drank Saaremaa beer."

"Sorry, Yankee. You're probably drinking Tartu instead. I don't drink that stuff. It's against my principles!"

"Saaremaa beer that's made in Tartu? Yuck."

"I agree, Yankee," he croaked. "I mean, it should be made here. At least it would give more people some work to do. Everyone leaves the island. Look at my son." He sipped his coffee bowl and stared at the prawns. "But, tell me, Yankee, what do you hate about Estonia?"

"Are you serious?"

"Go ahead," Epp winked.

Where to begin? Blood sausage? Salty porridge? Meat jelly? I could have named all these things, but one issue was more pressing. "I went to a pub today and they kept playing this goddamn accordion music about sailors," I leaned over the table. "And it was just *meremees* this and *meremees* that!" I tossed an arm in the air. "It drove me fucking crazy."

"I can see how that could get annoying," the Old Sailor leaned back in his chair.

"I always say that Justin could be a *saarlane*, though" Epp spoke up. "This is the only place where people look like him. Because of the pirates."

"Pirates?" he raised an eyebrow as he gulped his big coffee.

"Burning, pillaging, you know," I grinned.

"Justin, it wasn't like that!" Epp folded her arms. "He thinks they raided Kuressaare, like setting fire to the place and raping all the girls."

"What? No, no, I don't think it was anything like that," the Old Sailor munched on another prawn. "If anybody was doing that, it was us. You ever heard of the Vikings?"

"Well, yeah."

"In 1187, Vikings from Saaremaa raised the Swedish city of Sigtuna to the ground," he sipped his enormous coffee. "To the ground! Then the Swedes looked around and decided to become Vikings too. They took after us. They copied us, stole our ideas. So we were the real Vikings, the real pirates, we started it all. But Viking raids around here? In Saaremaa? I don't think so. No pirates would come here. We would have killed them!" He chuckled. "But I have a friend that looks a bit like you. His name is Peter Paat*. That's a real Saaremaa name. I am sure he has some Spanish or Arab blood in him. He's dark, just like you, Yankee."

The Old Sailor pulled the tail off another prawn and dipped it in the buttery pot water. Then he tossed it into his mouth. "Remember, there were so many shipwrecks on our coast, and there would often be a survivor or two, or ten, or twenty," he munched away. "They'd find him, nurse him back to health, maybe give him a job, he'd marry a local girl," he shrugged. "That's how it happened. And he never left the island!"

"Dead sailors were always washing up," Epp said. "On the coast, where my grandma grew up, in Pärnumaa, there is one sailor's grave we always take care of when we go to clean the graves. It doesn't even have a name on it. It's just a sailor's cross. No one knows who it is," Epp sipped her coffee. "But I think it's like this, that every family takes care of a sailor's grave – usually it's a dead sailor whom their forefathers found on the beach."

"The Estonian people are a sea people," the Old Sailor lit up another smoke. "And we islanders, traveled everywhere, to the Mediterranean and the Black Sea, even Africa. I'm sure some of them brought back darker girls with them. I mean, nobody is

---

* Paat means 'boat' in Estonian

ever all one thing or all the other," he tapped his cigarette ash in the lid of an old jar, "especially when you live by the sea."

The gentle morning light caressed Kuressaare. It fell upon the trees, the homes, and, most of all, the castle. As Epp and I walked along the harbor towards the castle, I thought about giving everything up and moving to Kuressaare, choosing one of the houses made of stone or wood or glass, it didn't matter, and settling down to raise a brood of little islanders And I would never leave this island! I had fantasies like that wherever we travelled with Epp, though, and the problem was that we were homeless, placeless; we were like gypsies, the possibility to leave was always there, always blinking, flashing, an easy way out, a secret tunnel, an escape hatch. Other people stayed. We left. But still Saaremaa felt safe. I could retire to such a place, I thought; sever all contacts with the outside world. I'd simply leave a note on our apartment door: Gone to Saaremaa. If you need something, you know where to find us.

I knew what Kuressaare castle looked like because it was in one of the old photo albums lying around our apartment in Tallinn. Epp had been here before, with some friends, the whole gang looking like some old U2 poster, with Epp framed by Bono, The Edge, Larry Mullen Jr., and Adam Clayton. There were chunks of gray ice bobbing up in down in the harbor, behind the shapes of Epp and her band mates with their denim jackets and wild hair. The gray ashy snow that blanketed the scene was appropriate, though, because the photos were snapped during the long, dull winter of the nineteen nineties, when it seemed as if history had reached its climax, and the only thing beyond the simmering horizon was the glowing embers of unachievable dreams.

But the castle had been there a long time, and it looked the same, whether in 1993 or 2003, in chilly gray or warm yellow sunlight. Most castles in Estonia were but ruins, destroyed by cannon in some long forgotten war. Walking through the dank, stone, tunnel-like gates into the castle complex you could smell its age from the dark moss on the wall. Still, the Kuressaare castle was whole, its towers capped with roof tiles that still shone red in the sun, it's giant gray facade lacking any visible signs of conflict. Protected by moats and sunlight, it didn't seem real, it was as if some down-on-his-luck Saaremaa mayor acquired one of Ingmar Bergman's sets and had it shipped from Stockholm as a tourist attraction. I would have believed it, had the castle not been so huge. The tiny tourists at its entrance were microscopic, atoms in the shade of antiquity; I stooped down and strained to squeeze the building – if a castle could be called such a mundane word – into one postcard-ready photo.

How did it survive centuries of war? I could only guess that Kuressaare's castle wasn't worth the blowing up. Saaremaa was so boring. There was no reason to even try storming its stronghold, let alone even building it. Maybe Epp was right about the pirates; maybe they really did show up with mandolins instead of swords. And why was the castle even built in the first place, to control the lucrative trade in Saaremaa beer and vodka?

We paid a few kroons to enter the castle and walked into a small courtyard, surrounded on all sides by light gray walls and Swedish tourists. "What's this?" I peered down through a set of metal bars into a crypt in the castle foundation. The underground room was not lit, but in the darkness I could see a skeletal shape slumped back in an old wooden chair, its bones covered in ancient attire: long boots, a cloak.

"Cellar of an immured knight?" Epp said reading a sign, and whispered: "You know what 'immured' means, right?"

"It means they walled him in."

The sign beside the crypt was in four languages: Estonian, Finnish, Russian, and English. In 1785, during the reign of Catherine II, a Russian engineer was drawing up a plan of the castle when he discovered the cellar, it said. In it stood the old table and armchair, and a skeleton, the bones of a Spaniard.

The Spaniard had been dispatched by the Vatican to Kuressaare as an inquisitor to help put down a shift to Protestantism among the local vassals. To test the Spaniard's piety, island rebels brought out their ultimate weapon: a pretty blonde maid. Of course, the Spaniard couldn't resist, the idiot fell in love with her.

When their secret love affair was revealed, the bishop decided that the inquisitor had broken his vows and would have to be immured, walled up in a closed space until he ran out of food, water, and oxygen. And there he sat until he drew his last breath, thinking about the choices he had made in life.

"Looks like I'm not the first foreigner to get stuck in Estonia," I said, looking down at the dummy skeleton.

"That bishop was just an asshole! He didn't have to do it," Epp said after she had read the sign. "He could have just let the Spaniard go back to Rome."

"But he was the bishop of Saaremaa," I sad sadly. "To let him go would have been against his principles."

FROM STUDENT
TO TEACHER

A year after I completed my university education,
I was back in the classroom, this time as a teacher.

Well, not exactly. Unless you consider the cellar of a medieval house in the Old Town of Tallinn a classroom. I had advertised myself as an English teacher in the ads section of a local newspaper and soon I had more private students than I knew what to do with, and I mean that because, with my limited teaching experience I really didn't know what I was doing. That didn't faze me. If Arnold Schwarzenegger could be a politician, I told myself, I could pass as a teacher of the English language. And so, I set out one summery Sunday morning at the end of August, walking with confidence across Tallinn's inspiring Town Hall Square on my way to my first language lesson of this new period of my life.

My first student of the week lived on Pikk Street, an artery of ancient dwellings on the north side of the old city. The medieval buildings glared down at me as I strolled towards the address written in my notebook. I looked back up at them, up high, following their facades to the blue sky. What kinds of people lived here in these magnificent buildings? I always had imagined that the Old Town was the domain of financiers and ambassadors and pimps. But for average people, normal people like Epp and me? What was it like to live in a UNESCO World Heritage site?

I checked the address and details again as I undulated over the old sidewalks. The lad's name was Mats. Age 15. Needs to brush up on his English grammar for a test. His mother Aet had arranged it all. 100 Estonian kroons for 45 minutes of my time. And bring paper and a pen. Mats might forget.

Young Master Mats was in luck that day. Not only did I have a paper and pen for him, I had brought along worksheets on the present simple and present continuous tenses, as well as exercises to test his knowledge of English prepositions, and an article on Californian politics to boost his vocabulary. And could you imagine? Me teaching others? If only my old professors could have seen me.

At precisely 11 am, I located the house on Pikk Street. It was tall and white, a four-storey Hansa skyscraper with soft-looking white stone walls that looked like they had been spackled with pastry dough. Beside its steps lay a closed wooden cellar, its doors painted a regal red. I jogged up the short flight of steps to the large wooden front door and pulled on its enormous bronze handle, but the door wouldn't budge. I looked around. There was no buzzer, no bell; no sign that said: "Welcome." What to do? I pulled out my mobile, a beaten-up, hand-me-down Ericsson, and called the one person who could sort this out.

"Aet kuuleb*."

"Hello?"

"Oh, Jonathan, how wonderful you're here!"

"Jonathan?" I responded, "But my name's..."

Before I could finish, the twin red doors to the cellar beside the steps burst open, and out popped a small woman with golden hair, a maroon shawl draped around her shoulders. "Come on, Jason, come down," she motioned to me. Then she poked her head back into the cellar and boomed: "Mats! He's here! Hurry!"

Aet was like no Estonian woman I had ever met. Like all Estonians, she looked a bit like an elf or dwarf or other fantastic creature, but still pleasant, charming. The fine lines around her blue eyes betrayed her age, but most of the middle-aged Estonian ladies I knew were country women with conservative haircuts who liked to dig up potatoes and watch Eesti Televisioon. Aet was different. She was fashionable, girlish. Her cellar was full of paintings and photographs, not jams and root vegetables.

"Mats should be here any minute," Aet said in a clipped British accent as she welcomed me into the cellar. She had scratchiness, an abrasive quality to her voice that seemed familiar, as if I had heard it before in some old movie. "And, as you can see, we run an art gallery," she tossed a manicured hand into the air, gesturing at the prints that hung from the walls of the cavernous underground room.

I looked at the prints, some color, some black and white, as Aet led me to the back of the silent, dimly lit space, the only

* Literally "Aet listening" in Estonian. It's how most Estonians answer the phone.

MY ESTONIA 2

sounds emanating from her black heels that clicked away on the stone floor. The large fat boulders of the foundation gave way to walls of brick that arched towards the ceiling. The fusion of the soft lighting and the red bricks gave the gallery an orange glow.

"How old is this place?" I asked.

"The house is from the 16th century, it used to belong to a wealthy Danish merchant," Aet said in her film star voice. "But the foundation? We don't know. Maybe 14th century? Just one moment, M A T S!" she screamed into the darkness.

I looked up at an old print of Town Hall Square as we waited. The image must have been 100 years old, but the square had barely changed. I squinted at the price tag. Did that print cost 100 kroons or 1000 kroons?

"Is the gallery your main business?"

"No," Aet replied. "But it's a good business, actually, a wonderful business. You'd be surprised how popular these pictures are. People just come in off the street and buy them, just like that. I'm terribly sorry," she peered into the darkness at the back of the cellar once more. "M A T S!"

"Mother, I'm here, I'm here, please," a young man emerged from the darkness. From where he came, I did not know. Perhaps there was a secret passageway into the house.

"This is my son Mats," Aet introduced us. "Mats, this is Jason, sorry, Jeffrey, your new English tutor."

"Right, how do you?" he said with a British accent and extended his hand. Dressed in a white button-down shirt, Mats was nearly as tall as me, thin and wiry with a long face and crown of long curly brown hair that gave me the impression of a tree in full bloom.

"Pleased to meet you, Mats," I shook his hand. I decided I would reintroduce myself as Justin later.

"How wonderful," Aet looked up at the two of us. "In a few weeks, Mats will have his high school entrance exams and there is an English language part to the test. Mats should be studying, but he needs help, and he sometimes is a little lazy."

Mats yawned.

"Oh, and, before I forget, this," Aet slipped a 100 kroon bill into my hand, my payment for the lesson. "Jeremy, can you come again on Wednesday at the same time?"

"Sure."

"Wonderful. Now I'll leave you two boys alone." And as quickly as she had appeared from the cellar, Aet disappeared into the darkness, the sound of her black heels clicking behind her.

6 6 6

How could it be that I was responsible for filling this young man's head with ideas, with the rules of language? How could it be that he would be relying on me for guidance, to soak up wisdom that would aid him on his quest for high marks? I hadn't been a bad student, but few teachers had inquired about me after I had gone. I never asked why.

The absolute low had come back in Denmark. We had arrived for the study abroad program on a warm August day, a day just like that morning in Tallinn, loaded from the airport into buses and then taken to our campus in the old city for a lunch, where the socially adept quickly began to separate themselves from the maladroit. I fell into the latter category and after a week of trying to secure for myself any kind of solid friendships, a week of the humiliation of trying to appear normal to others, to make small talk, to feign an interest in sports, to conceal the reality that I was an eccentric nutcase, I gave up and turned to beer for companionship instead.

Tuborg became my loyal sidekick, its taste mellow and soothing, like the Baltic Sea at sunset. I could drink gallons of Danish beer; oceans of the stuff. I had an enormous thirst. But I had to go to class. We had to learn about NATO expansion, EU enlargement, the Northern Dimension, the common currency, the four freedoms, and the two very important names we were never to forget: Javier Solana and Jose Manuel Barroso.

One day stood out from the rest. I had an itch in the back of my throat that day, way in the back that only a Tuborg could scratch. I was in northern Europe and Denmark was a permissive place, I reasoned. It was tolerant, free from the Puritanical fevers of my own. Surely Europe would permit me to drink one beer in my EU class?

I bought a bottle from the Turkish-owned convenience store beside the school and when I walked into the classroom, a dry, stale, chalky space on the second floor, I placed the drink on my desk. I would only be in Europe for only one semester and I was going to take full advantage of it. I had taken the first chug and was already feeling a little better when the teacher, a roly-poly Dane with old-fashioned spectacles, enormous cheeks, and a diplomatic background, strode over to my desk and wagged a fat finger in my face.

"Not here," he whispered loudly.

"But I thought Denmark was a permissive place," I protested under my breath. "I thought Europe was more tolerant!"

"It most certainly is, young man," he said with a throaty Danish accent. "But that doesn't mean that you can drink beer in my classroom. Go finish it the hall. Now!"

And so I finished my beer in the dry, stale second-floor hallway, looking out the window at the pretty Danish girls who passed on bicycles, the ringing of their bells echoing up from the street. I lost myself in the moment and finished the Tuborg, tossing the empty in a trashcan. Minutes later, I reentered the classroom, my face flush with alcohol, embarrassment, disgrace. When I opened the door, though, the other students surprised me with cheers. An eruption of applause filled the chalky air.

"Justin Petrone," yelled one of my fellow Americans at the back of the class as he clapped his hands together. "You are one class act!"

"So your name is Jason? Or was it Jeremy?" Mats sat in a pillowed alcove in the cellar, a pen in one hand, a sheet of paper in the other.

"Actually, I'm Justin."

"Oh dear. Just like Justin Timberlake?" Mats studied me with his green eyes. "But, tell me then, Justin, what does it mean, 'Cry me a river?'"

"What? Oh, you mean like in that song?"

Mats nodded.

Even in Estonia, I couldn't get away from Justin Timberlake. Whenever I spelled my name for a bank teller or taxi dispatcher, they had the same response: "Aha! Like Justin Timberlake!" It was inescapable. Timberlake was just there, always there. I imagined that if I tried to flee the pop star, maybe by rowing out into Lake Peipsi in the middle of the night, some old fisherman would still be there with a transistor radio, blaring out one of my namesake's number one hits. And the best part was that nobody even understood what Timberlake was saying. Sometimes I would stand in line at Kaubamaja behind little old ladies, listening to the boyband star coo about his sexual prowess. I found it kind of embarrassing, but Estonia's grandmas didn't seem troubled by Timberlake's pledge to "get them naked by the end of the song."

"Ok," I rubbed my face. "What Timberlake's saying in 'Cry Me a River' is that his girlfriend left him for some other guy."

"Oh dear," Mats chewed on his pen.

"And now she's, like, calling him up all the time, late at night. She says she wants to get back together with him, but Timberlake won't take her back. He says she can just go and cry; cry so much that enough tears will come out to fill a whole river."

"Hmm," Mats reclined in his seat. "So she cries so much that a river comes out. Cry me a river. Brilliant," his face lit up. "I've been trying to figure that one out for months," he said in his drawn out faux British accent.

Mats was a good kid, I determined, likeable, but, like his mother, a little different from the rest. While mother Aet sold antique prints, Mats said his art historian father Jüri was often away in the archives of some museum, trying to determine if a newly discovered snuffbox was baroque or rococo. Mats said he had an older sister "like him" who was studying in Austria. He also had a fun-loving older brother who had a taste for new girlfriends and designer shirts. "I don't even bother learning his girlfriends' names anymore. Every week he's got a new one," Mats sighed and shook his head.

"Really?" I asked. We were supposed to be learning about prepositions, but Mats' family life was more interesting.

"Oh dear, it is true. It's a bit different, really, but," he toyed with his pen, "that's family. What can you do?"

Was Mats really 15? Was he really Estonian? Watching him, talking to him, I felt like I was having tea with some precocious English Lord. Mats even brought me tea from the recesses of the dark cellar. I took mine with milk. He drank his with lemon, his legs crossed, one foot bobbing up and down in the air, as if he was waiting impatiently for a show to begin. According to Mats, he had learned most of his English from watching old James Bond movies ("Sean Connery was the best Bond, in my opinion, but George Lazenby wasn't bad either") and socializing with his parents' friends at the British embassy in Tallinn.

"When I heard you were an American, I almost told my mother not to take you," said Mats, gnawing on his pen, as if it were a pipe. "But your accent is actually quite good. A lot of Americans talk like cowboys, you know."

"You mean you don't want to learn to speak like Bush?"

"Oh dear, no, the British embassy people say they put their fingers in their ears when that man speaks."

"Yeah, I know what you mean," I looked away. "But, ok, what is really bothering you? What do you really need help with?"

"It's these prepositions," Mats banged a hand against his thigh. "We don't have these things in Estonian, you know. They are driving me mad. I don't understand, if I am watching a film, is the film 'on the telly' or 'in the telly' or 'at the telly'. No sense. No sense at all."

Telly. There it was. Once again, the Estonian Mats had cornered me with his British English.

"No, no," I said. "The film is 'on the TV', Mats, on its surface, the screen. At is a place, a location – 'at the TV' is like, 'Hey, Mats, where are you?' 'I'm here, at the TV.'" I folded my arms, pretending to hang out beside a TV set.

"Do people really say that?"

"No. But listen, 'in the TV' means you are actually, physically inside the TV box. So if we took all the stuff out of the TV, all the wires and circuits and everything, and put your head in it, then you'd be in the TV."

"Oh dear," Mats smiled and nibbled on the pen. "I don't suppose I'll be going in the telly any time soon."

Though Aet said her son was a little lazy, I came to feel that he was headed in the right direction. He was open, inquisitive; from Estonia's new generation. He had no memory of the Soviet era. Mats' Estonia had always been free. The sordid stories of the twentieth century were just tall tales to Mats, even if his grandfather August had fallen on the eastern front in 1944. All of it had happened ages ago. It was water under the Narva Bridge. Mats said his best friend was an Estonian Russian named Varennikov who everyone called Vare. "I do hope he changes his name soon," said Mats.

"Why?"

"Because he has to," Young Master Mats' eyes bulged. "I mean Varennikov? You can't get by with a name like that. It's just too long."

"But there are other Russians in Tallinn."

"But he's just Vare. That's who he is. That's what he's called. It's not like I am against minorities, or something, not at all," Mats folded his arms. "I want more of them, actually. Tallinn should be a global city, like London, you know, with all kinds of people."

I decided not to press him. Mats seemed confident in his opinions. I could see him ascending the ranks, moving swiftly from high school student to foreign minister to president of the republic. He would reverse Estonia's conservative migration policies and fill the city's empty lots with bustling bazaars and falafel shops and Bollywood shows. Though he was only 15, some part of me actually believed he could do it.

Towards the end of the lesson, Mats quizzed me on my Estonian. "14 cases," he smiled. "Difficult isn't it?"

"There is this one thing I can't say," I confessed.

"What? *Jäääär*? *Jüriöö ülestõus**?" his eyes brightened.

"No, not those. It's the words for 'Town Hall Square.' I can never get it right. Raeko... Raeko..."

"*Raekoja plats*?" the soup of vowels and consonants slipped from his tongue.

"Yeah. That."

"You mean you can't say it? But it's easy."

---

* "On the edge of the ice" and "St. George's Night Uprising" in Estonian.

"Rae. Rae-ko...," I tried.

"No, no. *Raekoja plats.*"

"Rae-ko-ja," I tried.

"Plats, plats," Mats chewed the pen and rocked his feet impatiently on the floor. "It's easy. *Raekoja plats.*"

"*Raekoja plats?*"

"Precisely," he smiled and crossed his legs. "Let's see if you can still remember how to say it on Wednesday morning!"

As Wednesday dawned, I rushed to photocopy Mats lessons at Epp's office in the Publishing House. It was just minutes before my lesson was supposed to start, and I was sweating, hyperventilating, running off the hot copies before tucking them into my bag. Then I took off, down the elevator, through the lobby, out the door, sprinting all the way from the office on Maakri Street across central Tallinn to the Viru Gate, and beyond it the Old City, up the sidewalks past the De La Gardie shopping center, past the Olde Hansa girls out selling roasted almonds, through the tongue-twisting *Raekoja Plats* where a rabble of British stag partygoers was busy playing an early-morning football match. I stopped a moment to catch my breath, then tore down Pikk Street, overcoming the early morning cruise ship tourists and their expensive cameras, almost knocking some of them over, past the Russian embassy, then the Swedish one, running or walking quickly the whole way, my feet bending and stretching over the uncomfortable cobblestones, moisture dripping from my forehead, doing everything I could so as not to be late. I didn't want to be late that morning, I couldn't be late, not only because it was rude in Estonia to be late, but because it reminded me of the person I used to be, the person I still was, the person I could never escape.

Tardiness was a central problem in my life. It all came down to some instinctive belief that anything could be accomplished in five minutes. Write an article, make it to an appointment across town, or prepare a gourmet meal, it could all be done in that amount of time. Five minutes. It seemed like an eternity, a galaxy of opportunities to get things done. It was not just one minute capsule of 60 seconds, I thought, but five distinct installations. Five minutes. I tried to pass it off as an inheritance from my Mediterranean forebears, but it was easy to blame it on the Italians rather than assume responsibility for the "problem" myself. And even though I was always late, I continued to believe in the possibility of five enormously long minutes.

"I can always tell when you decide to come to class, Justin," the voice of my old journalism professor Berg rang in my ears as I jogged down Pikk Street. "I can hear the door close behind me five minutes after I start my lecture."

Berg was a seasoned newsman, a media icon who had his first bylines when Eisenhower was still president. He was also my advisor in our journalism department in Washington, DC. I had spent four years down there in the capital of the United States of America, cornered by the World Bank and the White House and the State Department and the Potomac River, a resentful face in a crowd of egomaniacs, a foolish dissident swamped by budding politicians and diplomats and international bankers and human rights activists and other salty barnacles on the foundering ark of human irrelevance. And as much as Berg saw me as a nuisance, I still felt that he cared about me in his own seasoned newsman way, even if I was consistently five minutes late to his lecture, on the days I chose to attend.

"What's this? 'History of the Cold War?' 'European Union Politics?' These courses actually look interesting," Berg said wearily one April afternoon as he looked over my undergraduate coursework, preparing to sign off on my graduation application packet. "'Russian Past and Present,' 'The Scandinavian Welfare State' —You like this stuff?"

"Well, yeah," I said, my eyes drifting to the framed photo of Berg and his poker buddy US Supreme Court Justice Antonin Scalia that sat on his desk.

"Hmm," Berg snorted and pushed his dark glasses up his nose and looked over the application once more.

I crossed my legs and tried to relax, but I couldn't. Without Berg's approval I would stay in school. He was my advisor, my gatekeeper. My future lay in one swift stroke of his fountain pen. If he so wished, I could be stuck in the journalism program in Washington forever.

"Well, are you going to do it?" I asked after another minute had passed.

"Am I going to do what?" he croaked from behind the application form.

"Sign it?"

"Oh, of course I am going to sign it, Justin!" Berg cried out, and from his conservative, judicious, seasoned newsman mouth erupted a rare laugh, a volcanic plume of delight, one that not only filled his office, but echoed down the corridor. "Do you think I really want you to stay here? To have you in my class? Again?" I saw his stomach heave beneath his brown suit as he sought to restrain his laughter. "Oh no," he shook his head. "No, no, no. As of this May, you are going 'bye bye.'" Berg quickly scribbled his signature of approval on the application. "Then you can become somebody else's problem. Not mine."

"Thank you, sir," I said as he handed me the papers.

Berg snorted and replaced the cap on his fountain pen.

"Oh dear, don't tell me you ran here," Mats greeted me at the foot of the cellar.

"Could I get something to drink," I panted, out of breath.

"Of course," Mats said and turned, leading me deeper into the gallery. "You know, it's ok if you are a few minutes late."

The cellar was lit more brightly that morning than it had been a few days before. The cool harbor breeze blew down from the street and aired out the family's art gallery.

"You must be Jeffrey," said a gruff voice from a dark corner of the gallery, "Mats' new English teacher?"

"I am," I said and turned to see the origin of the gravely voice, the man in the corner, tall and lanky, just like Mats, but older and dressed in a casual, dark-green sweater and trousers that did little to conceal his long, stork-like legs. As he came into the light, I noticed the man's face was like Mats, too, but still different, older, sugared with a white mustache and framed by tufts of white hair that held a hint of strawberry blonde.

"Actually, my name is Justin," I told the old gentleman.

"And I am Jüri," his eyebrows leaped up and then settled back into place. "Mats' father. Come, come, sit down."

Jüri and I sat opposite one another in the alcove at the back of the gallery while we waited for Mats to arrive with something to drink. I studied his face, trying to place his age. He did not seem especially old, though there was something strange about the way he wore his hair, the bangs cut straight across his forehead, sloping down to cover the ears, like a knight from the Crusades.

"So, Jeffrey, are you from London?" Jüri squinted at me in the cellar light.

"I'm actually from New York." The flatness of my American accent surprised me when I said it, as if it belonged to someone else.

"Yes, well, everyone is learning English these days," Jüri's eyebrows leaped again. "Some people want to make it the official language of Tallinn. They say our language is too old fashioned. That we have to be new and modern and speak English."

"But this is Estonia. That would make no sense."

"I agree, it's a silly idea," Jüri smiled, his mustache arching upward in a sign of contentment and when I looked at him with his odd haircut and timeless face, something seemed familiar, as if I had met him before. "I speak Finnish, Russian, German, and French," Jüri said. "I mean when you work with archival materials you have to know at least several languages. And I have studied Latin and Ancient Greek. But Mats teases me. He says my English isn't so good."

Again I felt as if I knew him, but how? Then the image of Vana Toomas, appeared, Vana Toomas, the protector of Tallinn, a 16th century weathervane modeled after the city guard that stood atop the Town Hall on the hard-to-pronounce *Raekoja Plats*. I had even seen an Estonian psychedelic cult classic from the seventies where said Vana Toomas came to life backed by a rock ensemble dressed like bunnies with electric guitars. I could never forget Vana Toomas' face. And here he was again, in the flesh.

"Jüri," I looked across at him. "You look just like..."

"Like who?"

"Father, don't even open your mouth!" Mats returned holding a tray with a glass of water and two cups of tea.

"That's our Mats," Jüri looked up at his son. "See how he treats me?"

"Please excuse my father, his English is terrible," Mats faked a look of disappointment as he lowered the tray onto a small table. "And father, remember what mother said."

"Right, Jason was it?" Jüri pulled his wallet from a back pocket.

"Justin, Father," Mats corrected him. "Like Justin Timberlake."

"Oh, yes, I see," Jüri winked to me to show he had never heard the name. "Well, Mr. Timberlake, here you go," Jüri slipped another 100-kroon note into my hands. "Aet told me to ask if you could come again on Friday."

"Sure."

"Good. Mats needs practice."

I filed the money quickly away in a side compartment of my bag, so that the evidence of my financial relationship with this family would soon be forgotten. I didn't want Mats to wonder why I was being paid to talk with him about his brother's girlfriends or his opinions on cultural diversity.

"Very good, father," Mats smirked to the old man after the business transaction was completed. "Now you can leave."

I learned a lot about his family's history that day. They hadn't always lived in a Hansa mansion on Pikk Street, Mats said. Instead, Jüri and Aet had once lived in an apartment in Tallinn's dreary Mustamäe district. And when the family finally did scrape together enough money to move on up to the Old Town, it was in the late eighties and the ancient city wasn't exactly the kind of place you wanted to take your family.

"Father says that the buildings were run down, the windows boarded up," Mats said, sipping his tea. "He said it used to hurt him to see how the old historical homes were unappreciated and mistreated, that there was graffiti everywhere. It was a dangerous place."

"You're kidding me." I strained to imagine the Old Town with its gourmet restaurants and beauty salons and boutiques in the state that Mats described.

"Even I remember it," Mats said. "It wasn't so long ago. But," he yawned, "things are always getting better. Next year we should be in the EU, can you believe it, Estonia in the EU?

But it will happen," he sipped his tea again, "if the idiots don't screw things up."

"You think people might vote against joining?"

"Have you seen some of the flyers out there? There's one that says the Soviet Union is the same as the European Union. Then there is another that says there is the same number of letters in 'Soviet Union' as there is in "European Union."

I counted in my head. "But that's not true."

"That doesn't matter!" Mats wrinkled his nose in disgust. "Estonia does have its share of lunatics, you know, like any other country I suppose."

Our lecture went on, me explaining the dull intricacies of the English language to the gifted student, he explaining everything else to me. And over time, as Mats spoke, I began to feel sharp pangs inside my chest. He still had the confidence of youth, I noticed; there was a silent hum to him, a vibration. Mats was going places, and while Mats climbed the ranks, I imagined myself falling down, slipping through the cracks in the cellar floor, or even worse, reaching a plateau, stagnating, staying here in Tallinn, giving lessons on prepositions indefinitely, writing news stories about rebranding campaigns, going nowhere, repeating the same actions over and over again until they became a muscle memory, a routine, and I didn't even have to think about doing it anymore.

"So?" Mats asked. "Can you say it?"

"Oh what? *Raekoja Plats*?"

"See!" he laughed. "I told you it was easy. But is there anything else? Anything you need help with?"

"There's always *otsima*, *ostma*, and ot-sus-ta-" I rolled my eyes.

"*Otsustama*. To decide," Mats sipped his tea. "But those are easy. I mean, *otsima* is *otsima*, and *ostma* is *ostma*, not *otsustama**."

"Right."

"Like I said, it's easy. Much easier than awful prepositions. Much easier than French." Mats stuck his tongue out as if he had sunk his teeth into a bitter lemon.

"You are also studying French?"

"And Russian and German," he sighed. "But French, gross," he stuck his tongue out again. "That is the absolute worst. Do you speak French, Justin?" It seemed Mats would need a French tutor too.

"No," I looked at my shoes. "No French."

What did I speak? A little Danish, a little Spanish, some Estonian, maybe a handful of phrases from various other tongues. But I probably had more to learn from Mats than I did to teach him. And I envied Mats that morning. He was only nine years younger than me and seemed to be fresh, full of life. I felt old and used; like a mold settling into place.

---

* Otsima is 'to seek,' ostma is 'to buy,' and otsustama is 'to decide.' (In Estonian)

"SPRINGTIME" IN ESTONIA

I looked out from the eighth floor of the Olümpia Hotel with my trousers around my knees, a young doctor named Parts cradling my nakedness in her hand.

"Cough," she instructed. I stared out at the gray mist and the white sky, the tall buildings and the dark trees and beyond them the waters of the Gulf of Finland, and I coughed. Her cold hands then moved upwards and pushed at my lower abdomen, then retreated to her sides.

"You can put your pants back on," she said and in a second I buckled my belt and it was as if our whole little moment of intimacy in the sky never happened. Besides, I went to visit Doctor Parts because I felt ill. It was my first visit and that warranted an on-the-spot physical examination.

"It's like I said. We got the cat, and the cat had fleas," I told the doctor as she returned to her seat, tossing her long, brown hair over her shoulder, adjusting the sleeves on her blue scrubs. She was an attractive, round woman, Doctor Parts, but still a doctor and an Estonian one at that, which meant she had little interest in getting to know me.

"Then we got the cat medicine and that's when it started: the fevers, the back pain."

"I am going to write you a prescription," Parts said, looking at me briefly with dark blue eyes. "But have you ever been allergic to cats before?"

"No."

"Then I don't think it's the cat," she said. "You probably just have some kind of infection."

"Infection?"

Doctor Parts shrugged and handed me the paper and stood to see me out. In the doorway I asked her a question, something I had been waiting to ask. It was inappropriate, given the circumstances, but Epp and I had rehearsed it in Estonian that morning and I couldn't give up now.

"Doctor Parts?"

She looked up at me.

"Is Juhan Parts your brother?"

"No, he's not," she managed a smile, pulling the rubber gloves from her hands. "But you are not the first person to ask me this question." With that, she tossed her long hair over her shoulder again and returned to her office.

The cat connected me to Prime Minister Juhan Parts in some cosmic way. Estonia's thirty-something leader also had a kitten up in his office in Stenbock House, a ball of fur that nestled at his feet as he weighed new options to get his countrymen to say yes to joining the European Union in the coming referendum. And they had to say yes. If they didn't both Parts and the cat would probably have to find new work.

People said Parts took on the cat to soften his image. It caused a national debate, of course. "Some people think he should have taken a dog because dogs are more loyal and friendly and cats are too unpredictable and independent," Epp had informed me. "But maybe the cat is more appropriate. I mean Parts kind of looks like a cat." Did he really? At a glance, he looked like any other young conservative politician, with a clean-shaven face and a haircut you could set your watch to. But upon closer inspection Parts was a little different. The man's head was almost permanently cocked to one side, as if he was straining to hear a distant PowerPoint presentation. Behind his trademark squint was determination, order, respect, but little obvious empathy. Parts was an austere Evangelical Lutheran pastor of a prime minister, the man who supposedly had the flashy new computers in his office replaced with more generic ones because the existing high-tech systems were "not plain enough" for the Estonian people.

Parts' dedication to moderation, his battle cry to 'choose order' had won him the election. Still, his quirkiness began to irk even the Estonians after a while. So Parts' kitten was received as a pure PR play. Even if Estonia's leader wasn't exactly adorable, at least he had a cute pet, right?

But what about our new pet cat? She arrived in a different way. I had told my new friend Benny all about it as he drove me home the afternoon before I got sick.

"You said you have a new pet?" Benny asked, one hand on the steering wheel to his silver convertible, another hand dangling a cigarette along the door as he drove towards the city center.

"I came home and Epp – that's my wife's name – she took me down to the basement of our building. She said she found the kitten in the corridor and wanted to take her in, that if we didn't, someone might send it to sea school."

"Sea school?" Benny lowered his shades to look me in the eyes. "Don't tell me they have schools for cats in Estonia."

"You know, drown it in a bucket. Euthanasia."

"Shit," he pushed the shades back up his nose and returned his gaze to the road. "This whole country is crawling with homeless cats. Actually, the same thing happened to me and Mari – that's my girlfriend – recently. Now we have a little kitten. Adorable. Name's Miisu."

"That's our cat's name too!"

"Shit." Benny took a drag from his cigarette. "Mari says that half of all cats in Estonia are named Miisu."

"What's the other half called?"

"The other half," he exhaled, "is called 'Nurr."

"I think there's a chocolate bar called 'Nurr."

"There is indeed. There are also candies called Miisu," said Benny. "And there is Kitty candy too."

"I know that one. It's got a picture of a cat on the cover. The candies are kind of soft, beige. They look like some kind of cat food. Epp can eat a whole box."

"If you haven't noticed, the Estonians are a little weird when it comes to cats."

I studied Benny as our car rolled past furniture shops on Pärnu Road. To me, he was the embodiment of the Western businessman, the freshly cut gray hair, the tanned skin, the sunglasses, the cigarette, the face clean of any whiskers. At the same time he was inherently Swedish. There was a long, lilting wave to his English, and something ponderous and woodsy about his manners, as if his grandfather had felled trees for a living.

"Hey, Benny, what do they call cats in Sweden?" I asked after some time, the wind tossing about my hair as the convertible motored along.

"Well, remember, it is Sweden," Benny cleared his throat. "And in Sweden we call cats whatever the state tells us to call them." He chuckled a bit when he said it. Then he let out another puff of cigarette smoke.

🌢 🌢 🌢

I had met Benny at a hotel in the Old Town. He was interviewing young professionals for a project that had been advertised in the back of the week's paper. What the job exactly entailed, I did not know, but because the ad was so vague, it seemed interesting, like it might have some connection with intelligence work. Plus it was run by Swedes, all of whom, as everyone in Estonia knew, were rich. That meant the job might pay. We made the appointment by e-mail, and I arrived at reception at noon.

The receptionist ushered me into an unlit ballroom near the lobby where I was seated at a lone desk. Across from me sat three northerners, two male, one female; all blue eyed, all blond, all silent. No one shook hands. The interview simply started. The one on the left introduced himself as Benny, and he began to narrate a presentation about the project that he was undertaking, an attempt to build a network of "specialists" in Tallinn, a sort of crack squad of local mercenaries for Swedish entrepreneurs. Who was I? What were my talents? These were the things that Benny wanted to know. While we spoke, the others quietly took notes. At the end, I was invited to Benny's office on the outskirts of Tallinn. There I would meet the other mercenaries for the first time.

The next meeting took place three days later in the back office of the Estonian headquarters of a multinational transport company. The air smelled of rubber, the walls were covered by posters of trucks. I was rocked by internal waves of alienation the second I stepped through the door. Never had I ever aspired to be in such a place. I couldn't have cared less about tires or trucks, shipping or logistics. How of all scenarios had I been sorted to this one place at this one time? Yet if they had asked me to do something and promised a financial reward, I would have said yes. For how was writing about transport any different from writing about branding campaigns or from teaching teenagers about prepositions? It was all work, work and money, money that I, as an expectant father, thought I desperately needed.

The meeting room was well lit and modern. Benny poured coffee and talked. I was the only American there, which made me feel special. The others were mostly Estonians. They wanted to hear me mangle their language, so I tried a few sentences on them, like a trained bear. When I was done with my "foreigner who can speak some Estonian act" they were pleased and gave me the anticipated "did you know that some people have been living here for 50 years and still can't say one word?" routine. Like clockwork. At the end of the meeting, I still had no idea what the project was about. But I was not the boss. Benny was the mastermind. He said our team was off to a good start, and rewarded each one of us with a copy of Robbie Williams' new disc *Escapology*. Then he offered to drive me home, and we listened to the British pop singer croon about his desire to "feel real love" on the drive back into Tallinn.

I really wanted to believe that Robbie wanted to feel real love, but I didn't believe him. I suspected he was a bit of a liar, just like me. I didn't write about what I cared about, and Robbie probably didn't sing about what was on his mind. Maybe Benny actually didn't care about transport either. We were all in it for the money, for the money and for the illusion of a better future. Lying to ourselves was the fare we paid to board the express train to success. There was no shame in it, though. It was like my father had told me. Before my return to Estonia, the old man took me aside in New York, a hand on my shoulder and said, "Son, you're going to be a father soon and that means you are going to have to develop a hunger for money. You must be hungry for money. And no matter how much you earn, you should always be hungry for more." I had stood there nodding, eyes shut, searching every nerve in my belly, trying to feel the hunger.

And so to suit whoever it was that was willing to pay, I figured I should be willing to lie a little, to feign enthusiasm, all to feed this bottomless hunger that I was expected to have. Besides, journalism had kind of been a lie for me too. To get into the program at school I had padded my essay with earnest idealism, with references to my desire to better society and to spread the American way. The damn thing was so baked in bullshit I almost believed it. But it was, in its own way, not true. I didn't want to be some stuffy old news man. I wanted to be a gonzo journalist, like Hunter S. Thompson. But you couldn't say that in your application. You couldn't tell them what was in your heart.

Writing had always been an act, but I had learned to act well enough that people believed I knew what I was doing. If I kept it up though, I imagined that at some point, I would cross over, stop acting and simply become that what I had pretended to be. Maybe I would come to enjoy writing about transport.

I looked at Benny as he drove. Maybe he was once like me. Maybe he had crossed over long ago. I wondered if he had ever pondered such things, but he was too new an acquaintance to ask.

"How long have you been in Estonia?" I inquired from my new Swedish friend.

"Since the beginning; I was here in 1992. Or was it still 1991? Shit, you'll have to forgive me. I'm 53. My memory is like Swiss cheese."

"What was it like then?"

"In 1992? Oh it was a totally different country. It was just," he peered ahead into traffic. "Gray. Everything was gray or brown."

"Are you happy that you live here? Not in Sweden?"

"Shit, Justin," Benny raised an eyebrow. Maybe the question was too personal for a Scandinavian. "Sure, I am happy. I live with Mari, she takes good care of me, and we just built a new house in outskirts of Tallinn. Business is good. Life is good. I mostly like Estonia."

"Mostly?"

"There are only three things I hate about Estonia: the traffic, the so-called 'salads,' where you don't even see the salad due to all the sour cream, and the *'ma ei tea'* * attitude."

"The *'ma ei tea'* attitude?"

"You ask a guy a question, he answers, *'Ma ei tea.'* The other guys you ask just shrug and tell you the same thing. I mean, if you don't know the answer and he doesn't know the answer, then who the heck knows the answer?"

"Ma ei tea," I said, "but I do agree with you about the salads."

"The so-called cuisine here is a little off. I remember there was a Swedish Estonian family that lived in the flat below ours in Stockholm when I was a kid and they would always be cooking something awful. The stink would rise through the air vents. I've asked Mari what it was, but she doesn't know."

"You mean war refugees?"

"It was the fifties. There were a bunch of Estonian families on our block. But there were also Estonian Swedes around. They were different. These are Swedes from the Estonian west coast; they had been living here for a thousand years or something wild like that, before they evacuated in '44. Some stayed behind. Some have come back. Mari's got some Swedish

---

* I don't know. (In Estonian)

blood in her, you know. She took me down there some years back to pay a visit to a couple of relatives of hers."

"To where?"

"A place called Noarootsi. It's a tiny little place on the west coast. It was an old couple I met and I was totally stunned when they started to speak Swedish to me, I mean the way they spoke Swedish – it was kind of the same way I can hear people speak in old, black-and-white Swedish movies from the 1930s."

"Cool."

Benny took a drag from his cigarette. "And entering their house, the living room walls were totally covered with pictures of the Swedish king and queen and their kids. If they knew we were coming they would probably have put up the Swedish flag outside as well. Some of the houses have even got this typical Swedish red color on the exterior. Most of the road signs are in Estonian and Swedish. And Swedish noises are quite frequently heard at beaches there, I mean Swedes love the beaches here in Estonia. We just don't have sandy beaches like that in Sweden, and if we did, shit, there would be nine million people trying to squeeze into one tiny strip of land..."

A few moments later, the silver convertible, its new tires glistening in the sun, pulled up beside the metal gate that guarded the entrance to the American Embassy on Kentmanni Street.

"This is as far as I can go," he gestured at the gate. "But we should meet again. Soon."

"My wife and me, we are actually going to Stockholm and Oslo next week, after the European Union referendum," I told him. "Maybe we can meet there."

"I actually haven't been in Stockholm for two years," Benny said. "But it's a beautiful city. I grew up there. So say hello to it from me."

Two mornings later, I was watching the morning news in bed waiting for my medicine to kick in and take away whatever it was our new little friend Miisu had given me. Neither of us knew how old the scrawny black kitten with the soft white underbelly was, but it was definitely an urban cat, nervous and neurotic, with a habit for relieving itself in the most unlikely of places that quickly gained her the nickname Miisu "Shitty Paws" Petrone.

Our new scatter-brained family member caused such commotion at night that we decided to lock Miisu in the bathroom for the duration with some food and a litter box. Maybe it was a little cruel, but we had rescued her from getting terminated in someone's water bucket. Not that we knew who might do a deed like that in our apartment building. We had lived there for seven months and never even said so much as 'Tere' to our neighbors. Each morning, Epp would open up the bathroom door and proclaim loudly in two languages: "*Vabadus kassidele!* – Freedom for cats!" And little Shitty Paws would race down the corridor, bumping into furniture, happy to be free from her cell, perhaps even more screwed up than she was the night before.

Miisu lounged at my feet that morning, licking her shitty paws. It was a cool, gray day, and autumn had fallen on the city of Tallinn. The wind toyed with our white linen curtains through the half open window. Inside the television announcer spoke emotionlessly about the day's two main news items.

The first was the coming European Union referendum. In two days, Estonians would be asked to vote on joining Europe and the campaigns for and against this important step had become more bizarre, outlandish, and absurd as the day of reckoning arrived. In saner moments, when they weren't invoking numerology and astrology, the opponents asked why Estonia needed to join another union so soon after it left the previous one. Besides, the economy was growing faster than the EU average, the cruise ships packed the harbor with tourists, the real estate market was booming; adopting EU norms might slow the tiger down, they said. Estonia was like Norway, Iceland: a northern dynamo ahead of the pack. The EU obviously needed Estonia, they concluded, more than Estonia needed the EU.

In the Yes camp stood almost every single major Estonian politician of the past decade and a half. Former Prime Minister Siim Kallas told the people that if they didn't vote to join the EU, Estonia would be relegated to the geopolitical position of Finland in the Cold War, always forced to serve two masters, one in the West, the other in the East, with any premier in Tallinn playing the undesirable role of Estonia's Urho Kekkonen*, twisting himself into a diplomatic pretzel just to maintain sovereignty over his land.

---

* Urho Kekkonen was President of Finland at the height of the Cold War, from 1956 to 1982.

Posters paid for by Parts' Res Publica Party were less dour. One promised Estonian women access to "millions of sexier men," who were supposedly hard up, waiting across the Baltic Sea for some Estonian girls to come along and spice up their lives, so long as they were European citizens. Another poster made the choice jarringly clear. It read: "Is Russia Our Friend?" And below it listed all the wars in which Russians had fought for control of Estonian soil. This supposedly was put up to mobilize the ethnic Estonian vote behind the EU, but some of the Estonian Russians were offended by these posters. It was hard for them to conceive of their nation of origin as anything other than friendly.

I didn't dare discuss the poster with Ivan at the office. The whole Estonian-Russian issue was a minefield and my colleague, while a sharp and dispassionate writer, seemed a bit pricklier when it came to the topic. "Russia wasn't the only foreign country to invade Estonia, you know," he said once in passing, the words thick with meaning, and I turned the sentence over in my head a few times, trying to figure out what exactly he had meant to tell me. In the end, I had to agree with Ivan. It was true that Russian armies had marched across Estonian soil numerous times, sometimes as victorious conquerors, but hadn't there been other foreign armies fighting against the Russians in each one of those conflicts, sometimes Danes, sometimes Poles, sometimes Germans, and quite a few times Benny's Swedish compatriots?

Yet, somehow, the slogan "Is Sweden Our Friend?" didn't have the same sinister ring to it as "Is Russia Our Friend?" In fact, I could imagine Benny and me, driving around Tallinn, joking about such a sign. "Shit," Benny might say with a trace of a smile on his lips, "all old Swedish farts like me know that Riga was once the biggest city in the Swedish empire." But I couldn't make such jokes with Ivan, probably because him and Benny were just totally different people, but also because the wounds were fresh. It had been almost 300 years since the armies of Sweden trekked across Estonian soil. The last Russian troops had departed the country in 1994.

Even though the Soviets had run Estonia for almost 50 years, and the Russians for 200 years before that, the second news item reported on our old TV set affected me more than anything happening in Moscow. The Swedish Foreign Minister Anna Lindh died that morning, and her murder cast a somber shroud of sadness over the already overcast city of Tallinn. Though she had died across the sea, there was something tangible about her death. With her straightforward demeanor, blonde hair and smart glasses, Lindh could have been the Estonian foreign minister, the footage of the Stockholm mall where she had been stabbed could have been taken in downtown Tallinn.

The Estonian news showed photos of Lindh in the Estonian capital, buying pizza with then Estonian Foreign Minister Toomas Hendrik Ilves at a cafe the year before. It was the same cafe where Epp and I had bought pizza on my first day in Tallinn. Lindh and I had eaten pizza from the same oven in the same year! Our lives shared the same stage. Everything about Lindh's murder was palpable to me because of the increased symmetry between Tallinn and Stockholm. While still very different, the Swedish capital had become mentally closer to Estonia since 1991, while Moscow had drifted farther away.

"When my younger brother Aap had summer vacation a few years ago, I gave him a choice: we could go visit Novgorod or Stockholm together," Epp had said to me. "He said that Sweden sounded kind of boring, but Russia was more exotic. I was really surprised. When I was his age, there was nothing exotic about Russia, and Sweden was just unapproachable." In little over a decade, Russia had gone from familiar to exotic, and Sweden from unapproachable to boring. For average Estonians, with their Swedish-owned banks and Swedish-owned telecommunications firms and Swedish-owned TV channels, Sweden had become less and less foreign. Meantime, the border between Estonia and Russia, a nation that had been pummeled all year by suicide bombings in both Chechnya and Moscow, seemed more significant.

At its most basic level, I thought as I scrubbed the fur behind Miisu's ears, the EU referendum was a political decision. At some gut level, though, it was another way for the Estonians to keep up with the neighbors. Sweden had been Estonia's biggest investor since independence was restored. As Benny himself said, he had been there since 1992, if not 1991. The Swedes and Finns had acceded to the union in 1995, the same year Estonia applied to join. It was almost as if Estonia and its EU member neighbors Sweden and Finland had been in a common law marriage since that time. By voting to join the same union, the Estonians were merely making the relationship official.

🌢 🌢 🌢

Ivan was grumpy on the night of the referendum, his foul mood perhaps caused by the fact that he would be expected to write his story for *The Baltic Times* after the results were reported at 10 PM. His sourpuss was later reinforced by what the Latvian said.

The press center in the Estonian Foreign Ministry that night buzzed with foreign journalists. The brightly lit room was filled with the sounds of keyboards clacking and writers joking. The aroma of freshly brewed coffee hung in the air. To my right sat Ivan. To my left sat a gentleman from *The Copenhagen Post,* Peter by name tag, tall and angular with hair in his face, looking like a Scandinavian Beatle, typing away at his computer. Across the table I saw the Russian correspondent from *ITAR-TASS* mumbling into his cell phone, a scruffy beard on his face, his black cap still on, cloaked in a long trenchcoat, looking like a spy. What will he write? I wondered. How will he manage to spin this? We all sat before the press center's computer screens, impatient for the referendum results to come in. The room was thick with writers. I could barely move my elbows. And I felt extremely important. I was a foreign correspondent in a foreign capital poised to write about genuine foreign news. This was what I had wanted, wasn't it?

"You know, you can go home," Ivan said to me in his characteristic monotone as we waited.

"But the results haven't even come in yet," I said.

"I am the only one who is going to write this story. There is no need for you to be here tonight."

"But I want to be here. This, this is history," I protested. "And I can help you with the article. I can. That way you can get it done faster."

The first results had now started to trickle in on the National Electoral Committee's website and the buzz in the press center had grown louder. Most people thought the Estonians would said yes, though polls earlier in the year had shown lukewarm support for joining the EU. And no matter which way the vote came down, readers would want to know who had said yes, who had said no, and what the margin between them was. As I refreshed the committee's webpage, I noticed that the Ida Virumaa vote was tighter than the rest of the counties and Ida Virumaa was the most Russian county in Estonia. Perhaps the "Is Russia Our Friend?" campaign had backfired there.

"You know what," Ivan said and yawned as he looked at the vote tallies. "I suppose I could let you write a paragraph or two. But it's got to be really good, it will be on the front page of tomorrow's paper."

"Wait, did you guys say you write for *The Baltic Times*?" a tall blonde woman interrupted us from across the table. She had long, curving, pleasant features, looks I associated with Slavic women, and she wore a black pantsuit that looked more suitable for television than print. I couldn't read her name from across the table, but I managed to make out the word below it, *Diena*, which meant she was from one of Latvia's largest dailies.

"Yeah, we work for *The Baltic Times*," I answered her. "So what?"

"Heh," she tossed her golden hair back haughtily. "That newspaper sucks."

From behind his spectacles, Ivan Spengler, the young head of *The Baltic Times*' Estonian office, grimaced but said nothing. Sitting beside him, though, I felt his small body vibrate with inner rage. I also said nothing to the Latvian at first, but inside I thought severe, malevolent thoughts: I hope Latvians vote their referendum down next week. I hope they never join the EU.

"*The Baltic Times* doesn't suck," I managed to say.

"Yes it does," the Latvian beauty said and slurped down a plastic cup of coffee, pausing to wipe the moisture from her lips with a manicured hand. "I mean no one reads it. No one buys it. It's the suckiest, shittiest paper in the region."

At that, I looked away and refreshed my computer screen. The words from Riga hurt, but they were also kind of true. It's not that there weren't good people on staff at our newspaper. Gary, the American editor, was something of a hero having once worked in Russian papers in Kaliningrad. Tim, the British second in command, was a likeable chap who refused to believe that men in Estonia did not end their names in the letter 'S', like all men in Latvia do. Latvian men had names like Ivars and Pēteris and Kārlis, so Tim would ring us up on mornings before deadlines and ask to speak to 'Ivans' and 'Justins' about the status of pending articles. We would always correct him, and tell him that things in Estonia were different, but he would always forget.

I liked Tim and respected Gary. Beyond those two, though, was a mystery. Supposedly the owner was a retired Dane. An Odessa-born Jew was also involved. There were murky stories about the paper's financiers and different names at the top of the newspaper masthead, but I had no personal connection with those names. If I ever asked about them, Ivan would attempt to explain the complex, anonymous forces behind *The Baltic Times*, but I never quite grasped the paper's inner workings.

And we didn't exactly break news. We had our moments, but it was weekly, and week in and week out, I wrote up second-hand stories in English, stealing hooks and ideas from the local papers and marketing them as my own, like knock-off "Rayban" sunglasses or "Gucci" bags. Besides it paid comparatively so little that I jested to Ivan that the only reason it was still in business was because it relied on a steady stream of wandering expat writers like me, kids who would come and stay for a year or two in Tallinn or Riga or Vilnius and obtain a job at the proper-sounding paper to make their sojourns look legitimate to the people back home.

But was it really the "suckiest, shittiest paper in the region?" Probably not. Besides Gary and Tim, the paper also had Ivan and me, and we were journalists of the highest caliber, weren't we?

"Here take this and keep your fingers crossed," a young man with glasses handed me a crimson flag with a stripe of white down the middle. He was stocky and blond and his name tag said he was from *Latvijas Avīze*. I cautiously eyed the flag of the Latvian Republic in my hand, and twirled it around in the press center light.

"Our referendum is next week and the opinion polls don't look good," said the Latvian journalist. "We need all the luck we can get." There was a touch of humor in his voice, but also desperation too, and when I looked at the flag again I hoped that I hadn't jinxed Latvia's EU membership by thinking bad thoughts about his country. I also hoped that no one had cursed Estonia in a similar way.

At approximately 11 pm, two men – one old, one young – entered the press center's packed auditorium. Others may have been with them, but my eyes, and maybe everyone else's, were on the two dark suits.

The large room, filled with the Estonian press and representatives from news outlets across Europe, had been noisy, chaotic, warm and sweaty, its center a nest of video cameras and tripods, the air spiked by the hands of pushy reporters, each carrying a Dictaphone. But the room grew silent as the men took their seats, and when they did, I recognized them to be the highest-ranking Estonians in the land. To the left sat President Arnold Rüütel, his well-tended mane of silver hair glistening in the light, a look of vacant contentment on his handsome, soap-opera worthy face. To the right sat Prime Minister Juhan Parts, his square head cocked to one side, his smart squint magnified by his glasses, his square shoulders like boulders beneath his jacket.

When Rüütel was 12 years old, Estonia had been forced into another union, a Soviet Union, and in that union the agronomist Rüütel had become a communist loyal enough to ascend to the role of chairman of the presidium of the Estonian Soviet Socialist Republic. Now he was 75 years old, a gray grandfather, somehow at the helm of his country again, and leading it into a different kind of union, a European Union. Twenty years before, he had toasted the October Revolution. Now he praised his country's pending "full membership in the largest community of nations and richest common market."

133

Juhan Parts was 25 years old when Estonia left the Soviet Union, coming of age in the breakdown of the very system that Rüütel had seen established as a young man. And from those hard times, young men like Parts found themselves with immense responsibility for their nation's future. At 37, he was not Estonia's youngest prime minister ever. That honor still belonged to Mart Laar, who had been only 32 when he became prime minister in 1992. Thirty two! In less than a decade both Ivan and I would be 32. I doubted whether either of us could manage as the head of a country.

Rüütel and Parts took turns reading from a statement. The referendum, according to the men, was among the "most significant choices in the history of the people of Estonia and a setting-up of a guarantee for independence and national security."

Somewhere inside me, something began to vibrate. I was witnessing history. Years from now, my child might ask me where I was when Estonia voted to join the EU, and I could tell him or her, proudly, "in the same room with Arnold Rüütel and Juhan Parts!"

Ivan eyed me as I frantically wrote down the few Estonian phrases I understood. My hand was shaking as I wrote, either from drinking too many cups of coffee or pure excitement.

"You know, they'll provide you with English-language statements later," Ivan whispered to me. "I can handle it from here. You can go home."

Go home? Never. I wasn't about to let Ivan's sourness stand between me and history. I ignored my colleague and continued to write. When Rüütel and Parts were finally finished, the questioning began, and it was mostly in Estonian with a peppering of questions in English.

"Prime Minister Parts, I see here that you can speak English," a British journalist with long red curly hair asked from beside a camera tripod.

"Huh?" Parts grunted and leaned into the microphone.

"I said, your CV shows that you speak English fluently," she said, this time very slowly.

"Yes," Parts grunted again, and when he hit the 's' in 'Yes,' he lisped, so that it sounded more like he said "Yeth."

"How do you feel tonight?" she asked.

"How do I feel?"

"How do you feel that your country has voted to join the EU?"

"This shows that Estonian democracy has survived a test of maturity," Parts said, lisping all the way. Rüütel meantime looked on, silently smiling and staring into the audience. His only foreign language was Russian.

"How do I feel? One could very well say that spring has arrived in Estonia," Parts continued. Yes, yes," he nodded, as if to agree with himself. "Today, it is springtime for all Estonians."

"Then how come we don't see the Estonian people celebrating their decision?" the British journalist asked.

"What?" Parts grunted into the microphone.

"I asked, How come we don't see the Estonian people celebrating their decision to join the EU?"

It was a valid question. In Parts' mind it may have been springtime in Estonia, but outside the walls of the Foreign Ministry the city of Tallinn was silent, dark, the air cool and calm, not a soul in the streets.

"Huh?" Parts grunted again into the microphone.

"I was in Vilnius a few weeks ago when Lithuania voted to join. People were driving around waving EU flags and singing songs and celebrating. How come we don't see the same things happening in Tallinn?"

Parts relaxed in his seat for a moment as if in deep thought. Then he leaned back towards the microphone, tilted his head, and squinted at the British journalist.

"You don't know us, Estonians," Parts told the British journalist and bared his teeth for a rare smile. "We are slow to get started, but once we get started, we can't be stopped."

I scribbled the sentence down quickly, and I was prepared to fight with Ivan deep into the night over it if need be. Parts' profound words would find their way into the next morning's paper, no matter what.

A LOOK IN
THE MIRROR

We lost Sigrid at the Vigeland Sculpture Park.

The park itself was empty, save for a few camera-happy Japanese businessmen. It stretched out dull and orderly, a northern European masterpiece of manicured grass, spurting fountains, and seamless geometry, the indifferent faces of Gustav Vigeland's granite men and women and children looking down all the time, without empathy, without feeling, with only vacant stares, stares that reflected the gray sky above.

Epp and I indulged ourselves as tourists, like the Japanese. But Sigrid? Sigrid stayed behind on a park bench. She didn't feel like going, she said, and besides, she had seen the park before. Sigrid was also stinking drunk. She had requested two things from Estonia. One was a Norwegian-Estonian dictionary, and we had slugged the enormous *Norsk-Estnisk Ordbok* from Tallinn to Oslo. The other was vodka, and we had brought along two big bottles of the strongest drink one could find. It was a liquid menacing in its transparency; I imagined that the stuff might last Sigrid at least until Christmas.

"What happened to her?" Epp fretted as we returned to the empty bench from the park gates. "Where could she have gone?"

"Norway," was all I could manage to say.

Epp bit her lip and looked around. "She could be anywhere."

Sigrid was sober the night before when we met her at the Oslo bus station. We followed her to her apartment through the dark, lugubrious streets of the Norwegian capital, only to collapse into slumber on her living room floor. Epp's old pal Sigrid was small and a little mysterious, with jet-black hair and porcelain skin. Our initial exchanges were cordial.

"Tere," I had said in the bus station.

"Tere," Sigrid had sized me up, a bit of a dazed look in her green eyes. "But Epp, he speaks Estonian," she turned to her old friend. "I don't understand."

"He is learning," Epp had said.

"Huh. Jon couldn't even say 'Tere'," Sigrid had looked away. "It was just some weird Eastern European language to him."

The day dawned, gray and cool, and from Sigrid's third-floor windows I watched the Osloans go to work, silent, blonde, and neat, the ringing of mobile phones echoing in the street, like Tallinners only richer. Epp left to do an interview and I went out to find breakfast. Sigrid stayed behind, curled up in the kitchen, silently sipping a coffee. When I returned to the apartment, though, our hostess was not there.

"Sigrid?" I stood in the abandoned kitchen, the milky September light flooding the small room.

No response.

I looked around. All of Sigrid's living space was modern and wooden, smooth and white, like a page out of an IKEA catalogue. It almost seemed too decent for a 34-year-old Estonian painter. She would not have had it as good in Tallinn. No, back home she would have been stuck in some dull Soviet apartment block or one of those rambling 19th century wooden ghettos. Here she lived a life of comfort, of normalcy, of self-assembled furniture. Sigrid had become a Western European.

"Sigrid?" I called out again, this time a bit louder, inflecting the second syllable. From the bedroom, I heard a snort and a cackle.

"Go away!" she whispered.

I glanced down at the kitchen table. There was the dictionary we bought her, as sturdy as a coffin, beside a half-eaten chocolate. Then I noticed that one of the two bottles of 80-proof vodka was half empty. But how was that even possible? We just gave them to her last night.

Unless.

"You bloody bastard! You have ruined everything!" Sigrid exploded into the kitchen, a blur of white and black. "I haven't seen Epp in years. Years! This was supposed to be a special time for us. But then you," she snarled at me, "you had to come along and steal her from me!"

"Steal her?" I stepped back, "but I didn't."

"Yes you did, you thief! I hate you!" Sigrid stammered and moved closer to me, the stench of alcohol creeping out from behind her pearl-like teeth. Epp had told me that Sigrid was beautiful and crazy, that pretty much all the guys who worked with her had been in love with her. Now as I peered down at Sigrid with her wet eyes, the roots of her dyed black hair showing gray, I tried to imagine being attracted to this volcanic mess. And I was, because she made me so mad.

I said in a low voice, "I'm sorry, Sigrid."

"'I'm sorry, Sigrid,'" her face contorted as she mocked me and stepped back. "Oh my," she froze and studied my face, as if I was a subject for one of her paintings. "Yes, now I see it quite clearly. You're a Mama's Boy, aren't you?"

"A what?"

"Yes, you are," Sigrid took on the subdued tone of a doctor. "A Mama's Boy. I can tell just from the way you stand. From the way you talk. He was like that too, you know. Always listening to that witch and not to me," Sigrid clenched her fists at her side. "And you are just like him!" her whole body shook with rage. "Just like fucking Jon!"

And as soon as she said "Jon" her face collapsed into her hands and she began to cry.

"Sigrid?"

"Your love with Epp will fail!" she squeaked as she sobbed. "Love is like a drug, you see. Today, you and Epp are high. You are high on this drug of love. But what happened to us will happen to you too. Yes, I can even see it now," Sigrid looked up at me, her pasty face an obscene mix of torment and disgust. "Your love will fail like all others."

I said nothing.

"Just go away, Mama's Boy!" She wiped a tear from her eye. "I need to be alone."

I walked around the block until Epp returned. When she did, waving, as if nothing bad had happened, as if everything was the same, dressed in her green pregnancy outfit, glowing with life, I decided naturally to hand my Sigrid problem to her.

Epp and Sigrid were like the sun and the moon, I figured. The two would have to balance each other out. For the rest of the day, I would say nothing to Sigrid. She was Epp's "special friend," and that meant she would have to be Epp's "special drunk and verbally abusive friend," too. As the old girlfriends disappeared into the bedroom together for a therapy session, I waited in the kitchen, thumbing the *Ordbok*.

After fifteen minutes, Epp emerged from Sigrid's room.

"Sigrid says she's sorry," she bit her lip again, like a nurse bearing disappointing news. "Her husband sent her a text message this morning. That's what this is all about." In the distance, I heard water running. "She's taking a shower now."

"Don't you mean her ex-husband?"

"They are still legally married," Epp sat down beside me. "That's how Sigrid can get this apartment. She has a paper that says she is psychologically unfit to work. As long as she stays married to a Norwegian citizen, she gets to stay here and she gets quite good money from the state."

"She's nuts."

Epp shrugged. "Her cat died a week ago and she loved that cat. After she broke up with Jon, it's all she had left."

"She told me she hates me and that our love will fail, like all others."

"Honey," Epp folded her hands in her lap, "Sigrid is like a beautiful bird stuck in a golden cage. She's stuck here. And besides, she's drunk."

"I don't say things like that to people when I'm drunk."

"Well, Sigrid always did drink like a man, but she is a sweet girl anyway," Epp said and bit her lip again. "Anyway, I told her I would order a taxi. We have got to get her out of here."

An hour later we were searching the sculpture park for Sigrid. The shower had apparently done her alcohol-ravaged body little good. For all I knew, she had hit the other half of the bottle in the shower. And I couldn't get the image of her staggering from the taxi out of my head, especially the moment when she cursed at that innocent Norwegian grandpa who was crossing the street. After we dumped her at the park bench, it seemed impossible that she could leave that spot, but she did.

And with her gone, I felt a satisfying wave of relief wash over me.

"Sigrid? Sigrid!" Epp scurried everywhere, looking for her friend under trees, beside stone walls. I pretended to look too, but I just as well would have let her slip into one of those fountains, never to return, her wicked vibrations bubbling up like some underwater earthquake. Mama's Boy! Why did she say it? If there was one red button that no one was allowed to push, it was that one. Mama's Boy! To hell with her! Let her rot away, slurping at the teat of social welfare like all the others! You hate me? Well, the feelings are mutual, my dear Sigrid. So piss off. Piss off to the bottom of the fountain of the Vigeland Sculpture Park. And what a place, it is. Oslo: quiet, cool, gray, provincial, indifferent, everything Tallinn is but hundred times more. Why, it's the perfect place for a suicide. Congratulations, Sigrid. In your failure of a life, you found the right place to die.

"I found her!" Epp crowed in triumph from across the park. I could see two shapes standing in the distance, next to the museum door, one leaning against the other.

So Sigrid wasn't dead after all. Emotionally bruised, yes, and physically crippled by 80-proof vodka, but still on her two feet. Epp had rescued her old pal. They returned to our original meeting point with Sigrid limping and staggering like a wounded solider, their arms linked tightly.

"Hello," she straightened her posture before me, trying to look normal, as if she was meeting me for the first time.

Epp helped her to the bench again, and slid between us.

"She was in the museum," Epp whispered in my ear. "I found her crying in the toilet."

"Oh."

"She's not usually like this," Epp whispered again. "She's just drunk. And her heart is broken."

"Come here, sweetheart," Sigrid said to her old friend in a raspy, smoky voice, and wrapped an arm around Epp's growing waistline. "Have I told you lately how gorgeous you look?"

"It's the pregnancy," Epp chuckled, and gestured at her growing belly. "All the hormones," she blushed in the gray light.

"I missed you, sweetheart," purred Sigrid.

Epp pecked her old friend on the cheek and squeezed her tight and in that moment I abandoned most of my ill feelings towards Sigrid. Even if her breath stank of vodka and she had verbally abused me, she was still Epp's special friend Sigrid. That kind of meant that she was my friend too.

But Sigrid's misery haunted me. I knew personally what Oslo's soul-sucking gray sky was capable of, and I was nervous being back, but I didn't know the city could do the same thing to someone else. There was something wicked about Oslo, something evil. It ate away at the goodness in people, burning them in sad tones of blue and gray and black, like some kind of frozen-over Scandinavian hell.

In my mind, it was already like a dream, how I arrived there two years before, off the overnight bus at 5 am, into the blue cold of the north. I knew Norway was supposed to be cold, but I had no grasp of how cold it could be in October, and the cold weather was always the first and easiest culprit for my sudden illness. I had trudged through Oslo's frosty streets that forlorn morning, a heavy backpack on my shoulders, the sounds of the electric trams my only company.

Now, two years later, I could see how much this city reminded me of Tallinn in its cruel silence. There was something that stitched these two places together, but what was it? The weather? The people?

The Estonians had long tried to convince the world of their northernness, to explain this nameless ingredient that connected them to the Norwegians. It was a struggle. They cringed as foreigners took them for Russians, plied them with drink, toasting a jubilant *nostrovia**, only to be introduced by their new Estonian acquaintances to the toast *terviseks***.

---

* Cheers! (In Russian)
** To your health! (In Estonian)

Searching for a new word to define themselves, to set them apart, to provide the outside world with some prism through which to interpret their country, they settled on an old one: Nordic. It was a word with multiple meanings. For Americans, it brought to mind images of skiing and reindeers and polar nights. To Norwegians, it captured all that was good about their superior social welfare paradise. But to the Estonians, Nordic summed up all that set them apart from other easterners, the fondness for melancholy, the embrace of quiet, the unsexy stoicism that led Latvian and Russian women to make ironic jokes about "hot-blooded Estonian guys."

So Estonia was Nordic, the Estonians said. It was Nordic like Oslo. It was there in the milky sky, the cold glare of a Vigeland sculpture, the dull horror of an Edvard Munch painting. It was neither in Rome nor in Delhi or Beijing or Moscow but only here, in the air, in Oslo, in Stockholm, in Reykjavik and Torshavn and Oulu and Odense and Kärdla and Tallinn. I thought Anatol Lieven nailed the idea in his 1993 book *Baltic Revolution*, when he wrote that being in Tallinn was "like finding oneself in the cold, clear, bracing air of the Scandinavian mountains." At first it comes as a great relief, he wrote, but later "you begin to notice a certain chill in the emotions. They turn blue, go numb, and one begins to fear they will die out altogether."

Estonia was the "world's only post-communist Nordic country," Toomas Hendrik Ilves, Estonia's former foreign minister, tried to convince the Swedish Institute of International Affairs in 1999. "Brits, Scandinavians, Finns, Estonians consider themselves rational, logical, unencumbered by emotional arguments," Ilves said. "We are businesslike, stubborn and hard-working. Our southern neighbors see us as too dry and serious, workaholics, lacking passion and *joie de vivre*."

Dry? Lacking passion? No *joie de vivre*? Ilves clearly had never met Epp or Sigrid. But he was onto something, and yet the definition, the hidden cable that linked Oslo to Tallinn eluded even him. I thought Ilves was right, though, because if there was one place where a human being felt more atomized, more detached, more alienated from humanity than Tallinn, it was Oslo in dark autumn, with its silent blondes *snakker*ing quietly into the latest telecommunication devices, its machine-like tram drivers plowing ever forward, its drunks sleeping anonymously under bridges, like tired elves.

And I had now returned to Oslo like a triumphant king, back to a place I had once fled.

The memories flickered in and out of those days. While strolling the following evening with Epp and a very hungover Sigrid through the city's sterile walking streets, I could still taste the past. The feel of the cold white toilet against my fevered body that first night two years ago, the silver garbage tin in the corner, the dim lighting of the hostel bathroom, and the sick conviction that I had come to Oslo to die. By that time I had spent two weeks on the road and fiction had become insidiously intertwined with reality. Behind I left Berlin and Prague and Copenhagen. I kept thinking of Ursula in Germany, lighting up her hash pipe and talking about Marxism, September 11 and the end of Western civilization, talking about how she used to sell ice cream behind the Berlin Wall.

At night, she stood behind the bar, her black hair up, a mystery. In the mornings she would scurry about her apartment, prodded onward by some Germanic pagan god of work.

"What time is it?" I would ask, one groggy eye open.

"8 am." Ursula would grunt, as if I should know what time it was.

"Go back to sleep!"

"I can sleep when I'm dead," Ursula would say. What a woman! What a German!

Ursula was beautiful. But she was rotten inside, just like me.

A week later I arrived in Oslo, only to fall ill for days. The disease was ambitious and brutal. Only later, when the high fever broke, when my weakened body summoned the courage to right itself, when I found the cunning to pull myself away from the unearthly demons, the hot jungle sweats, I knew I had to get the hell out of Norway, away, to anywhere, somewhere. Maybe Stockholm could save me. I had it in my drug- and disease-addled mind that some superior being was out to destroy me for what I had done. I knew it with the same certainty as my own birth date. Something wanted to crush me like a pulpy fruit between its metaphysical fingers and Stockholm was the right place to give it the slip. God would never look for me in such a godless place.

And that's how I escaped Oslo the first time, in the back of an overnight bus, a polite middle-aged Norwegian woman with a gigantic chest beside me babbling on about the weather, like some kind of life-preserver of sanity.

"Are you okay?" Epp asked me.

"Yeah," I said. We had taken a seat on one of Oslo's regal central squares.

"You haven't said a word for half an hour. What are you thinking about?"

"Prince Haakon," I answered.

"Huh?"

"I feel bad for him, you know. His cousins get Copenhagen, Stockholm, and he gets stuck with Oslo. I mean, imagine, you grow up here in this lousy place and one day your father, who's a king, tells you, 'Someday, Haakon, all of this will be yours.' And you look out on Oslo and you would like to say, 'Eh, tell you what, Dad, you can keep it.'"

"Oslo is not like Stockholm," said Sigrid, puffing on a cigarette, the ash glowing in the shadowy early evening light. "Stockholm is an international city. Oslo is provincial. Nobody talks to you here if they don't know you. My only friends are foreigners," she exhaled.

"It's the same for me in Tallinn," I told her. "I don't think I have even one real Estonian friend. I don't know why. I am surrounded by them every day, but they just ignore me."

"Well, we northerners aren't the friendliest people," Sigrid sighed. "But I think it's a little easier to be an American in Estonia than an Estonian in Norway. Like when I tell Norwegians I am from *Estland**, they assume I'm some kind of Russian prostitute."

---

* Estonia. (In Norwegian)

"How is that possible?" I asked. "Your name is Sigrid. It's the most Scandinavian name you can have."

"Oh yeah, 'Sigrid,'" she shrugged. "It was recently my name day here, there was a big spread in the newspaper about Sigrids, but it doesn't matter!" Sigrid flicked the ash from her cigarette to the ground and continued: "They can tell instantly that I'm not Norwegian so they ask where I'm from, and when I say *Estland*, they just assume I sell drugs or I'm a hooker or something. Jon's mother would barely even talk to me when she heard I was from *Estland* because he's from a rich family and she expected him to marry some proper Norwegian girl and I can't even speak Norwegian correctly."

I nodded when Sigrid spoke and thought about Epp's family and how they saw me, this strange foreigner who would most likely never master their language.

Sigrid paused to light another cigarette. "And it's so sad, you know," her voice quivered, as if she was about to start sobbing again. "Jon is a good person. But he has been sidetracked, sidetracked by drugs and his mother's psycho tricks."

Epp rubbed her friend's back and we looked out into the square. Across the gray granite park was the students' bar.

I remembered how I had tried that first night two years back to calm my oncoming fever with a beer. I recalled the bartender, young, blonde, tall, pleasant and familiar. I could see once again the shape of her figure in the red lights of the bar as she bent over to fetch me a drink. When she surfaced from behind the counter, she saw my face.

"What is it?" she was dressed from head to toe in black, the uniform of the northern urban woman.

"You remind me of someone," I told her. "A girl I knew when I was a kid. We used to play together."

And then the surprise: the bartender wrapped an arm around me and kissed me on the cheek. It was wet and soft and it made me think that maybe underneath Oslo's tough, indifferent exterior there was warmth and forgiveness. "You don't look good," she whispered in my ear. "You should go home."

My home that night was a hostel on top of a barren hill on the outskirts of town, a bunk in a four-person room shared with other wandering minstrels and sociopaths. It was raining in Norway on that distant evening in 2001, and in 2003 in the square that night, Norway started to rain again on me, on Sigrid, on Epp, on our unborn child.

"Perfect Norwegian weather," Epp smiled and held her hands out palms up.

"Perfect Estonian weather," I winked to Epp and the murky loneliness of the past dissolved into the raindrops. What had I done right? I wondered, looking at her. What did Sigrid do wrong? Why did her love fail?

"Another shitty Norwegian day," Sigrid sighed heavily in the rain. "Let's go back to my apartment, sweethearts. I'll make dinner." We started to walk through the rain and darkness.

🌢 🌢 🌢

I never did see Jon or his mother, but I couldn't get that "evil witch," as Sigrid called her, out of my mind. I imagined her to be tall and gray, eyes a dead blue, hair silver blonde, and her elegant, black-booted foot all the time pushing down and away, down at Sigrid's unworthy Eastern European face and away, like the Norwegian delegation to the Estonians at some Nordic Council gathering, telling them that they could attend meetings but would never, ever, become full members. Norway would always be first, Estonia would always follow. A Norwegian girl was assumed to be royalty; an Estonian girl was probably a prostitute or a drug dealer. Such was the pecking order of the Nordic world.

In her IKEA-furnished kitchen, Sigrid chopped tomatoes and offered us wine. She was now in fine form, grumbling curses here and there like an old, Italian man, making Epp laugh.

"Did I tell you that you look gorgeous?" Sigrid teased Epp.

"Once or twice," she blushed.

"And how old are you again?"

"Twenty nine," Epp said.

"That's right. I'm a few years older than you. And Justin, you look young, you can't be my age."

"I'm still 23," I said. "Almost 24."

"Wait," Sigrid slowed her chopping. "You're 29 and he's 23? What are you two, some kind of perverts?"

"Wasn't Jon older than you?" I asked.

"Yeah, he was," Sigrid said. "So what?"

"So, you're a pervert too."

"No, no, no. It's normal when the man is older," Sigrid said. "But you two, you two are just weirdoes, perverts!"

"Whatever you say, Sigrid."

"Justin, I have something important to ask you."

"What?"

"Are you happy now?" Sigrid's green, cat-like eyes met mine.

"Happy?"

"You are only 23 years old and you already have Epp, you are going to be a father. Are you happy now? I mean is this all what you wanted?"

Was it what I had wanted? It wasn't exactly what I had planned. But the idea that life could be neatly planned out and followed to some horizon of certain happiness like the plot of a Disney movie seemed bankrupt when one considered the circumstances of how I had found myself discussing happiness in Sigrid's kitchen. If I had actually yearned to eat pasta with Sigrid that night, it probably would have never happened. But some greater tide had brought me to Sigrid's Oslo kitchen, and when I thought again of the city, two years before, the hostel bathroom, the hot sweats, the bartender's kiss, the rain, the loneliness, an answer came to me. "Of course, it's what I wanted. I am really happy."

"Good answer!" Epp cheered, and when she did, a strong gust of wind hit the window, making its glass rattle.

"You have to promise me something then, Justin," Sigrid was now chopping black olives with her knife. "You have to promise me that you will never hurt Epp."

"Um, ok," I said.

"No, no. You can't just say, 'Um, ok.' You have to say, 'Yes, Sigrid, I promise that I will never hurt Epp, ever.' Can you do that?"

"Yes, Sigrid, I promise that I will never hurt Epp, ever."

"Good," Sigrid pushed the diced tomatoes and olives onto a heap of steaming pasta. "What are you planning on calling this kid anyway?" she asked.

I looked to Epp. She looked at me. "Marta," Epp decided to reveal our secret.

"Marta?" Sigrid dropped her knife. "Marta?" she tried it in her mouth again and her face contorted, as if she had just sunk her teeth into a lemon. "But Marta is like some old lady's name. I think I had a teacher named Marta. She was just old and smelly and terrible. Marta? You're really thinking of calling your daughter that? You might as well call her something even worse, like Marfa. How about that? Marfa Marta!" Sigrid's voice grew louder. She cackled, as if she had just thought up a name for a new venereal disease.

"Well, I was also thinking of calling her Mia," Epp whispered, waiting for Sigrid's judgement.

"Mia?" Sigrid's face contorted again. "No, no, that's just some bullshit new name. Mia. Hmph! Nah! Tell you what. You two should give her a real name, like Maria. Can you imagine if your name was Maria Petrone? Oh my God, you could just shout it from the tops of buildings, from the tops of mountains: 'My name is Maria Petrone!'" She jumped up, knife still in her hand.

"I don't know," I said. "I kind of liked the name Marta. We found it on Hiiumaa.

"Oh, don't tell me you're going to name your sweet little daughter after some *vana mutt**, some frigging old fart from Hiiumaa!" And when Sigrid yelled it, I swear I saw the Old Hiiu Lady leap up behind her, her snow white hair tied up in a scarf, her eyes ice blue, whimpering, imploring me to give my child her name.

---

* Literally 'old mole'. (In Estonian)

153

"But, but we saw it in a very special graveyard." Epp looked confused.

"A graveyard? Yeah, that's where all the Martas belong," Sigrid hopped onto a stool and then onto her kitchen table. She looked down on Epp and me, a lamp dangling in front of her face. "No, Justin, no Marfas or Murfas or Martas or whatever awful old lady's name you found in the graveyards!" she shouted. "Your child already has a name and I have named her. Her name is Ma-ri-a Pet-rone! Say it with me: 'My name is Maria Petrone!'"

"My name is Maria Petrone," Epp and I murmured, looking up at Sigrid as she cried into the air, shaking her fists at the ceiling.

"Louder, like you really mean it!" Sigrid cried and her head hit the IKEA lamp, causing her shadow to dance on the wall.

"My name is Maria Petrone!" we chanted.

"Once more! Louder!"

"My name is Maria Petrone!"

"Good," Sigrid jumped down from the table. "Now, that's settled."

"Aww, Sigrid, you are so inspiring, we miss you in Estonia," Epp laughed. "You should move back. Little Marta, eh, Maria will need a babysitter."

"I left Estonia behind," Sigrid slid into her seat. "Tallinn's so provincial. It's even worse than Oslo. I can't go back to that place, to all those people. If I went back, I would feel like a failure."

"But what are you going to do here?" I asked.

"I don't know, paint, write poetry," she shrugged. "I can only go forward. I can't go back, and I don't have to work here, right?" She poured herself another glass of wine. "Shit, the bottle's empty. I have to go to the store and get some more. You two are leaving tomorrow. I have to celebrate your visit," she put an arm around Epp.

"I'll go get it," I volunteered.

"Are you sure? You don't even know where the store is."

"I'll find one," I stood up from the chair. "Let me leave you two alone for a while."

I walked down the block. The night was windy. On my way, I heard a young Norwegian woman talking behind me. I figured she wanted directions, though I didn't understand what she was saying. I turned to answer her. She was dressed in a blue windbreaker. It ruffled in the cold air.

"Can I help you?" I said.

The woman kept walking and talking.

"I'm sorry, do you need help?" I tried again.

Her blue jacket brushed against my coat as she walked into the night, oblivious to my existence, still talking to herself, her boots clicking on the sidewalk into the black streets. Then I realized she was wearing a mobile phone hands-free headset. Through a small earphone, she could hear her invisible friend. From a tiny microphone on the earphone cable, her friend could hear her. I was right next to her all the time, and yet she didn't notice me. To her, I was as significant as a tree or bench or street lantern. Two seconds later she disappeared into the darkness.

In a nearby supermarket, I obtained a bottle of red wine and tried not to think of the exchange rate as I handed over my last kroner to a bored-looking Pakistani clerk, who silently handed me the wine back across the counter without saying a word.

Sigrid was waiting for me in the stairwell when I came back, the door to her apartment closed behind her.

"You left to buy wine because of what I said yesterday, didn't you?" she said in her coarse voice.

"I just thought you two had some catching up to do," I said and handed her the wine.

"Thank you," Sigrid said and took the bottle. "I don't hate you anymore."

JEWELS IN
THE NIGHT

We got to Stockholm at 5.40 on a cold September morning.

We had left Sigrid behind in Oslo's cavernous bus station, and by the time we crossed the Norwegian border, she and her dead cat and Jon's mother were but faint memories. The bus rolled on all night through the Swedish mountains and countryside, and from its windows I saw mostly nothing, only dark forests and blue lakes reflecting the beams of the moon, then here and there the phantom lights of cities I had never heard of, Karlstad, Örebro, Eskilstuna, Södertälje, and finally, Stockholm, glowing in the morning blackness in blue and red and white and yellow, like jewels in the night.

The Swedish capital was built on islands and peninsulas, a spider web of bridges and underground trains, castles, museums, shopping centers and apartment blocks, all of them shooting out of the bedrock like mountain chains in pastels of orange and yellow and gold. I arrived the first time the same way, two years before, rode the trains to my hostel, where I collapsed into the lobby still broken and ill, alone, sleeping off a light fever. The ladies at the desk wouldn't check me in until 1 pm, so I just sat there and slept and downed orange juice and tried not to think.

And nobody disturbed me because it was Stockholm, it was big and sprawling and international. When Epp and I arrived, two years later, the markets bustled with Arabs and Persians and Turks calling out in garbled Swedish. It was mushroom season in Sweden, and here and there were mountains of golden chanterelles together with ripe fruit that glistened in the sun.

Along the waterfront later, where Baltic waters lapped at the floating city, a huge battleship had moored flying the green and gold and blue of the Brazilian flag. From unseen speakers loud samba music blared. The sailors lined the docks, waiting for the admiral to disembark. The music was danceable, riotous. "*Bom dia**!" I yelled to the sailors. "*Bom dia!*" they echoed back, grinning, probably thinking this chocolate-headed fellow with the huge backpack was an errant boy from Rio that had followed the stink of womanhood all the way to the top of the world. And then the pompous admiral came down the steps, dressed all in white, his mustache hilariously curled on either end, like some extra from a Latin soap opera. But that was Stockholm. It was alive, it moved, even in its misty tones of gray and blue, its giant buildings and hard soil, the heart of the north kept pulsating, never resting.

The city was like a powerful, silent octopus, I reckoned, a tentacle stretching in every direction, under the sea, surfacing in the harbors of Oslo and Copenhagen and Reykjavik and Helsinki

---

* Good day! (In Portuguese)

and now even Tallinn and Riga, with Stockholm at its head, its brains, its eyes, and its jaws.

In the vacuum that accompanied the fall of Soviet power, the Swedes had made a move on the Baltic once again, this time with money instead of warships. Close to half of all foreign direct investment into Estonia was Swedish in 2003. Only 1 percent was Russian. Nearly any enterprise you considered in Estonia had some Swedish capital behind it. The banks, the newspapers, the TV stations, the garbage collectors, the milk, the sausages, the telecommunication networks, the phones and chocolates and IT startups and building supply stores and insurance firms: somewhere at the end of the line sat an old gray-headed man in Stockholm named Bengt or Björn, counting his kroner, hoarding his wealth, a Baltic robber baron of the 21st Century.

I had actually had the idea to interview some of these dukes of Nordic capitalism, but all my plans fell by the wayside as Epp and I took the city. In the morning we lay by the giant red Stadshuset near the water, sipping coffees and eating pastries from a cafe, our moods high. I kept thinking about *The Seventh Seal*, the dark elegance of Bergman's classic film, and how something powerful in it had made me want to come north, even when I was a teenager. When I had applied to study abroad in Copenhagen, my pals at school in DC were perplexed. Go to Brazil, to Australia, to South Africa, they said, to some place warm, some place exotic. But I chose the north. I had to go north.

"Wait, what? You saw that movie and it actually made you want to come up here?" Epp cocked an eyebrow in the sunlight.

"I think I had a crush on the actress who played Lisa, the blacksmith's wife." It was a pathetic answer. But it was true.

"You know, you're a real weirdo," Epp looked at me with pity. "It's a film about death, shot in black and white, set during the Black Plague. Most people think that movie is depressing. Most people would never want to come to Sweden after seeing that movie."

"Sigrid said we're two weirdoes."

"No, you're the weirdo. Not me. And what's all this about Sigrid? You liked her, didn't you?" Epp teased me.

"Not like that."

"You and crazy women, eh?"

"Shut up!"

"I like crazy women too," she said and sipped her coffee. "I collect crazy people. You and Sigrid are two of the shiniest jewels in my collection."

Epp began to flip through her notebook, which she had pulled from the abyss of her backpack, going over numbers, going over names, going over appointment times. That's how she was, always planning, always involved with the next project, her inner locomotive surging forward with the buzz of caffeine.

"When are you ever going to take a break?" I asked her.

"What do you mean?"

"You know, when will all your big projects be finished?"

"That's just who I am," she tipped the coffee cup to swallow the last of its contents. "I will always have new ideas."

"Take a nap, damnit. Get some rest!"

"Hush!" she said and concentrated on her notebook. "I can sleep when I'm dead."

During the day and into the night we skipped from interview to interview, every muscle, every movement proceeding according to plan. First there was Lena Endre the respected actress, and then there was Jonas Gardell, the raucous comedian. The half-Estonian Endre was polite, well-oiled, smooth as a fish, ready to have her picture taken. Gardell was opinionated, funny, and vain. "I love getting older," the bald, tanned, denim-clad forty year old proclaimed in a downtown cafe. "I get more beautiful with every wrinkle."

Gardell was not just a comedian and acclaimed novelist. He was also Sweden's best known gay man, the most out of the closet, a kind of homosexual messiah who lorded over the annual Pride marches as if to give each his blessing. Living in Estonia, I had nearly forgotten that people like Gardell even existed. Sure there were gay celebrities in Estonia too, and everyone knew who they were, and they all knew that everyone knew, but at the same time nobody talked about it, it was a topic beyond the bounds of polite discourse, even the Estonian word for "homosexual" – *pede* – had a sort of dirty ring to it, so most used the English word, "gay," instead.

Epp would whisper in my ear from time to time that "so-and-so's gay," just so that I knew, usually pointing out some fashion photographer or TV host, and it was whispered because it wasn't like in the American press where rumors would circulate in the tabloids before the stalked celebrity issued an urgent press release on his or her sexual preference, or in Sweden where stars like Gardell appeared openly in public, holding their partners' hands, celebrating the joys of gay parenthood. You could say that Estonia was still in the closet about its gays. It had Swedish banks and Swedish TV channels and Swedish everything else, but it still did not have Swedish openness. There was no Estonian Jonas Gardell.

Later in Odenplan, a square north of the city center, we sunned ourselves in the plaza like sea lions, breathing in the crisp autumnal air under the low, blue sky. Stockholm was cozy and anonymous, ancient and progressive. If it were sunny there every day, I told Epp, I could stay forever. But we both knew it wasn't so. Soon it would be winter and Stockholm would be just as glazed over as Tallinn. Soon it would get darker and everything would look like Antarctica again.

We came to Odenplan to meet Rita Ahonen. While Lena Endre and Jonas Gardell were clearly stage people, at ease before a camera, Rita showed up quietly in the square, a bush of dark curly brown hair above a round pleasant face pierced by two green eyes, a lightweight jacket around her, saying little other than "Tere," and suggesting we follow her back to her place. We would be more comfortable there, she said. We could speak more openly.

Rita didn't talk much to me but Epp and her leaped into a conversation in Estonian and that's how we walked, Rita first, Epp second, me in the caboose. Rita walked with certainty, her bushy head pointed into the future, like she knew exactly where she was going, and in her airy silence I imagined that she belonged to some secret Estonian sect and was guiding us back to her temple. From Odenplan, our muse led us across the sunny square up the hill to the Stockholm Observatory, and as I looked down on the red and blue and silver roofs of Stockholm, the trees still hanging desperately onto their summer colors, I remembered something. I had walked this all before, two years prior, with Elizaveta, a Russian student from the program in Denmark who had had found me wandering Stockholm's walking streets during our October break.

Poor Elizaveta. I could see her again in the sunlight, her soft, sweet Slavic face, her dark hair, the shopping bags in her arms, like the melody to an old song. She was a nursing student from St. Petersburg and she always corrected me when I said Leningrad by accident. "It's not Leningrad anymore!" she would say with her Russian accent and stomp on my foot. Only in hindsight, I could see that she really liked me, and she followed me around almost all of that night in Stockholm, crawling through restaurants and pubs, and across squares and parks, but I was toxic in those days, and I knew all along that it wasn't meant to happen. I would have to dump her and quickly, for her own good.

I exhaled in a second-floor kindergarten near the Observatory, looking at the childlike handprints on the walls, the tiny hooks where they hung their jackets, the little multicolored plastic chairs where they sat each morning. You could see the children of Stockholm in the streets, parading, dressed in fluorescent orange vests. Children! And I was soon going to be a father to one, back in this world of finger paints and scissors and glue. It was the children that had kept Rita in Stockholm, she said, but she hadn't come to Sweden to be a teacher. No, Rita Ahonen had come to Stockholm fifteen years before as the wife of a dissident.

It was all there in the photos on her desk, their private war against the Soviet Union. And how did she wage it? With photographs of supermarkets and shopping malls.

"We used to send these photos back to our friends in Estonia," Rita said, pointing to an old photo of her standing in front of a mountain of polished apples in a supermarket. "And no one could believe it. No one could believe that this is how it was in the West. So we had to show it to them ourselves."

Only when I saw the man beside her in the old photos, when I glimpsed his nose, did I put it together, that Rita Ahonen was married to a former Soviet dissident Heiki Ahonen, and I knew Heiki. I had met him that spring to interview him about plans for the new Museum of Occupations they were building in Tallinn. It was a hot day and his office was warm and stuffy, overflowing with huge stacks of studies. Heiki had a marvelous nose around which it seemed his whole face orbited. It supported dark-rimmed glasses, and behind them, his eyes smarted with humor. While Heiki's manner of speech was direct and flat, I felt that he was deeply amused by something the whole time I was there.

"Is it true that they sent you to Siberia?"

"Yes," he answered with a polite smile on his face.

"I didn't even know they still sent people to Siberia in the Eighties."

"They did, indeed."

"So, um, did you make any friends while you were there?"

"Oh yeah," he let out a light chuckle. "I made plenty of friends in my Siberia days. Azeris, Armenians, Georgians..."

And so on. Was it my naive line of questioning that amused Heiki, or the fact that he had gone up against the Soviet empire as a young man and, by some measure, won?

Heiki had been one of the organizers of the Hirvepark demonstration in Tallinn in 1987 where Estonians had stood to denounce the Molotov-Ribbentrop Pact* and Soviet rule. In 2003, it was already history, a black and white photo in a school textbook, but back then, the thirtyish Ahonen had already been in and out of prisons for years, so the Soviets finally gave up and "emigrated" the problematic Ahonen family to Sweden, where they continued to be difficult by fighting back in that very Swedish way, by using wealth to their advantage.

Sweden was a fitting pit stop for the Ahonens. From 1945 to the restoration of independence, it was the home of Estonia's government in exile, founded by Jüri Uluots, the country's last legitimate prime minister who had gone underground in 1940, appointed a new Estonian government during the Nazi retreat in September 1944, and later made his way to Stockholm himself, where he died as a refugee the following year. While Swedish neutrality forced the Estonian exile government to officially meet in Oslo, its members lived and worked and pressed their case for Estonian independence from the Swedish capital for nearly 50 years, writing books and pamphlets and organizing parades and meetings, all to draw attention to the unjust fate of their country.

Still, Rita's photographs of supermarkets could do things that post-war exposés with titles like *Baltic Eclipse* and *The Drama of the Baltic Peoples* could not do. While the exile community appealed to those who would listen in the West, the Ahonens made their case to the Estonian people themselves.

---

* The Molotov-Ribbentrop was a non-agression pact between the Soviet Union and Nazi Germany signed in August 1939. The treaty included a secret protocol dividing Northern and Eastern Europe into German and Soviet spheres of influence, anticipating the "territorial and political rearrangements" of these countries.

"People simply could not believe how well the Swedes had it," Rita said. "Remember this was the time of rationing in Estonia, when you had to wait all day in line to get a loaf of bread or some meat. When we first got here, I would spend two hours in the stores just looking around because the packages were so interesting. In Estonia, you could basically make two meals: they sold sometimes chopped meat and sometimes chicken, that was all. Here, in Stockholm's supermarkets, I panicked. An old Estonian lady finally gave me an excursion around the supermarket to teach me what was what."

As I looked at Rita's old polaroids that she had taken in the shops when she arrived in Sweden, the images of fruit and walls of milk cartons and piles of sweaters, it was easy to see why she had been overwhelmed, because Stockholm was just brimming with material wealth. Every street housed stores that were bursting with things, books and candleholders and yogurts and computers and baskets and pillows, couches and chocolates and guitars and mirrors and cabinets and kitchen utensils, baguettes and nightstands and TVs and sinks and refrigerators – just stuff, everywhere stuff, Stockholm was overstuffed.

And it was all coming to Estonia now, too. In every neighborhood of Tallinn, new palaces of stuff were being built. The derelict real estate of the Soviets was plowed under, while rapid injections of Scandinavian money brought forth shimmering shopping oases, erecter sets of rotating neon signs and automatic glass doors that rose into the night, sparkling from wall to wall with shiny new things.

Estonian dissidents of the late 1980s like Heiki Ahonen had fought for freedom, but to convince the people of its merits, they had to show them its fruits. And now Estonians could finally enjoy those fruits: succulent mangos and pineapples and pomegranates imported from Morocco and Costa Rica and Mexico. Looking at Rita's old photographs in that second-floor kindergarten, I suddenly realized what they were. They were postcards from the future.

"Färgerna på den estniska flaggan är: a) blått, vitt och svart, b) svart, blå och vit, c) blå, svart och vitt, eller d) vitt, blått och svart*?"

The students' house at Stockholm University smelled of youth, of flat beer, rotten eggs, perfume and hair gels, leather and vinyl and jeans and cosmetics. The dark wooden floor of the place had been smoothed by armies of boots and its tired sagging couches gave comfort to those brave Swedish souls who yearned to learn Estonian as a foreign language. A young Swedish woman, plump as a pigeon, held a microphone and quizzed the audience about the colors of the Estonian flag.

"A? Blått, vitt och svart**?" a young man with spiked orange hair finally answered from one couch.

"Nej***," the plump Swede shook her head, pushing her long brown hair from her shoulders, and then re-read the options.

---

* The colors of the Estonian flag are a) blue, white, and black; b) black, blue, and white; c) blue, black, and white; or d) white, blue, and black. (In Swedish)

** Blue, white, and black. (In Swedish)

*** No. (In Swedish)

"The answer is C." I whispered to Epp and Andres. *"Blå, svart och vitt."*

"Now, Justin, I am amazed," said Andres, sipping beer from a plastic cup. "You've only been here a few days and you can already understand Swedish."

"I've always had a knack for languages," I brushed off his compliment.

"Don't be fooled by him," Epp gestured at me with her thumb. "He's lived in Denmark and been to Sweden before."

Andres was about thirty, lean, and dressed in black. He taught Estonian to Swedish youth, and he lined the students up outside to speak with us for journalistic purposes. Some were young guys with Estonian girlfriends who wanted to learn how to whisper sweet nothings into their ladies' ears; others were grandchildren of refugees who wanted to relearn their forebears' forgotten tongue; and a precious few were just weirdos out for kicks. Why learn Estonian? Why not?

"So, tell me, Justin, what do you like about Estonia?" Andres asked as we watched the quiz.

"I like how it keeps developing," I told him. "Like behind our apartment last winter there was a big hole in the ground. Now there's a huge apartment building."

"Huge ugly apartment building," added Epp.

"Yeah, I don't know who designed it," I said. "It's big and white. The thing looks like *The Love Boat*."[*]

"The love what?" Andres leaned in, as if he had misheard me.

---

[*] "The Love Boat" was an American television show produced from 1977 to 1986 that was set aboard a cruise ship.

"Never mind."

"I hear that from a lot of Swedes," Andres nodded. "They say Tallinn has this kind of special energy."

Across the room, the plump girl with long hair announced a new question through the microphone.

"Estlands president är en a) Mart Laar, b) Toomas Hendrik Ilves, c) Lennart Meri, eller d) Arnold Rüütel?"*

The orange spiky haired kid's hand went back up. "Lennart Meri?"

"Nej," the long-haired girl shook her head and smiled, satisfied that she had stumped the crowd again.

"I wish it was still Lennart Meri," Andres whispered to us. "Can you believe our president is Arnold Rüütel? Arnold Rüütel! This young, energetic country that is about to join the EU has some old Communist as its president?"

"I was in the room with him last week," I informed Andres. "He was seated, like, only fifteen feet away."

Andres frowned. He was not impressed.

"Parts was there too." I retold the story about the prime minister and the British journalist who couldn't understand why Estonians weren't partying in the streets.

"Yeah, yeah, once we get started we can't be stopped," Andres said and rolled his eyes. "That's an old joke."

"I like to ask people where they were when they found out Arnold Rüütel was elected president," Epp said. "Where were you?"

---

* Estonia's president is a) Mart Laar; b) Toomas Hendrik Ilves; c) Lennart Meri; or d) Arnold Rüütel. (In Swedish)

"Oh, let me think," Andres said. "I was here in Stockholm in the university library. I couldn't believe it. And you?"

"I was working on a TV program in Tallinn," Epp said. "It was that same bad September. September 11th and all those other things."

"Two thousand and one," I said. "A weird time."

None of us said anything for a moment.

"Well, only three more years until they choose the next one," Andres said.

The Swedish girl at the center of the room asked the group of students again if they could name Estonia's president and when one student finally identified Arnold Rüütel, the students applauded and it seemed all so familiar to me, so normal, as if I was back in America. We had passed mounds of flowers outside the Swedish foreign ministry that morning, and while the nation still mourned its fallen foreign minister, most people here in Sweden seemed worry free, as if nothing bad could ever really happen to them. None of them had done time in Siberia. No one had been forced to leave the country. No one had ever had an old Communist for a president. No one had ever had a panic attack in a supermarket. Life in Sweden just rolled on as it had before, moving to the dull tempo of democracy, mellowing with age.

"Sweden feels different from Estonia," I said as we watched the students.

"How so?" Andres shot back, curious.

"I don't know. It feels stable."

"Oh yeah, Sweden is totally developed. It's stable, it's done," he smiled like a teacher. "But at the same time, Estonia keeps changing. It's dynamic," his eyes brightened. "I miss it."

And so we moved on, just like old times, on the road, moving from hostel to hostel, loading up on free coffee in the morning, stuffing all our possessions into our bags, and then out the door, onto the next destination. One night we slept outside the city in the archipelago, tucked into a small private red cottage, listening to the geese honk in the water. We forgot to bring towels, so we used the room's curtains instead. "When they dry," advised the expert traveler Epp, "they will look totally normal." Another night we put down our bags on a floating hostel operated on a boat in the city harbor, staring out the portholes in the black of the evening at the lights of the Old City, Gamla Stan, glittering like diamonds in the distance. On our last evening in Stockholm, we sat by the pacific waters, eating chocolates and watching people cross the bridge from Södermalm to Gamla Stan.

"Sometimes you can just tell a person's nationality by looking at them," Epp said. "Like these ladies are definitely Swedish." She gestured at a group of four women, each with short blonde hair, smart glasses, blazers, rings glistening on their fingers, some holding white shopping bags from Södermalm's trendy boutiques. Each one had an understated silk scarf tied loosely around her neck, the badge of the middle-aged Stockholm female.

"How about these women?" I pointed at the three ladies who followed them. They had mostly dark, curly brown hair, pretty blue eyes that reflected the city lights. Each was engulfed in a thick fur coat that floated above her knees. The party walked with grace and confidence across the bridge, as if they

171

owned it. I imagined they were on their way to an exclusive restaurant.

"Ha. That's easy. Those are Russians," Epp said. "This is kind of a fun game."

For the next few minutes we watched more people come over the bridge: a gang of young Turkish guys, their hair slicked black, a trio of rotund Finnish ladies with short haircuts and dark glasses, and, of course, Swedes, Swedes, and more Swedes, most on foot, some roaring through on bikes.

I kept waiting to spot an Estonian, but then I remembered that I was seated right next to one.

"Oh, I am just so exhausted from this trip," Epp yawned and stretched and rubbed her tired eyes. "Let's go home."

I helped her to her feet and we started off across the bridge to our lodging on the boat. As we walked I looked back over my shoulder at the lights of the city, breathing in the lustrous image of Stockholm one last time. It was a beautiful city, big and international, but I felt a heavy road weariness overtake me on that bridge. As provincial and Oslo-like as it was, I was eager to get back to Tallinn, back to our little one-room apartment on Kentmanni Street. I imagined our newest family member Miisu Petrone was sitting there right at that moment, waiting patiently by the window for our return, looking out into the darkness, all the time licking her paws.

OLD
WOMEN'S
SUMMER

It had only officially been fall for a few days, but summer was already long gone, a hazy memory of bike rides and forest hikes.

A cold snap in early September had brought color into the trees, and dry golden leaves crumpled underfoot on Tallinn's sidewalks. The Old Town enjoyed its final gasps of touristy glory, playing host to groups of retired Germans and Swedes and Italians, all of them still struggling to capture the Hansa city's medieval magnificence with their high-end cameras.

Only a few cafes still had outdoor patios, and those that did had in recent days begun to stack the chairs and fold the umbrellas. But a strange thing had happened one morning. The sun came out strong, the temperature rose, and the streets were full again. Estonian ladies tore off their colorful scarves and let their hair down. "Kids" – many of whom were probably the same age as me – picnicked in the shadow of St. Nicholas Church, drinking beers and making romantic connections.

And from nowhere, a British stag party mobbed the Viru Gate, loud, boisterous, and wasted at 11 am, marching along as if to proclaim, "Summer's not dead yet!"

Epp called the reappearance of warmth and sunshine that morning *Vananaistesuvi* or "Old women's summer." She was at home sorting her things with the windows open, while I made my way across the Town Hall Square to a pub called Molly Malone's to meet my new friend.

"Justin! Over here!" I saw Benny's arm rise from the outdoor cafe and wave in my direction.

I still had no idea what this Swedish businessman Benny saw in me or why he wanted to meet, but I was beginning to suspect that he liked me as a person. Maybe he was trying to hammer together some kind of friendship. Whether I could reciprocate was something we would both find out.

"Have a seat," Benny pushed a chair out from the table. He dined alone: a plate of runny scrambled eggs, gray, undercooked bacon, mushrooms and beans from a can, and half a tomato that reflected the sunlight.

"What did you get?" I eyed the plate.

"Full English breakfast!" Benny smacked the bottom of a bottle of ketchup until it spurted out in thick red gobs all over the eggs. "Delicious! Not bad for Estonia, eh? Want some?"

"I already ate," I said. "I'll just have a coffee."

"Ah, I see." Benny shoveled a heaping forkful of Englishness into his mouth. "So, how was Stockholm?" He chewed.

"Just as I remembered it," I said.

"You've been there before?"

"In a previous life," I said. "As a backpacker."

"Ah, I backpacked around Europe too," Benny dabbed at the corners of his mouth with a napkin. "Nineteen seventy three! Shit, you should have seen us back then."

"I can imagine." And in my mind I saw Benny decked out in platform shoes and bell bottoms, sideburns and a scruffy beard. 1973! It reminded me of my father and the stories he would tell of how he had bummed around Barcelona and Amsterdam and Athens, sleeping on benches, of the old pubs in Munich where the crippled middle-aged veterans would sit, drinking away the bad memories of the Eastern Front. My father had a bushy mustache back then, shoulder-length hair, a pair of shades, and a flat cap. He was staying in Athens in 1973 when a murder took place. The police stopped every suspicious character on the block, and that of course meant that Dad and his friends were questioned because they looked like criminals. Sometimes a black and white picture of a nameless European girl would find its way to the top of the pile of old photographs. "Oh yeah, I remember her," my father would say holding the old image, a gleam in his eye. "She was nice."

"My father was backpacking around Europe the same year," I said to Benny. "Maybe your paths crossed."

"Entirely possible," he said. "Those were the days."

Indeed they were. How those "stories from Europe" inspired me as a kid. How I wanted to do it all too, to have stories to tell a hundred times at the dinner table to remind my innocent children that before the days of televisions and VCRs, kitchen tiles and washing machines and hairdryers, there was something worth remembering.

But it was gone now. My father was different. He was like Benny – deep in middle age, his face shaved, his hair cut, creases at the corner of his eyes from days spent managing sales managers and product shipments. What had happened to the boys of 1973? What force had turned them into the men of 2003?

"What does your old man do now?" Benny asked.

"He sells computer hardware."

"Ah, computers, now that's a good business to be in," Benny sunk his teeth into a piece of toast. "But anyway, what's up with you? How's little Miisu?"

"Little Miisu is fine, but she got us in some shit, Benny."

"Oh no, what did she do?"

"Epp's cousin was visiting and feeding her while we were away. I guess she used the toilet in our apartment and for some reason it didn't stop running. Our neighbor somehow heard it through the wall and called the building owner and they had to get a plumber into the apartment to turn our water off. The owner lives in Florida. So, right now, we are in the process fighting with her via e-mail over the water bill."

"Shit, that's terrible. But how's Epp?"

"Epp is, well," I paused to think. "She's pregnant." I blurted it out and when I said it, I felt as if I had confessed my deepest secret, the one that Ivan, the colleague I sat next to almost every day in the office, still didn't know.

"Shit," Benny laid his fork down by his plate and extended a hand. "I had no idea. Congratulations. When's she due?"

"First week of January," I said. "I keep dreaming about it."

"What kinds of dreams?" Benny lit a cigarette and reclined in his seat.

"Like, last night I had a dream she gave birth in the woods."

Benny exhaled a puff of smoke, the scent tickling my nostrils.

"But when I held the baby up to the light, it had, like, antennae growing out of its head."

"Antennae?" Benny snorted in amusement. "Now that is what I would call an anxiety dream. Listen, Justin, you have nothing to worry about. Babies are cute. They eat, sleep, and shit. That's it. Wait until your kid becomes a teenager," he nodded. "Then you'll have real anxiety dreams."

"You speak from experience."

"I have a 21-year-old daughter who is studying in Uppsala," he said. "She was just here visiting me a few weeks ago. It was really nice," he exhaled again. "Much better than it used to be. I mean teenagers, and especially teenage girls, are the worst. They get in your face. They say the things that no other person would dare say to you. They can be nasty, really nasty."

"But this isn't Mari's daughter, right? She's not Estonian?"

"Oh, no, I was married to a Swedish lady before," Benny said. "But you know Swedish women. They expect you to do exactly half of the work. But if you only do 49 percent," he shrugged to show his indifference, "you're on your own."

"And Estonian women are different?"

"Estonian women are like Swedish women were when I was a kid. They are very strong but," he struggled to find the right word. "More understanding? I don't know."

"Maybe they just have lower standards," I said.

"Right, right," Benny said and chuckled. "I don't want to get in trouble here. I mean Mari is really strong. She tells this story about how the Communists were trying to storm the parliament building here and she went down there with her kids, and they were little babies then, and they all held hands to form a barricade around that building. Whenever she tells that story she starts to cry. And that was only like 12, 13 years ago, shit, can you believe it?"

"It was."

"But this whole country reminds me of the way Sweden used to be, the way it was 50 years ago. It's the way the people act, what they talk about, in their body language. Estonian guys are sort of tough and silent and handy and, shit, that's how Swedish men used to be. That's how my father and my uncles were. Even the pork chops taste like they did when I was a kid."

"The what?"

"Oh, that's right, you're American. You don't know this. In Sweden there is some dumb regulation on how much fat is allowed to be in a pork chop. But Estonia doesn't have that regulation. Therefore Estonian pork chops have more fat. They are tastier, just like the ones I used to eat when I was growing up. Whenever we have Swedes over here, we serve pork chops."

"What do they think?"

"Oh they just can't believe it. They say, 'Shit, Benny, now that is a good pork chop!'"

All day long I rambled among the elastic crowds of Old Town, thinking of the me of '01, thinking of the boys of '73.

"Those were the days!" "You should have seen us!" "Epp's pregnant." "Shit, congratulations." I used to dream of becoming who I became, but it was never a want or a need but an image, an idea. It hummed all the time in the distance, like a faint radio transmission.

At night, I returned to Kentmanni Street. When I opened the apartment door, Miisu bounded down the hall before me, a clumsy blur of black and white. Then I saw Epp in the little Krushchevka kitchen. She was dressed in parachute-like yellow pants, big plumes of light, billowy things she had probably acquired from Malaysia or India or China or one of her other eastern haunts. They were like clouds, airy, almost translucent. A choir of Buddhists was chanting on the stereo, one of those long elusive songs that goes on and on and has no beginning and no end. The smell of incense and warm food was in the air, the whole scene an ointment, caressing my muscles, pulling me apart and putting me together again, except this time the right way.

"Tsau," she said.

"Tsau," I answered. "What did you make?"

"A little experiment. Indian curry," she wrinkled her nose. "I am not sure how well it came out."

"My intuition tells me it's good."

"You and your intuition."

She returned to the stove, her pants floating above her ankles, candles all around her aglow, trickling red wax onto an old dish. A glass of wine. Glossy wooden cabinets. A pregnancy magazine. Bowls of grapefruits. The ancient painted radiator. Tiles broken at the corners. Black windows. The nag, the itch,

179

the knowledge that she was about to tell me something. Probably something about her plans. Plans, plans, she always had plans. Names, numbers, dates, lines scribbled in notebooks, on tiny pieces of paper, a crossword puzzle of contacts and ambitions and visions and question marks, things that had to happen the right way at the right time. But for what? To what end? What do you want, Epp? Tell me. Something was about to happen, but I didn't know what it was yet.

"Did you say something?" Epp asked me suddenly.

"What? No," I answered.

She gave me an odd look and then shook her head and returned to stirring the food.

FIRST
SNOW

---

*I lived a corporate life in those days or at least
I like to think I did.*

I had a long green coat. I shaved. I carried a briefcase. In it were
lessons. Lessons for Mats. Lessons for Antero and Lii. Lessons
for the gang at Budget Rent-a-Car. I wrote them out by hand
at night, photocopied them in the mornings, whiling away my
time at the Publishing House, drinking free coffee, refilling my
cup at the water cooler, reading fresh copies of the tabloids,
and talking to Rein, the forty-something layout designer at
Epp's magazine, who sported a long brown ponytail and was
into progressive rock. King Crimson, Deep Purple, Yes – it all
arrived by airmail to Rein's desk, ordered via Internet. Epp liked
to work in the early mornings, before her big-bosomed bosses
assumed their positions. That just happened to be when Rein –
the only man in this magazine – worked too.

"Hey, Justin, have you ever heard this?" Rein would say,
headphones buzzing in his ears. "It's by a group called Genesis.
The Lamb Lies Down on Broadway."

"I've heard about this record," I'd say. "And I've heard it's good."

He would nod, pleased. Rein had thirty years of Western music to catch up on and he did it with gusto. A few more listens to the album *Machine Head* and he'd be able to sing along drunk to "Highway Star" when Deep Purple hit Tallinn's Saku Suurhall in November. Rein had seen Robert Plant sing recently at one Estonian music festival. In the seventies, when Rein was young, to attend a Led Zeppelin concert would have been but a pipe dream. Plant never sang "Stairway to Heaven" at the VI Lenin Palace of Culture in seventies, the sun sinking into the Gulf of Finland, naked kids diving off the rocks into Tallinn harbor. But now Plant and other aging British ambassadors of rock had enlarged their tours east. Estonian fans like Rein were waiting.

Rein was a beam of light, a rock of testosterone in the estrogen nest that was the Publishing House. I had always thought that Epp was the epitome of the strong Estonian woman who could run a business, keep house, and take care of six kids and a drunk husband, but when the editor-in-chief Tiina and her right hand woman Aita showed up, I felt as if I was in the presence of blinking, thermonuclear devices. Do not cross this line! Danger! Tiina and Aita stepped into the office like grande dames, dressed in high-end clothes with hairstyles that seemed to change every fortnight, necklaces bouncing off their cleavages, hands smoothed by moisturizers, crimson lips, a ring on almost every finger, in clouds of perfume. You could always hear them when they left the elevator and walked down the corridor towards the office. Their high heels made a powerful sound.

It has been said that an Estonian's favorite food is another Estonian, and it could also be said that Estonian women have a terrific appetite. But Tiina and Aita were officially tolerant of Epp's young slacker husband who drank their coffee and used their free Internet and refilled at their water coolers. I always did it with a smile too, and a "Hi, how are you?"

Dark-haired Aita rarely talked to me. She only talked to Epp and Rein. Aita would walk right by me, her remarkably big boobs bouncing all over the place. Warning! Warning! Nuclear attack!

Tiina's life had started in a small provincial seaside town called Haapsalu. Now she lived in an opulent Tallinn suburb, indulging herself in the caviar of publishing life. Blonde and curvy, Tiina to me looked like some kind of Estonian Brünnhilde. I could imagine her up there, standing on the roof of the Publishing House, a Viking helmet on her head, spear in hand, commanding her underlings: "I want November's cover story! I want it now!"

I had never met anyone like Tiina or Aita before. They made my mother's colleagues across the sea in the cutthroat world of New York real estate look like pussycats. Sometimes I wondered what it would be like to be married to a woman like Tiina or Aita, a real *eesti naine**, a walking thermonuclear device. Then I remembered I was already married to one. Epp may have been less intimidating, but she was definitely just as strong.

---

* Estonian woman (In Estonian)

From the Publishing House, I'd be off to my lessons, turning tricks for 100 kroons for an hour of my native English-speaking time, a scarf tied loosely around my neck, my green coat trailing in the wind, like I was actually heading somewhere. Winter officially would not begin for almost two more months, but the temperature had already dipped below zero, and the muddy soil of Tallinn's parks and construction sites was cracked and hard, like old bread. The trees reached out of the earth, like the hands of drowning men.

My new students Antero and Lii fell prey to my snake oil English teacher routine earlier that month and for some reason had taken a liking to me. I met them in the morning when it was still dark out. Their office was in a concrete iceberg of a building near the National Library on Tõnismägi, set in a pack of postwar structures built strong so that they could withstand that ultimate of art critics: the atomic bomb.

Stateless Estonian Russians were learning the national language on the third floor, and sometimes I would see the Russians in the corridor on the way up to Antero and Lii's office on the fourth. There they waited in the dusty hallway, a nervousness in the air, jittery, as if they had been plucked off the street for a crash course in geophysics. "Where are we?" "What are we doing here?" Maybe they just wanted a proper passport so they could move to Paris. But first, what is the difference between *ostma, otsima,* and *otsustama**? Can you prounounce *jää-äär***?

---

* To buy, to look for, to decide. (in Estonian)
** The edge of ice. (in Estonian)

And *Jüriöö Ülestõus**? I always smiled when I passed the Estonian Russians. We were all in it together. Once in a while, one would even smile back.

Antero was in it with us too. Originally from Helsinki, he had mastered the Estonian language enough to run his own business. He took Estonia seriously too, his bookshelf was lined with treatises on Estonian-Finnish cooperation, the fur-hatted battalions of Finns who crossed the frozen Gulf of Finland to fight in the Estonian War of Independence in 1919, swords raised; the *Soomepoisid***, Estonians who crossed the frozen Gulf again to fight in the Finnish army in 1943 "for Finland's freedom and Estonia's honor." The burly Finn Antero always wore thick sweaters and talked about the bad old 1990s when he tried to make his way in an Estonian metals trade that was infested with mafia who would kill you if a business deal went sour. "I carried a gun," he said. It still made him nervous.

That was before Antero turned to the safer business of running a language school instead, and the Estonian girl Lii was his number two. She was young, long and lean with black hair and long finger nails. I would watch her extravagant manicure as it dipped into her desk to fish a few Lydia Koidulas free. Sometimes she would give me a Carl Robert Jakobson.***

---

* Jüriöö Ülestõus – The St. George's Night Uprising (In Estonian) was a very bloody and unsuccessful 14th Century revolt by indigenous Estonians against their Danish and German landlords and rulers.
** Finnish boys. (in Estonian)
*** Estonia had its own currency, the kroon, from 1992 until 2010, when it adopted the euro. Poet Lydia Koidula (1843–1886) was featured on the 100-kroon bill, while prominent national awakening figure Carl Robert Jakobson (1841–1882) was featured on the 500-kroon bill.

Antero, like a lot of Finns and Estonians, had problems with making a 'th' sound in English, because there is no corresponding sound in their languages. Wherever he saw a "th" he substituted a "t" or, more often a "d." I spent my nights designing tongue twisters to get him to speak the right way. Things like "the thoughtlessly thunderstruck thoroughbreds thumped through the thoroughfare" and "I think the thing is that there's nothing to thank them for." But when Antero's hand went up in the classroom, he couldn't help but start his sentence with "I tink," instead of "I think."

Lii wanted help with her business English, and one glance at her e-mails revealed the problem that plagued all Estonian communication – the exclamation point. For Estonians, the exclamation point was always handy, an old pal that could always be counted on to show up and make it a party. Any letter penned by an Estonian might read, "Hi! How are you?! I'm fine! The weather really sucks today! Let's meet after work!" Lii was disappointed when I told her that, in English, she was only permitted to use an exclamation point on very special occasions.

Then there was the bluntness. Estonians had no time for niceties. They always got straight to the point. As dumb as it may have seemed to the Estonians, English speakers liked their correspondence flowery and sweetened up with "I hope you are well" and "So wonderful to hear from you!" It took some convincing to get Lii to spike her letters with such emotive embellishments, but I promised her it would pay off in the end.

Both Antero and Lii also suffered from what I called the *Noh* factor, in that Finns and Estonians say *noh* (Estonian "well") to buy time when they are thinking of the rest of the sentence. To them it seemed harmless, but this threw off English speakers like me because *noh* sounded like "no," introducing negatives into places where they never should have been. Antero might say something like "Estonians are closer to Europe, they are, *noh*, an Old Hansa country. When Tallinn was in the Hansa League, Finns were, *noh*, still living in the trees." I tried to do the same thing in Estonian, only then did they understand what their precious *noh* was doing to me.

Our lessons were spiced by Antero and Lii's opinions about Estonia. Antero was convinced that Estonians were very good language learners. "My friend's daughter surprised me the first day we met. When she heard I was from Helsinki she started speaking Finnish, and it was just flowing, *noh*, fluently from her mouth."

"Antero! What did I tell you about *noh*?"

"I am sorry, sorry, so sorry," he said, blushing. "So I asked her where she learned Finnish and she said from watching television. Fluent Finnish! It was, *noh*, like a miracle."

"Oh yeah, my wife told me that everyone in north Estonia used to watch Finnish TV all the time," I said. "Whenever she came up to visit her uncle and aunt in Tallinn they would watch Finnish TV. She liked the commercials most. They didn't get the Finnish stations down in Karksi-Nuia."

When Lii heard that Epp came from Karksi-Nuia, she leaned back in her chair in the office, leveled her eyes on me, and whispered, "Ah, so you married a Mulk?"

"A what?"

"A Mulk."

187

"Huh?"

"What's a Mulk?" grunted Antero.

"You mean you don't know what Mulks are?"

"No," I said, pausing to contemplate if my wife was a member of some secret society. Maybe those nights she said she was going to Tiina or Aita's house to discuss the magazine, she was really meeting with these so-called Mulks?

"Mulks are people from southern Viljandi County, on the Latvian border," said Lii. "And Mulks are very, very rich."

"They are?"

"And they wear long black robes and they think they are better and smarter than everyone else."

Hmm. Epp didn't own any black robes as far as I knew. Did she think she was better or smarter than everyone else? She did tend to think she could do things better than most people.

"Maybe you are onto something," I said. "But what do Mulks do?"

"Mulks sit on the porches of their big farms in their long black robes stroking their cats," Lii narrowed her eyes, as if she was an arrogant Mulk herself. "All the time, they are looking at the neighbor's property, thinking of a way to buy it," she kept squinting and then broke character, revealing a smile. "Because of there's one thing Mulks like even more than money it is real estate!"

"But what does Mulk even mean?"

"Not sure," said Lii. "Someone told me it means 'fool' in Latvian."

As the month wound to its close, the days grew shorter, the orange sun hovering in the haze of the sky, then retreating slowly into the distance. Half the working day was dawn, the other half twilight. In the black mornings I would summon a taxi to our home street and ride it out into the darkness.

Budget Rent-a-Car was a client of Antero and Lii's firm. The building was set back in the woods under a canopy of tall pines along Lake Ülemiste. Inside I always made for the company kitchen to load up on free coffee from their machine, lightened with powdered milk and served in a tiny brown cup. At that hour, I usually took a refill. It would have been my third cup of the day and there would be more.

When it came to Estonian students, the Budget-Rent-A-Car gang, they all aimed to please. Give them a homework assignment, and they would complete it on time, their handwriting legibile, everything in its right place. Ask them a question, and they would respond with succinctness, hands folded in their laps, like good children. Sometimes they even dared to make eye contact with me, but only for a moment. But what I could not get them to do was converse with one another. I tried everything, any kind of interesting situation I could dream up, but usually it led to about three sentences being spoken.

To get the Budget gang to talk, I once asked them what Estonian celebrity they would most like to meet. Eve said she wanted to meet Jaan Tätte, a puppy dog-eyed, long-haired bohemian singer who I had once seen on TV. When he wasn't sailing off the coast of Saaremaa writing poetry, Tätte could be found bumming through the markets of Morocco in search of his muse. I suspected a lot of Estonian women wanted to meet Jaan Tätte. Even Epp.

Ülo, the only male in the group, wanted to meet Markko Märtin, the rally driver, and it was no surprise because most Estonian men didn't just want to meet Markko Märtin, they wanted to be him. Märtin was a top gun, a dispassionate daredevil, a strutting middle finger to danger. Estonian men would gather around TV sets on the weekends to watch their hero Markko behind the wheel. And when Märtin defeated Marcus Grönholm at the Neste Oil Rally Finland that summer, guys like Ülo erupted out of their living room chairs, pumping their fists in the air. Not only had the Estonian Martin defeated a Finn on Finnish territory, he also set a record for the longest jump in a World Rally Championship when his battered Ford Focus flew 57 meters in the air at a speed of 171 kilometres per hour. As always, British co-driver Michael Park, nicknamed "Beef", was by his side. Märtin liked Park, he was quoted as saying, his only flaw being that he couldn't speak Estonian. Then again, the daredevil Märtin himself didn't live in Estonia anymore. He lived in Monaco.

And I understood why. After my lessons at Budget, I would walk the three frosty kilometers to the newspaper office, sometimes pausing to get a fourth coffee in the gas station across the street or read up on Estonian celebrities. My personal favorite was Anu Saagim: a leggy middle-aged blonde with a crazy gleam in her eye and a mission in her heart to look as ridiculous as possible. She had recently posed nude for a magazine, covered only in milk with a hand thrust in her underpants, and a mad "kiss this, Estonia" grin on her face. Saagim was an extreme extrovert in a land full of people who looked at their hands when they spoke for fear of what others might think of them. Estonia was lucky to have her.

One morning, I came out of the gas station and noticed there was something different about the parking lot. It was covered in a fine layer of something white. Hmm. What could it be? Hail? Frost? I leaned over and ran a naked finger through the sugary substance on the ground. Snow. It was the last week of October, and it had already snowed. Christ. Growing up in New York, I had never seen snow on the ground in October before. November, sometimes. October, never. But here it was. If the temperature stayed beloved freezing, the morning's snowfall could stay on the ground until May.

How did I wind up here of all forsaken places? Why couldn't Epp have been Greek? Ah, Greece. Standing there in the cold parking lot, looking at the frozen pines, I imagined me and Epp the Greek eating calamari every night, drinking ouzo, swimming nude in azure waters. Then a snowflake landed on my nose. It wasn't so. My heart had never yearned for a Greek goddess from a sunny isle, anyway. It had asked for a northern woman. I had wanted *The Seventh Seal* and got it. Again I could see us walking together through the blustery snow on the way to the maternity ward, then trudging back with our vulnerable bundle to the little one-room apartment on Kentmanni Street.

Or maybe not?

Because when I concentrated on the image, the black shadows in the snow, I actually couldn't picture us returning to our small home after the delivery. That part of the future was out of focus.

It troubled me.

191

Pärnu Road rolled by, furniture stores, a police station, abandoned houses, the wind wrapping itself around my legs. I was crossing an overpass close to the city center later when my mobile rang. I picked it up. It was Epp in the office. At first I figured she was alone, but then I heard noises in the background. Rein was there too, probably listening to Genesis.

"I have an idea!" It was the way a lot of her phone calls started. "Justin, I just realized that I am so tired of fighting with the neighbors and the owner over this water bill. Let's pay the bill but let's get out of this place!"

"Ok."

"And I don't want to mess with these landlords anymore, so I was thinking, maybe that, well, maybe we should buy our own apartment, you know. And if we decide to leave Estonia in the future, then we always have a place we can stay when we come to visit."

"I was just thinking the same thing," I said.

"What?"

"I was just walking here and thinking that we shouldn't stay on Kentmanni Street any longer."

"Ha! Really?"

"My intuition says we should leave."

"So I don't have to convince you that we need to move?"

"No, I think it's a great idea."

Epp paused, perhaps shocked that her risk-averse husband was willing to do something as dynamic as buy an apartment without a few weeks of constant brainwashing.

"Wow," she said finally and laughed. "Well, I've already been looking at apartments online. I've found a few places. I'll print out the ads. We can look at them tonight."

"What about money, though?"

"Well, I think we can get the down payment money together somehow. Everyone else seems to be taking bank loans and buying apartments. It can't be so hard!"

I stood at the crest of the concrete overpass and looked off into the distance. The orange sun was rising above the rooftops of Tallinn, cloaking the city in early morning shadows. Old chimneys punctured the horizon, smoke curling to the sky. Empty trams glided like ghosts below me. Somewhere down there in the jumbled jungle of the city our new home was waiting.

REAL
ESTATE
FEVER

*I wasn't enamored with our Kentmanni Street
apartment, anyway.*

It had two pluses: it was centrally located and had central
heating. Beyond that the old Khrushchevka was nothing
special. We put down carpets to cover the broken tiles in
the kitchen. In the bathroom, we fought rust with paint and
a strategically placed laundry basket. The place only looked
normal at first glance. Stay awhile and you would see it for
what it was: a centrally located, centrally heated dump. While
Nikita Khrushchev was long dead, his cursed architectural
legacy lingered. Sometimes they would turn off the water in
the building, and when it went back on, the faucets would belch
out brown muck for hours. I thought we were the only ones
with this problem until I heard Ivan complain about the same
thing in his building in Lasnamäe.

The neighborhood was lifeless. Other people lived in
districts with personalities, places like Kristiine or Kalamaja

or Kadriorg. Our address was "across from the American Embassy." On our street and the next one over there were a pair sex shops with faded red signs that I never saw anyone enter or exit. They looked so forlorn that even I never fantasized about going in. A family of stray cats lived across from one of the shops, a mother and her offspring, nesting in the dirt. In the spring, we had watched the adorable kitten roll by his mother's side, suckling at her underbelly. In autumn, the male cat was grown and still nursing in the leaves. Everytime Epp saw the scene she said it reminded her of our neighbors: an old woman who lived with her middle-aged son.

There was no future in Kentmanni. It looked like a screen-hot from *A Clockwork Orange*, its Stalinist and Khrushchevka windows staring down on us with the rigid gaze of dead fish, old newspapers tumbling down the sidewalks with the wind. I imagined there were dozens of cozy apartments for sale out there in the city, better places where the faucets didn't cough rust and the tiles weren't broken, places without sex shops and incestuous cats and middle-aged men who lived with their mothers. They were out there waiting for us, centrally located and centrally heated, at the right price. All we had to do was pick one.

"Honey, are you a Mulk?"

Epp shrugged in the dark, as if to say, 'Don't waste my time.'

I stared at her.

"Justin, why are you asking me this? We have to find a place. Could you please focus and talk about real estate?"

"Are you Mulk or not? It's a simple question."

"No, it's not," she said, frustrated. "Am I a Mulk? Not a real one, okay? My roots aren't from there, you know, my grandparents roots come from North Estonia and from the West Coast and from Russia. But I was born in Viljandi, which isn't the real Mulgimaa, and moreover, officially I was born in Tallinn, so in that way I am not a Mulk. But at the same time I grew up in Karksi, and that's in the very heart of Mulgimaa. In this way I am one.

"Thank you."

We stood on a corner waiting for a real estate agent. It was only 5 pm, but by this time of the year everything had reversed, gone into the black, cut only by a few hours of midday sun. We had already been searching for our new home for a week and a half. The search started on that hazy orange afternoon when we went to see the first apartment on our list, a one bedroom in Kristiine that promised a "view of the Old Town," and sure enough, if you stood on the tips of your toes in the kitchen you could see the spires of St. Nicholas' and St. Olaf's churches poking above the tram lines and overpasses that cut Kristiine from the city center.

From that point on I familiarized myself with the tricks of the Estonian real estate trade. If it took you 45 minutes to walk to Old Town, then it was within "walking distance of the Old Town." If, by contorting yourself into some awkward position, you could catch a glimpse through the bathroom window of St. Olaf's spire, you had a full-fledged "view of the Old Town." And everybody wanted a view of the Old Town. It was one of the few nice parts of the city.

"So what do you know about Mulks?"

"Well, they eat *mulgipudru*," Epp said and shrugged again.

"What's that?"

"It's like mashed potatoes with barley and pork rinds."

"Do you like it?"

"Sure."

The real estate agent finally arrived to whisk us away into the night. His name was Tanel. He was in his thirties, dark hair, glasses, clean shaven, and professional. He spoke in the flat tone of a news anchor. Tanel's car was clean, and its cleanliness, his professionalism stood out to me because of the places he was to later show us. In my memory, these places existed far away, on the other side of town, but where they actually were in physical relation to the heart of the city was lost in the inky black of the night as we zoomed around, illuminated by headlights, cool air and shadows, like the negatives of photographs.

"Listen, I don't want to buy from Russians, ok?" Epp said to me in the backseat. "Then we might have to make up the contract in two languages and then there is the question of what their contract says versus what our contract says. It can cause all sorts of problems."

"That's ok with me."

I had lived for nine months in Tallinn and Russian to me was still as alien as Chinese or Hindi, maybe because I was trying to master Estonian, and I would accept nothing less from myself than total fluency. But out here on our real estate hunt, Russian was inescapable, it rose to the surface. Forty percent of the city spoke Russian, and it seemed like all of their apartments were for sale. Epp had drawn on her Russian skills at the second apartment we checked out earlier that week. It was on Kotzebue Street at the mouth to a district called Kalamaja, northwest of the Old Town, beyond the drunk-infested *Balti jaam**.

We had gone on a rainy, miserable morning. The house was fortress-like, a Stalin-era castle with high ceilings and big rooms. The owner was a little old woman with short hair who was born in Moscow and was about to return. The house had been built by German prisoners of war, she said, and it was actually one of her selling points. "Made by Germans, made by Germans, good German quality," she said it over and over again, as if I wanted to be reminded of how the Soviets worked the POWs to death in the construction process. The little old lady from Moscow kept Epp and me in the big, high-ceilinged, POW-built kitchen for a good 45 minutes chainsmoking and talking about the benefits of living in a German-built home, while Epp translated it all to me. *Nemetski, nemetski, nemetski, nemetski.* After a while even I came to understand that *nemetski* meant German.

"Well, what did you think?" Epp said when we left.

I closed my eyes, trying to imagine us in the muddy backyard with our newborn child, but the only picture that came to mind was of gaunt, overworked German POWs. "Nah," I shook my head. "It's not the place for us. Even if it was built by *nemetski* people."

"Do you even know what *nemetski* means?

---

* Baltic Station (In Estonian) – the main train station in Tallinn.

"It sounds like some famous Russian guy. You know, Tchai-kovsky, Dostoevsky, Nemetski."

"It comes from the word 'nemoi' which means 'mute' and 'not ours.'"

"Why did she keep talking about Germans, anyway? Who cares who built it?"

"Some people think German-built houses are better. Germans are known all over Europe for their workmanship."

Germans didn't build the houses Tanel showed us that night. I had lived for months in Kentmanni thinking it was among the worst Tallinn had to offer. It was only when I stepped outside my little box did I see how poor some Estonians really were, and when I say Estonians, I mean Estonian Russians. They lived on the edge of the city in dormitory-like apartment complexes, the buildings in various stages of ruin with rotten balconies collapsing, spraypainted with swastikas and swearwords. The whole environment sick, a melange of old ladies with plastic bags, broken bottles, amputees in wheelchairs, 24-hour kiosks, and abandoned cars.

Tanel led us to one of these houses, a first-floor, super fixer-upper with an advertised "sea view." Its occupants were an old man and his pet dog. The old man barely took notice of us when we entered, his eyes fixed on some old, Russian military documentary. Tanel spoke to him, politely, professionally. He looked like he should be selling new offices on Maakri Street. Instead, he peddled ruined apartments.

I looked out the window into the night, at the lights of ships twinkling in the bay. A sea view, yes, but from where? Inside, the dimly lit apartment, the dog continued to bark and jump at the man's feet. It was angry, frustrated. Why are we living here, old man? The dog seemed to say. The apartment was dim, dank, musty. It smelled like it hadn't been cleaned since Khrushchev's Secret Speech. The old man just kept watching television, the tanks rolling by in black and white, the grainy sounds of ancient air sirens and machine guns and grenades, ignoring the intruders, his hair sticking up over his ears. The little dog barked and rolled in the dust, miserable. Where did this man come from? I wondered. Where was his family? How long had he been here? How much longer would he stay?

"This place stinks," Epp whispered to me.

"I guess you don't want to take it?" I whispered back and winked. It wasn't like the old man could understand us. I just didn't want to offend our real estate agent.

"I'm sorry," Epp told Tanel. "It's not for us."

Tanel shrugged and blinked behind his glasses and said *sbasibo** to the old man who nodded and kept watching TV. Judging from Tanel's expression, the apartment had been on the market for a long time. The little dog barked at our heels on the way out the door. What would happen when the man died? I wondered. What would happen to all the others like him, packed away in these crumbling apartments, watching military documentaries? If they had any sense, his children had probably moved on to London or New York. Maybe he still had a sister or a cousin somewhere. But here, in Tallinn, he lived alone and he would probably die alone. I imagined the old man's corpse being wheeled out the door, the little

---

* Thank you (In Russian)

dog taken to a shelter or thrown out on the streets, the TV set sold to a pawnshop. The wrecking crew would descend to tear the condemned building down, and then there would be nothing, as there once was before. Just a plot of land with a sea view.

More apartments and sellers paraded before us that night, glum and dispossesed, as if they had been plucked from a long-winded BBC World Report. "Sergei is an unemployed engineer who lives with his wife Marina and their four children in this three-room flat in Kopli, on the outskirts of Tallinn, the capital city of this tiny former Soviet republic." "Natasha lives in this two-room apartment in Pelgurand with her eight-year-old daughter Anastasia. Natasha is a single mother and works as a school teacher, but her salary is low. The family is poor and the house is heated by wood furnaces."

Wood heating. It had already sparked a minor clash of civilizations. It happened after we saw the apartment on Laste-kodu Street earlier that week. It was between the bus station and the Central Market, its backyard filled with rotten boards and plastic containers. The century-old wooden structure looked out on a rundown corner grocery. The house was a patchwork of colors, as none of the tenants could agree what to paint it, so each painted his or her section alone. One part of the building was orange, another gray. The floors of the house on Lastekodu Street were warped. Walking around you got the sense that you were at sea. I could imagine taking a small marble and setting it at one side of the apartment, only to watch it roll down to the other side. Still it had new-ish looking floors, a functional kitchen, a toilet that looked fit to use, a shiny metal furnace. Maybe it was the best we could do.

"So, what do you think?" Epp asked later that day. "I think we should take it." We sat in a cafe eating cake and drinking coffees. Outside, it was raining.

"I don't know. I can't see us living there. I mean, my intuition –"

"You and your intuition," she cut me off. "Come on! It's a good price. It's in an okay area. We could rent it out to a Finn when we leave Estonia."

"To a Finn? You really think that some Finn is going to rent that place?"

"Why not?"

"Everytime it gets cold in the winter he's got to go outside and get more wood for the furnace. No way! It's not the 19th century anymore. At least in Finland."

Epp looked away for a second. Then she trained her look of anger and disgust on me. "We aren't rich, Justin," she snapped. "We can't afford to be snobs."

"I'm not being a snob."

"Yes, you are."

Was I? I was. My great grandfather was an Italian immigrant bootlegger, my grandfather sold insurance, my father sold computer hardware, and I was the cherry at the top of the cake of American social mobility, the professional journalist, the one with the college education, the snob without money. The Petrones had gone from poverty to snobbery in four generations.

"I'm not sure about the house," I tried to bypass the wood furnace issue. "It's not in good shape."

"But it can always be renovated."

"How can you renovate it? If I drop a marble on one side of the kitchen it would roll to the other side. You can't fix that."

"Hmm," Epp said and stared into your coffee. "Okay, maybe you are right," she looked up. "I just got excited, that's all. I thought finding a place would be a little easier."

At around 7 pm, Tanel returned to the same street corner from where we had departed with a stoic look on his professional face. Was he disappointed we hadn't liked anything? Was it because we were looking in the wrong places or was it because, God forbid, we were snobs?

"I don't think these were the right apartments for people like you," Tanel said in his TV news anchor voice as he turned off the car. "You should check out apartments in Kalamaja. It's an up and coming area, and a lot of people like you are moving there."

"Kalamaja? But we already looked there," I said. "Remember the huge house built by Germans, on Kotzebue Street?"

"That's not real Kalamaja," Epp said. "Real Kalamaja starts a little further beyond that street."

"You can probably get a good deal in Kalamaja," Tanel reassured us. "The neighborhoods that we saw tonight – Kopli, Pelgurand – they just aren't right for people like you."

What I came to like about Kalamaja was that most of the houses were pre-Soviet instead of post-Soviet. The district was bruised and worn, yes. Some houses stood abandoned, their windows blown in by the wind, the upper floors blackened by fire. Gangs of wild cats congregated beside dumpsters hungry for their next meal. But the shabbiness gave Kalamaja its charm. The district had survived two world wars, a backward economic system, and still looked salvageable.

Nikita Khrushchev's architectural legacy was absent here. Instead there were wooden houses, not apartment blocks, but real homes, two-story, boxy "Lender" buildings named for the local architect who designed them, and three-storey, curvy "Tallinn" houses with art nouveau-influenced domed roofs, all of them lining the district's streets in red and green and yellow, one after the other, like toy soldiers. Most of the houses followed the same pattern: a staircase in the center opening out to apartments on every floor. Lenders had four one-room apartments per story, while the bigger Tallinns had four two-room apartments per floor. The houses had been built at a time when Baltic Germans ruled the city, and the Kalamaja district, called Fischermai before 1918, retained a distinct Teutonic flavor.

For the first time on our real estate hunt, I could close my eyes and envision myself pushing our little baby in a carriage down the street. The fact that there were other people pushing baby carriages down the streets of Kalamaja, "people like us" as Tanel might have said, may have guided my intuition along. Whether they were Estonians or Estonian Russians or even the last remnants of the fabled Baltic Germans, I didn't care.

What mattered to me was that they were young, employed, and walked as if there was a future, as if they too believed that Kalamaja could be rescued, that the money that had saturated the city center would soon infiltrate this adjacent district, bathing everything in fresh paint and new plumbing and silvery tin roofs. There was a smattering of hope in Kalamaja, hope that was less in the ruined apartment blocks of Pelgurand.

The apartment we found the first day on Väike Patarei Street was close enough to the sea that you could smell the salt in the air. A three-story yellow wooden house with a tin roof, its stairway was tiled in white and black, the walls stripped down to their wooden base. The owner met us at a door in a long gray coat, her hair wavy and brown, tucked under a black beret, looking as if she had made herself up to match the old building. Her husband was a lanky architect with a thick beard who sat at a desk and tried to be inconspicuous. Their three year-old child – a little towheaded boy – greeted us when we entered the apartment. "My daddy draws houses," he said from behind a tiny toy desk.

Epp was smitten. "I like this place," she whispered to me as the owner showed us around. "And I like them. They're like us."

I liked the Väike Patarei apartment too. It had just come up for sale that morning and Epp had arranged to see it directly. With its white walls, wood floors, functional kitchen, it stood apart from so many other Tallinn apartments in its normality. This begged the question: what exactly constituted "normal" in Estonian real estate? Väike Patarei was the first apartment I saw in Tallinn where I felt I could move right in. And while

I still couldn't understand most of what the owner was saying as she gave us the quick tour of the place, at least she spoke in Estonian, a language I now found familiar and comforting. I liked the way the owner addressed us too. Her hands would point out a detail, but never did her body come within a meter of ours. The woman was fundamentally Estonian, polite and yet distant. She was expecting a second child and they needed more space, she said. Everything was startlingly normal.

Until I asked, "Where is the shower?"

"It's in the kitchen," the owner said.

"It is?"

And there it was, a white shower cabinet with glass doors, right between the sink and the refrigerator. How could I have missed it? Maybe I thought it was some kind of pantry. I tried to imagine taking a shower there while Epp made breakfast. It wasn't the most private space in which to wash oneself I figured, but at least if you got hungry, you could fix yourself a sandwich while taking a shower. My heart sank when I saw the shower cabinet in the kitchen. Väike Patarei, the most normal apartment we had seen, wasn't so normal after all.

"I think we should take it!" Epp said outside, rubbing her hands together. "We are not going to find a better deal than this!"

"I don't know," I said, kicking a pile of leaves off the sidewalk. "Do you really want to take a shower in the kitchen?"

"But we're the only ones who will be living there! What did I tell you about being a snob? Let's go back in there and make them an offer. In real estate, you have to be quick!"

I almost said yes, but the tiny hope that we could find an apartment just as nice as the one on Väike Patarei with a shower cabinet in any room other than the kitchen restrained me.

"Let's look around a bit more," I pleaded. "If we can't find anything better by tonight, we'll make an offer."

In the evening, Epp called the owner of Väike Patarei to inform her that we had decided to take the place, but in polite yet distant tones, it was relayed to her that the apartment was no longer for sale. Someone else had gone through right after us and bought the apartment on the spot, she said. Epp was disappointed. I felt ashamed. My reluctance had cost us Väike Patarei, and who knew how long it would take us to find another place as good. Epp had been right. In real estate, you had to be quick.

LANGUAGE
SCHOOL

Estonians enjoyed nothing more than bellyaching about how people never bothered to learn their language.

"I can't believe you speak Estonian," a real estate agent had said to me. "Some people have been living here for fifty years and can't say one word."

"Fifty years?" the apartment owner had retorted. "More like sixty years!"

What was even more hilarious was that I had had them all convinced I understood everything they were saying! It was easy to fool these Estonians. All you had to do was say "Tere" and they would welcome you into the tribe. But while pretending to understand Estonian could win you praise, it could also get you in trouble.

When Epp's sister Eva and her daughter Simona came to visit us one day in Tallinn, Epp and Eva decided to go shopping and then had left little Simona with me. The five-year-old had golden hair, blue eyes, and the adorable face of a seal pup. Eva's apartment in Tartu didn't have a tub, so when Simski, as she was called, saw ours, she wanted to take one immediately.

I agreed and drew the water and Simski took off her clothes and hopped in. Happy in the tub's warm water, she looked up at me and splashed a little water in my direction, playfully. "Paljas porgand! Paljas porgand!" *she said and laughed.

"Huh?"

"Paljas porgand," she repeated, her little eyes twinkling.

"Oh, *porgand*, a carrot," I recognized one of the words. "Are you hungry?"

"Paljas porgand! Paljas porgand!" Simski said and shook her head, this time a little louder.

"Do you want something to eat?"

"Ei!" she cried, frustrated. "Paljas porgand!" she said again, this time slowly, as if I was hearing impaired and that would help me to understand her. "Paljas porgand! Paljas porgand!"

"Okay, okay. I'll go get you a carrot."

As soon as I left the bathroom, I knew I had made a mistake because Simski started crying, jumping up and down in the tub, bellowing the same phrase over and over again in agony: "Paljas porgand! Paljas porgand! Paljas porgand! Paljas porgand!"

"I'm getting you one!" I shouted to her, peeling a carrot over the sink. "*Üks moment***!"

"Paljas porgand! Paljas porgand! Paljas porgand!"

"It's almost ready, kid!" I peeled faster.

---

* Naked carrot. (In Estonian)
** One moment. (In Estonian)

"PALJAS PORGAND! PALJAS PORGAND! PALJAS PORGAND!" Simona was bawling now, hysterical, howling and splashing, getting everything wet. There was water all over the corridor floor, Simski even splashed little Miisu, who sprinted down the hall and went to hide under our bed. If she screetched any louder, I feared our neighbors might call the police and I would get into trouble for child abuse.

"Oota! Oota! Wait!" I yelled to her from the kitchen, my head throbbing from her voice. "Please!"

"PALJAS PORGAND! PALJAS PORGAND! PALJAS PORGAND!" she screamed, the sound of her shrill voice like daggers in my ears. "PALJAS PORGAND! PALJAS PORGAND! PALJAS PORGAND!"

"Fuck!" I cut my finger slicing the carrot and cursed. Simski howled and cried even louder. Finally the carrot was peeled and sliced, ready for consumption. I raced back to the bathroom. "PALJAS PORGAND! PALJAS PORGAND!" "Here! Here's your porgand, Simski! "PALJAS PORGAND! PALJAS POR-GAND!" "Please take it."

The little girl was suddenly silent. She took the vegetable in hand and eyed it, puzzled. Then she tossed it on the floor, screamed "Paljas porgand!" and splashed me, soaking my pants.

"Why did you do that, Simski?" I thundered. "You said you wanted a goddamn carrot!"

"PALJAS PORGAND! PALJAS PORGAND! PALJAS PORGAND!"

"Oh Christ."

I jumped to the phone and speed-dialed Epp, my hands wet, shaking.

"Epp kuuleb," she answered.

"Where ... where are you?"

"We're in the Old Town. What's the matter, you sound upset?"

"Can you come home? Please? I have a bit of a problem on my hands."

"What? Is Simona okay?" Epp asked. In the background I could hear Eva ask her, "What's going on? What's happened?"

"She just keeps screaming 'paljas porgand' and splashing me," I stammered. "I gave her a carrot but she just won't stop shouting at me."

"Oh Justin," Epp's voice became soft and she and began to laugh. "Could you put her on the phone?"

"Hold on. Simski?"

"PALJAS PORGAND! PALJAS PORGAND!"

"Aunt Epp wants to talk to you."

Simski took the phone in her hand. When she spoke, and it was more like a whimper, I saw she had little tears running down her cheeks. Eventually Epp and Eva managed to calm her down. Simski handed me back the phone and sat down in the tub, her eyes and cheeks red with exhaustion.

"She was just frustrated that you couldn't understand her," Epp said to me. "That's why she got so upset."

"But I got her a carrot."

"No, Justin, 'Paljas porgand' means 'naked as a carrot.' It's just a thing that kids say sometimes."

"How the hell was I supposed to know that?"

"Well, maybe you should take some Estonian classes."

"Classes? But ... but everyone thinks I'm fluent!"

211

Epp laughed softly to herself for a moment and then she regained her composure. "I don't want to offend you, Justin, but you're not even intermediate. If you take Estonian classes, you are probably going to need to be in a course for beginners. If you want, I can look around."

I looked down at puddles of water on the floor and said, "Okay."

There were seven of us in the beginning, all foreigners, all male. We sat around a table in the basement of the Tallinn Language School on Endla Street, down the hill from the National Library.

Other than our foreignness, it seemed at first glance that we had little in common. Manuel was tall and dark and soft spoken, an IT wizard from Barcelona. Next to him sat Joris, a Belgian with curly brown hair and spectacles who taught European politics at a local university. Then there was gray-headed Manfred. Based on his accent and his name, I imagined he was German, but he didn't say where he was from when he introduced himself. Just another foreign businessman, I presumed. Across the table sat three more eager students: Simeon, a lawyer from Bulgaria with a cherubic face; Lutz, a young EU bureaucrat originally from Dresden with the dark-framed glasses of an intellectual; and Sebastian, a flannel-clad bohemian from Budapest who bore the romantic pout of a man who knows he is devastatingly handsome.

Any time one of the dialogues in our lessons made use of a female Estonian character, Sebastian's lips would tremble and he would be moved to speak. "Ah, yes, Piret, I know Piret, I met her at Club Privé last night," he would say and softly chuckle to himself, or "Siiri, oh yeah, I remember her. She was at Club Hollywood last Saturday."

But while Sebastian was the only single one in our class, it turned out we had all been moved to study the language by Estonian women. "Reelika said she found classes for beginners online and, well, here I am," Manuel said in his soft Spanish accent. Manuel had met Reelika while studying in Germany, had moved to Tallinn to be near her, and had been commuting to Helsinki during the week for work until he had recently found a steady job in Estonia.

Joris' story was similarly European. His wife Esta was raised by Estonian émigrés in Sweden and she now held an EU post in Tallinn. Their two-year-old daughter Aino was being reared in a multilingual environment, with Joris speaking Flemish to her, Esta speaking Swedish, and Esta's parents Estonian. While little Aino already understood the language of Estonia, Joris said he was having a harder time fitting in. "Whenever I go for a walk with Aino in the park, old women are always coming up to me and telling me to fix her scarf or that it's too cold to play on the grass," he complained. "I told Esta that it would be nice if I could tell them that I am Aino's father and I know what I'm doing, so she suggested I take some classes."

Simeon's wife Kati had made a similar suggestion, as had Lutz's girlfriend Liisi.

"So all you guys are with Estonian women, huh?" our teacher Mai said, looking down on us from the head of the table, almost in pity. "What about you, Manfred?"

213

"I met a young lady at a conference on international politics," the gray-haired man looked up. "When I moved in with her, to Tallinn, I thought, 'Ok, great, I'll learn Russian and I can get by in all three Baltic States.' So I learned Russian. But when I tried speaking Russian to people here, I quickly learned that this is not the right language to speak."

"Well, most people in Estonia speak Estonian," I said from across the table.

"Ja*, ja, that's true," he said. "But I always tell my Estonian friends not to forget their Russian," Manfred shook his finger in the air. "It is a very useful language to know." He chuckled a little when he said it, as if he had really meant to say, 'keep your friends close but keep your enemies closer,' and I was reminded of the EU referendum poster, Is Russia Our Friend?

"Don't worry, Manfred, I haven't forgotten Russian yet," Mai said. Our teacher hadn't forgotten English, French, German, or Swedish either. Mai had a mane of yellow hair and always wore scarves with dramatic colors. She was quick, a blur of yellow, blasting through the lessons. "We have so much to do! We have so much to learn! We have to move on!" she would say. With her many languages and flamboyant style, Mai seemed well traveled, international, but to look at her face was to see a person unmistakable in her Estonianness. With thin Asiatic eyes, broad cheekbones and thick lips, she reminded me a bit of Epp.

Mai drew upon her vast vocabulary to teach her multinational class. Sometimes she would tell Manfred the definition of an Estonian word in German, or explain a phrase to Joris in

---

* Yes. (In German)

Swedish or French, two languages that the Fleming knew well. I was the only one in class who wasn't fluent in a language other than my native tongue, but I was determined to leave all the others in the dust when it came to Estonian. If the real estate agents thought I was fluent, I must have some potential, I told myself.

Our textbook was called *E nagu Eesti**. The book consisted of dialogues and vocabulary exercises, grammar charts and puzzles, but the illustrations were what grabbed me. From end to end, *E nagu Eesti* was filled with educational cartoons, caricatures of stereotypical Estonians doing Estonian things like shoveling hay and skiing, except instead of portraying her countrymen as humans, the artist had rendered these fictitious Otts and Kärts and Krõõts and Atses and Antses more like scheming elves or wily dwarves. With their long noses and beady eyes and expressions of inhuman detachment, the Estonian dwarves and elves looked at first like pure fantasy. Sometimes when my caffeine high began to peak, I imagined them talking back to me from the page, chattering on in little cartoon voices about saunas and cross-country skiing and meat jelly, all the things Estonians loved. But then I would notice that a cartoon resembled my father-in-law Andres, or Epp's Uncle Tiit or her grandmother Laine. Maybe the artist wasn't so creative after all, I wondered in these moments. Maybe Estonians really did look like dwarves and elves.

Once I showed the strange pictures to Ivan at the office. "Look at that one," I had pointed at a character in the book.

---

* E as in Estonia. (In Estonian)

215

"It looks just like Epp's Uncle Tiit!" "Let me see what they are teaching you," Ivan had said and took the book, flipping through the twisted images of troll-like caricatures that were meant to represent the people of his country. He looked for some time and then wrinkled his nose and tossed the book back to me. "I just don't understand Estonians!" he cried in a rare burst of emotionality. "Why do they have to be so scary and Nordic?"

Scary and Nordic, they were, but also darkly funny. The more I learned the Estonian language, the more I began to feel like I was becoming privy to some secret joke I didn't yet understand. On the outside, everyone kept a straight face, but inside, it seemed they were laughing. It was there in the dry dialogue, the fantastic drawings, in Mai's detached but amused glare. Something was extremely funny in Estonia, rib-ticklingly hilarious, but what was it? During our lessons we would take turns reading the short poems that were featured in the book. And so seven guys named Justin, Manuel, Joris, Manfred, Simeon, Lutz, and Sebastian read aloud the works of poets like Hando Runnel and Leelo Tungal, Jaan Kaplinski and Heljo Mänd, Paul-Eerik Rummo and Tiia Toomet.

We would go around in circles, each student taking a line:

Õuna kodu on õunapuus, pirni kodu on pirnipuus, kirsi kodu on kirsipuus...*

Mai would sit at the head of the table, nodding, quietly entertained as she heard poetry read in her language by a Spaniard, a Belgian, a Bulgarian, a Hungarian, an American,

---

* An apple's home is in the apple tree, a pear's home is in the pear's tree, a cherry's home is in the cherry tree... (In Estonian, a poem by Heljo Mänd)

and two Germans. At the end of class, our teacher would rocket out of her seat and shout *"tubli"* and *"on teil veel küsimusi**?"* but usually we didn't have any questions for her. I didn't even know where to start. Every word was new. Every rule had an exception. After learning Estonian for an hour, one's feeble Indo-European brain would throb.

We would all stumble out of the school basement into the soft morning light and stand around in the parking lot for a few minutes telling jokes before going our separate ways. As we talked, I imagined Mai looking down from us at from her office on the second floor, a knowing gleam in her eye. For centuries the Estonians had been desperate for people to learn their language. At last, they had found seven idiots who were up to the task.

◊ ◊ ◊

Well, five, actually. Within two weeks of the start of our lessons, Sebastian the Hungarian Casanova abruptly skipped town to chase tail in some other city, and Lutz found a sudden reason to report back to Brussels for his next assignment. That left Manuel from Barcelona, Joris the Fleming, Simeon the Bulgarian, and Manfred, the gray-haired German. Of my classmates, I came to know Manfred best. He lived in Kadriorg and we used to walk together to the city center before he caught his tram home.

Manfred spoke little of his past at first, but that didn't mean

---

* Do you have any more questions? (In Estonian)

he was quiet. Actually, he never shut up. Whether it was radical Islam, the rise of China, or Russia under Putin, he had strong opinions. We would stroll along Endla Street, over Tõnismägi, down Pärnu Road, and across Tammsaare Park to the Tallinn Department Store, where Manfred's tram would take him home.

"But what can be done to secure peace in the Middle East?" Manfred would exclaim with his finger in the air, as we crossed the city.

Manfred liked to point when he spoke. He came from that older, more opinionated generation, I figured, the one that was still convinced in the possibility of a better future. When Manfred's peers came of age in Germany in the 1960s, they went up against the authorities with Molotov cocktails and slogans. Young men like me or Manuel or Joris or Simeon tried not to bother ourselves with the ailing world's chronic problems in 2003, but Manfred still had that idealistic sparkle in his eyes.

"How can we secure peace in the Middle East?" I repeated the question as we crossed Tammsaare Park. "Maybe Arafat and Sharon have to go first. I mean, they are both so old!" I noticed Manfred wince when I said it, but I continued anyway: "They've been fighting all their lives, so they probably just know how to keep fighting. They don't know how to make peace. Once those two are out of the picture, maybe then things will get better."

"Ja, ja, the hope of a future generation, that's what they said when we were young," Manfred said. "But what about all these young suicide bombers, eh? These jihadists? Do you think that once Arafat is gone, they will stop blowing themselves up? No, no. I don't think so!"

218

Manfred gave me the address of his homepage on the Internet, but when I looked it up later I found it was all in German, plastered with apocalyptic articles about *Der Terror-krieg* and *Der Inner-Islamiche Konflikt**. When I asked about it one day, he told me he had been in Jerusalem for half a decade in the German embassy. He had also lived in New York for five years before that, working at the United Nations. These days the retired diplomat spent most of his time writing analytical pieces for German newspapers.

"I get a lot of angry letters, you know," he boasted. "I'm a popular guy!"

Manfred loved to debate, he loved to argue. Though his head was gray, he had the energy of a little boy, all excitement, all movement. His favorite Estonian food was *lasteviinerid*, little pink sausages made for children. "I have Astrid fry them up for me. I can eat two bags!" he said. "Delicious!" And the more I walked with him, the more he reminded me of the city of Berlin itself, the lightning quick trains shooting out like stars, everywhere construction, jackhammers and scaffolding, cranes and hardhats. It was in the brash way he spoke, the way he seemed so convinced of his opinions, the hunger he had for life, as if he really could only sleep when he was dead. Maybe all Germans were like that, Saxon firecrackers, always moving, always doing, arguing on and on and on about *der krieg* and *der krise* and *der konflikt*. Ja, ja.

Manfred said he spoke English and French fluently and had a basic command of Arabic and Russian. "But Estonian,"

---

* The Terror War and the Inner Islamic Conflict. (In German) he shook his head, "this is the hardest language I have ever learned. I mean the grammar is completely different from our thinking. Everyone talks so fast. Pop! pop! pop! pop! It sounds like a machine gun. Let's just say it's not like French or Italian or any other language based on the Latin system."

"But there are a lot of loan words from German, at least," I said. "Like Mai said, *mantel*, coat, is *mantel*."

"And *gabel*, fork, is *kahvel*; *krug*, a mug, is *kruus*. All the household items have similar names. There is no denying the German influence here and the mentality is very similar. It's something I noticed immediately. The Russians are easy to approach. The Estonians? It takes time to get close to them. They are like Germans, stiff and shy. But, here's a big difference," he wagged his finger in the air again, "contrary to Germany, life is more liberal here."

"How so?"

"Because in Germany the whole of life is regulated by rules! The individual is tied up in a strict social system. It's nice, for some, but there's no fun, no risk. But here, when Astrid and I go out to our summer house, I can drive my jeep on the beach and nobody bothers me. In Germany, I would probably be breaking the law and some old woman would call the police."

Manfred's eyes sparkled again. He was lost in visions of himself behind the wheel of his jeep, zooming down that wild beach, but all I could think about was the fact that Manfred even owned a jeep, not to mention a home in the wealthy district of Kadriorg, a place we could simply not afford to buy into, let alone a summer house. I watched him as he got ready to board his tram. Maybe his Astrid had been right to take a chance on this erudite diplomat. Maybe Epp had been mistaken to invest in a penniless wannabe journalist like me.

"Hey, Manfred, where is your summer house, anyway?"

"In Salmistu, about half an hour east of Tallinn on the coast," he said. "Astrid and I really got a good deal on it and, oh, it is a beautiful spot. I've been thinking of buying up some more land around there too, you know. We are going to take a look this weekend, before it gets too cold."

"We're looking to get a place too."

"What? Where? In Salmistu?" Manfred's blue eyes fixed on me with intense interest, as if I was a potential competitor.

"No, no. In Tallinn."

"Ah, ja, ja," Manfred relaxed his shoulders and licked his lips. "I tell you, real estate is one of my passions in life. And now is the time, Justin, now is the time! It's the off season and prices are just starting to rise with EU accession coming. The prices in Salmistu have just spiked since I bought our place there last year, and, oh, believe me, they will get higher. You'll see. Just wait until next spring, Justin," he wagged his finger in my face as he stepped into his tram. "You will see!"

SEARCHING
FOR A NEST

At night, we lay in bed, thinking of ways to finance our real estate endeavor.

We still had money tucked away from our wedding gifts and Epp had her salary. There were also my wages from teaching and writing articles, though they were barely enough to keep our kitchen stocked with milk and chocolate and cat food. But after turning the issue over, we arrived at a solution. There were other financial resources we could count on. One was my parents. Another was the Estonian state.

I had expected my father and mother to be cool to the idea of helping us with the apartment. They had blown thousands and thousands of dollars on my university education with the hope that it would earn me a six-figure salary right out of school. In Tallinn, I was earning three figures, three Estonian figures, 100 kroons an English lesson. But when I presented the idea to my folks, Mom and Dad astonished me: "Makes sense," they said. "We might be able to loan you the down payment."

And not only were they willing to loan us money, they were interested in the process. They wanted to give us advice. Given all the nights I had spent listening to them talk at the dinner table, I was surprised by how quickly I had forgotten my parents' twin passions: money and real estate.

My father was the one who loved money. It just had a way of finding its way into his pockets, he said. Once we were in New York City and a twenty dollar bill floated down from a skyscraper into his open palm. When I was a kid, he helped me organize my first business: collecting used bottles from neighbors and bringing them to the bottle depository. Even with a full bag, I might only earn five dollars a week, but it was all in coins, and dad loved the coins, the way they jingled. When I told him what my new friend Manfred had said about rising real estate prices, he believed me. "I know the Germans and the Germans know money," he said. "That Manfred sounds like he knows what he's talking about. My kind of guy!"

My mother was the real estate agent. At night, when Epp huddled by the landline's receiver, talking to her, it came back to me, how my mother had always collected real estate catalogues everywhere we went and spent her time gazing out windows on vacations, talking of relocating to the sunny Florida Keys, or the remote islands of New England, or the river towns of Pennsylvania. "It's just a fantasy!" she would say defensively, dreamy eyed, staring out the window.

I had spent my youth waiting for my mother: yawning over old magazines in antique shops, wasting away in paint stores, flipping through color wheels where the colors had names like "salmon" and "lemongrass." "What color do you think I should paint the living room, peanut or caramel?" my mother might say, holding out what looked to me to be two identical shades of brown. "Uh, caramel?" I would respond, unable to distinguish between the two. "You sure?" she'd squint at me. "Maybe peanut?" I'd try again. "Wow!" her eyes would brighten. "I was thinking the same thing!"

So my parents agreed to loan us the money, but how could we pay them back? Enter the Estonian state.

Since regaining independence, little Estonia's population had dropped while the population of all other northern European countries, save Latvia and Lithuania, had risen. The old guidebooks from the early nineties still said that 1.6 million people lived in Estonia, but there were only 1.4 million souls in the country in 2003, down 13 percent from 1991. Across the water in Finland the population had risen a healthy 4 percent during the same period.

Where had the people gone? The answers were as scattered as stars. Some left mother Estonia for mother Russia, others had found new mothers with names like Great Britain and Germany, Australia and the United States of America. Others were in the cemetery, underground or ashes. Others remained unborn, but not at their own urging. Terminated was the word. Or not even created at all. At night, hustling through Tallinn's stacks of wooden and cement boxes, in search of a home, one could imagine that from every dark window once shone a light, in every crooked ruin once dwelled a happy family. Most of the lights were still on, but in Estonia, in a dozen years, 200,000 people had disappeared. Poof!

Yet help was on the way. The government had a solution. The state's secret weapon, its remedy for the population free-fall, was parental compensation. New mothers, or fathers, could be paid their full year's salary in monthly installments while they were on parental leave, the government had ruled. If the economic instability that followed the collapse of the USSR had caused a decrease in the number of Estonians, there was now a new juicy financial incentive to make more of them.

Since mostly women went on leave, most people referred to parental compensation as the *emapalk* or "mother's salary." To me it sounded fantastic, a pipe dream. Pay people to have children? It would never pass muster in the US, where any politician who supported such a policy would be branded a wild-eyed "socialist" and publicly shamed. But here in Estonia, the "socialists" enacting the policy were none other than Prime Minister Juhan Parts' merry band of conservative Friedmanites. Estonia was championed by economic liberals the world over for its flat tax. They looked askance when it came to parental renumeration.

"The state needs new tax payers," Epp had said to me when I raised the discrepancy. "The mother's salary is not a bad deal for them when you think about it."

The new law was scheduled to come into force on January 1, 2004. And lucky for us, our little golden egg was expected to hatch exactly one week later.

Otsime Pesa – "Searching for a Nest." Each letter told who we were and what kind of place we were searching for. The bottom of every letter contained Epp's e-mail address and the number of the mobile phone we shared. We printed out a hundred of the signs early in the morning in the Publishing House and then headed out to distribute them. As a real estate agent, my mother's soundest advice was to avoid other agents and go direct. Our plan was to stuff mailboxes in the neighborhoods we liked, with the hope that our nest would be found.

It was deep in November by then, damp and gray. The early snow of October had long melted. Now there was just rain and gloom every day, punctured by infrequent bursts of sunlight. The sidewalks were covered in a carpet of wet leaves, the moss on the old roofs of Kalamaja was rich and verdant, my cheeks slick with moisture. Every night after work we went out hunting for apartments, the night air so wet you could see your breath. Some owners had read our "Searching for a Nest" flyers and called us back, babytalking on and on about how sweet it was to see a young couple looking for a nest. But none of the places we saw compelled us to buy.

We looked mostly in Kalamaja. This area had grown on us though it had some rough patches, which is to say that in some places, it looked like the war had just ended. At one house near the harbor we encountered a pair of grizzled old drunks, their faces black with dirt, passed out in the stairwell doorway, strewn about like corpses. Half the house was black, and Tallinn's drunk community was responsible for most of the half-burned houses, I was told, as the inebriated were prone to accidentally starting fires. I tried to steer clear of especially run-down streets when we were flyering, but Epp insisted on putting a flyer in every postbox of every house, even the ruined ones, ever optimistic, because someone who had something good to sell might find the paper. "Never mind that," she would say, pointing to an abandoned building or a heap of trash. "All of it will be gone in five years."

And I believed her. By this point I believed in real estate more than I believed in anything else: music, the written word, the future of the European Union, let alone any class I taught or article I wrote. Real estate! It had sutured itself to my soul. I believed in Epp and I believed in Manfred and anyone else who would tell me that we were doing the right thing. "You've got to be quick, Justin, quick!" "I know the Germans and the Germans know money." "Prices will rise, Justin! You will see!" Everything to me was now an apartment. Everything was doors and windows and chimneys and radiators, floors and walls and plumbing. The Lamaze classes we took once a week at the Tallinn Central Hospital seemed like fragments of a dream. Prospective apartments were all Epp and I talked about at night. Real estate was our reality.

Some of the apartments we looked at though were less than real. More than once we walked into a place that shined with patterned moldings and ceiling panels and bathroom tiles, fit for polite company. But when I touched the molding, it was soft and gave way, and when I ran my finger along the bumps in the bathroom tiles, I found that the air bubbles below smoothed themselves out. That's because the moldings weren't made of wood, they were made of styrofoam, and the tiles weren't ceramic, they were vinyl. These apartments were made to look normal, but underneath, they were not. Pull off the styrofoam and see the rotting logs. Pull up the vinyl and see the crumbling cement. Epp had a word for renovation jobs like these: *Euroremont*, which translated roughly as "European renovation."

But *Euroremont* was a manifestation of something bigger than moldings and tiles. *Euroremont* was born of the acute desire to look European, to appear normal. Indeed, it was a time when Europe was in the air, and the prefix "Euro" had gained a special popularity in the heady days before EU accession. "Euro" had that trustworthy ring to it, a sound of seriousness, sturdiness, stability, quality, reliability. In the center of Tallinn you could leave your car at the Europark. In the supermarket, they sold Euroleib*. All around Estonia's capital, shops sprang up with names like Eurofoto and EuroPrint and Euro Furnituur.

And among them all was Euroremont, apartments made to look like any apartment in Antwerp or Trieste or Stuttgart, except they weren't really in Antwerp and they weren't in Trieste or Stuttgart. These apartments were in Kalamaja, one of Tallinn's "up and coming" urban districts, and what "up and coming" really meant was that it was still down and hadn't arrived yet. All the European styrofoam molding and vinyl bathroom tiles couldn't hide the truth, that Estonia was headed West but hadn't reached it yet, that the land was in limbo. Europe was out there, the lights of Stockholm almost visible, glowing in the distance, looming ahead, blinking, the new normalcy. But Russia was still in the rearview mirror,

---

* Eurobread. (In Estonian)

crumbling, corroding, combusting, flaring out in a bust of dead journalists and suicide bombs, secret service intrigues, assassinations, plane crashes and greed, the old discord. And all the time, Estonia was zooming along on the road in between, its eyes fixed on the horizon. When would Estonia finally get to normal? In five years? Ten? No one could say.

It wasn't all bad.

Once in a while, an apartment would charm us with wooden floors and exposed beam ceilings and a decent view to park, or maybe even a view of the Old Town. But it would be too far. Or it would have no kitchen. Or I might have reached up to touch one of the charmingly exposed wooden beams only to discover it was really made out of plastic.

I kept on waiting for the right place to surprise us. I thought it would come as one big "Aha!" a real estate thunderbolt: we would just step in and the loud bells of my intuition would sound in my ears. Epp was more practical than me. She took her time, examining things from every angle, peppering every owner with her questions. "How big are the utility bills?" "How old are the electrical wires?" "Have you redone the plumbing?" It typically took me about 30 seconds to determine that a place wasn't for us. I just knew it. But she would stand there asking questions and taking notes. "Why do you waste your time writing that stuff down?" I would say. "You know the place isn't for us." "I treat every place as a potential future," she would answer. "I have a good imagination."

A few more times we bounced back across the city, desperate, again at the mercy of real estate agents, and I never really trusted the agents. They seemed like the kind of people who could tell you a cardboard box was a luxurious penthouse. And, of course, the houses would not stay in their present condition. Oh, no. They had potential. Any chimney could be turned into a fireplace and any garbage-strewn lot could become a nice back yard. A huge renovation project was always being planned, one that would make the rundown house new again, one that was expected to commence right after the agent received her cut from the deal.

We had been searching for almost a month and found nothing. One apartment on the harbor had a sea view that looked out on cranes and cargo containers and would soon be obscured by the concrete wall of a new parking garage. Then there was the Stalinist fortress near the Central Market with the high ceilings and old-fashioned, stove-heated bathtub.

"It looks right out of an old Russian movie," Epp had said, amazed that something so foreign could be so close to us all the time. "It's kind of cool, but I could never imagine living here."

"I'm not heating that bath stove anyway," I told her.

"Nah, this place isn't for us. It's for Russian aristocrats," she said, "and by aristocrats," she added a second later, "I mean poor aristocrats."

We searched everywhere in Tallinn for normalcy in our price range but couldn't find it. At night, under the moon, drifting through the mist and moisture, I often blamed myself. If it hadn't been for my high standards, we might have taken that apartment on Väike Patarei Street. All the contracts could have been signed. We could have been out shopping for furniture by now. Epp had been right that day. I was a snob, an American elitist. I couldn't deny it. It was true. When it came to apartments, I was the snobbiest, snootiest, most arrogant elitist you ever saw. But it was all for my family. And that to me was the ultimate excuse.

The night we bought the apartment on Valgevase Street, I ran between the ATMs of Hansapank's downtown office beside the SAS Radisson hotel and Ühispank's towering headquarters across the street, an intergalactic postmodern Scandinavian rocketship of geometric curiosity, steel and glass. Estonia's previous conquerors had built fortresses and naval installations and air bases. Its new bosses built legoland hotels and banks from outerspace. I had collected as much money from my American account as the Hansapank ATM would allow me to withdraw and then raced to Ühispank to collect the second half. Epp and I later fed the thousands of Estonian kroons into her bank account at Hansapank, and she was able to make our payment online. "We booked the apartment!" she said and hugged me afterward. "We found our nest!"

Valgevase. It meant 'white copper' and it was wedged between Tööstuse, or "Industrial," and Vabriku, or "Factory" Streets. Kalamaja used to be a working-class district and houses on Valgevase were all from the turn of the previous century, all made of wood, solid and sturdy as tanks, some with scaffolding around them, the true symbol of the "up and

231

coming" neighborhood. There were a few stragglers, such as a rotten house on the corner, its top half black with soot from a fire, leaning to one side like an army vet with a bum hip. But the people on the street did seem okay, young, urban, professional, like us, and even the vagrant cats that congregated at the nearby dumpsters looked better fed and fluffy, almost domestic. Everything that was good about Kalamaja was present on Valgevase Street.

But then, why had it never rung the bells of my intuition? An agent had shown it to us and the small attic-level space aroused little of anything, no passion, no delight. There was no "aha" on Valgevase. But it hooked us quietly, it reeled us in. We came back to see it once more, just in case, and then we came again. And each time we returned, we were surprised by how normal it was compared to the others. The house was frog green, a "Lender"-style building of big one-room apartments, freshly renovated, sheetrock dust in the air, paint drying, with only two places left to buy on the third floor, each with a skylight. I favored the one in the back. From its window, one looked out on a picture of Astrid Lindgren-like coziness, slanted tin roofs, colorful houses, crooked windows, old chimneys puffing smoke, kids playing on the wood piles. Everywhere else it was dark and raining, but in this litle appartment, it always felt a little bit like Christmas. It made you want to drop your bags, drink a hot cup of *glögi**, and take a nap. Honey, I'm home.

Epp said the place won her over when she started thinking about what dishes might go with the apartment: "I would like to

---

* Mulled wine. (In Estonian)

buy two big yellow cups and sit there and have tea and snuggle!" But I suspected that, perhaps subconsciously, I had known all along that it was the right place for us. Drop a penguin anywhere in the sea and he will find his way back to land. Set an expectant mother and father in Tallinn in November and they will find a nest for their offspring.

That Valgevase was an unfinished apartment was a blessing and a distraction. A blessing in that, as part of the deal, we would be able to select everything: the bathroom tiles, the sink, the flooring; we were even able to convince the contractors to make us a closet. This meant that there would be no shower cabinet in the kitchen, there would be no styrofoam moldings or plastic beams in the ceiling, and there would be no stove-heated bathtub, which was good.

The downside was that Epp and I began to spend most of our days in home improvement stores debating what color the tiles in the bathroom should be. There was also the issue of furniture, and in many Estonian furniture shops, the beds and tables and chairs all had been given personal names to distinguish them from one another. A coffee table might be called a "Laura," for instance, a certain bookshelf a "Paul," a basket a "Susanna." I imagined how we would stand at the counters of these shops, ordering away, "We'd like one Laura, two Pauls, and three Susannas, please." "I'm sorry, we're out of Susannas." "Okay, well, do you have any Marias left instead?"

When we debated how best to furnish Valgevase, Epp's opinion typically prevailed, but I managed eloquent, stirring defenses of wooden floor panels and lighting fixtures. My inner John F. Kennedy passionately endorsed shower curtains and bathroom tiles. "I don't think these tiles will be easy to clean," Epp would protest. "They are too rough. Run your fingers on it. Dirt will get stuck in those grooves." "But this is the only one that moves me, this is the one I feel belongs there!" I would argue back. "All these others look like Euroremont!" – "But Justin," she would lower her voice to its most rational tone. "The other ones make more sense." – "Then why do you even bother asking my opinion? Just take the ones you want!" Then she would fold her arms and walk away. "I am not talking to you until you calm down."

What had happened to me? What had happened to us? The carefree backpackers had been replaced by a tireless woman in the manic eighth month of her pregancy, eager to build a practical nest, and her husband who was ready to die for bathroom tiles, a man who was so amazed to learn from a fellow shopper that it was best to get a Swedish-made toilet as it could withstand the high-water density of northern countries like Estonia, that he wrote about it in his diary at night.

In looking for a place to live, I had been hooked by the boomerang of time. I had traded a mother for a wife, childhood for fatherhood, a crumbling apartment for one that had yet to be finished. Again I was tinkering with faucets and spinning colorwheels. Again it was time to decide between the "lemongrass" and the "salmon," the "peanut" and the "caramel". We had finally found our nest. Now we had to fill it with stuff.

SCOFFLAWS

If Ülhispank's downtown headquarters was a rocketship, then Järve Keskus was a lunar base.

Perched on the pine-lined edge of Lake Ülemiste, the shopping center glared down on the vast, sea-like parking lot, stories of rectangles and squares, metal and glass, granite and plastic, red and silver, its name like 'Hollywood' across the top, visible in soft white:

J Ä R V E.

Inside, Christmas music already, Christmas lights, the scent of instant coffee, body odor and perfume, escalators, elevators, mobile telephones, bicycles, pillow cases, pasta strainers, oven mits, sauna cleaners, cereal boxes, play corners, squadrons of TV screens buzzing above, beaming advertisements in Estonian and Russian, and people, throngs of people. People in Estonia may have had different living standards and different mother tongues and different favorite songs, but in the palaces of capitalism, they rubbed shoulders, thighs, plastic bags, they became only one thing, consumers, united in their lust for goods.

The northern money men had bankrolled it, naturally. Men like Benny only richer, counting their kroner, the faceless barons of the Baltic. The well-heeled merchants of Sweden's Hansapank and Ühispank had trading posts in Järve Keskus, as did the intrepid lenders of Finnish-owned Sampo. The telecommunications giants were there, too: Elisa of Finland, Tele2 of Sweden, and Eesti Mobiiltelefon, EMT, with its cute trademark ladybug, at first glance purely Estonian, but, if you followed the money, a subsidiary of Stockholm-based TeliaSonera.

But who could really tell what was Swedish and what was Finnish and what was Estonian anymore? With Nordic money a kind of creeping placelessness had arrived. Or was it the fulfillment of place? For, had Estonia never been Soviet, wouldn't it have looked just like this? Kreenholm had a shop in Järve Keskus and if the new Estonia was like any shop then it was this Narva-based textile and clothing firm, a company whose employees spoke Russian, whose marketers spoke Estonian, and whose bosses spoke Swedish.

The Danes were in it too, those Napoleon-complexed, jazz-loving, open-faced sandwich-adoring narcissists. If a Swede was in on something, one could always bet on a little Dane to follow, trailing like a yipping dog, shaking its tail. But while the Swedes provided the lollipop housing loans – to people like us – and mobile phone networks, the Danes supplied private security, and private security was in in Estonia, a country where the gospel of Friedman had left a trace on every leaders' lips like confectionary sugar. Of the private security firms, Danish-owned Falck was the most visible. One watched them from afar, cautiously, the big guards stomping around like Mexican paramilitaries, shrouded in dark uniforms, walkie-talkies beeping, heavy boots, medallions suspended from their necks with the trademark fearsome falcon in flight, glaring in red and white. Falck.

Whenever I think of that bird, I think of my pregnant wife crying. Then I get angry.

Tallinn's buses were green, the seats within gray, the handles black, as innocuous as a doctor's office. Unlike the inner-city trams with their mudbath floors, the buses were newer, cleaner, upholstered. The cost of admission was 15 kroons. You bought your ticket from an R-Kiosk and punched it when you climbed aboard. The drivers never checked it but, then again, they never spoke, they never smiled, they barely feigned humanity. The enforcers of the punched ticket rule were the plain-clothed Falck guards, the ones who hid the insignia of the red and white falcon under their jackets. If they caught you with an unpunched ticket, something supposedly happened. What that something was though no one had ever really told me.

We rode the bus to Järve Keskus because we didn't have a car. We didn't have a car because we had spent our borrowed cash on a tiny attic apartment in Kalamaja. Our remaining cash supplies had dwindled and my pockets were becoming full of punched tickets that had never been checked. Fifteen kroons! It was enough to buy a decent-sized candy bar or two bags of milk. I might as well have dropped it in the gutter. It depressed me to waste good Estonian money like that. So I took to smoothing out old punched tickets to make them look fresh, recycling them if you will, then punching them anew. And no one noticed, because no one ever checked. Fifteen kroons! Gone! After some time, I stopped punching my tickets altogether. I figured that if a Falck guard really did check our bus, I would have time to quickly punch it before the guard asked to see mine. They would probably enter the bus at either the back or front entrances, so I always rode in the middle.

And I never really thought anything bad could happen to us, even if we did get caught. For one, I spoke Estonian, beginners' Estonian, but, still, the national language, the one that supposedly glued everything together. Without the Estonian language there would be no Estonia, and to learn it was to become a true believer, a fellow traveler. Just imagine that some Estonian security guard had been forced to speak to Russians in Russian his entire life and then some fresh-faced American kid showed up one day on a bus and said, "Tere!" to him? What Estonian could resist it? Estonian was Estonia's most valued currency, its most prized natural resource. And it could get you out of trouble. Manuel from Barcelona had said so.

"One day I was driving near Tallinn and I was pulled over for speeding," Manuel had told us after class in the Language School parking lot. "I said, 'I'm sorry, Mr. Officer, I did not notice the speed limit sign,' but I said it in Estonian, you know? And do you know what the police said to me after I showed him my license?" Manuel looked around at our blank, international faces. "He said, 'Oh my God, you are from *España* and you speak Estonian?' – 'Yes, Mr. Officer,' I said, calmly. He was shocked. You could just see it. His face was all white. He said, 'Some people have been living here for 50 years and can't say one word.' And then he let me go. No fine. No nothing. *Nada.*"

So we had Estonian on our side. We also had my wife's belly. It was big, and it had a baby in it, and everyone loved babies, even security guards. Pregnant women, it seemed, ruled the world. People opened doors for them, bus passengers gave up their seats for them, even other women gave up their seats. People loved to loathe each other, but they couldn't be a jerk to an unborn baby. No matter who you were, a criminal, a lush, a waitress, a politician, a Sunday school teacher, a journalist, if you were pregnant, you got to cut to the head of the line. People might have despised the mother, but they had nothing against that fresh innocent soul, gurgling away inside, the one that hadn't done anything wrong to anybody. Yet.

We had our bases covered. I thought we were invincible. My Estonian skills. Her pregnant belly. Together we were set, we had a skeleton key for calamaties and yet it was an illusion, for we had not yet met Sirje. And Sirje was a walking calamity.

🌢 🌢 🌢

When my great grandfather Salvatore died, they cleaned out the house and in the process found hundreds of dollars hidden, some of it in books, most of it inside a mattress on the second floor. The speakeasies, the quick money from the construction jobs in Greenland and Bermuda, it had all added up, it was all there, tucked away from the banks and from the government.

I wondered where the money in the mattress had eventually gone on the bus to Järve Keskus. We were going there to buy a bed for the apartment, on credit. We had boarded near some furniture shop on Pärnu Road.

"Justin, did you punch our tickets?" Epp asked me, seated.

"I'm not sure if this is the right bus. I'll only punch it if it's the right bus."

"But what about Falck?" She asked and looked concerned with her big fat lips and mesa-like cheekbones, staring at her cheap ass, spawn-of-spendthrift-immigrants husband.

"What about them?"

"Do you want to get a fine? It could be like 1000 kroons." The sum sounded enormous. "Don't you think it's worth it to pay 15 kroons so that you don't have to pay 1000 kroons?"

"But they never check."

"Tickets, tickets!" The woman in the red jacket surprised me, and it really was a stick up, a bank robbery, the way she did it. "Tickets, tickets," she stared up at me through her glasses, and showed me the gun she had in her hand, except it wasn't a gun, it was a badge, a fearsome, very pissed-off looking red and white eagle. Falck.

I fetched the slender pair of blue and white paper tickets from my wallet, each with an old-fashioned "15" embossed upon them. "I was just about to punch them," I told the woman in Estonian and held the tickets out. "We just got on."

"You and you," she gestured at me and my pregnant wife. "Come."

"Let's just punch them here," I said to her. "We weren't sure if this was the right bus."

The woman in red hit the red buzzer near the door with her palm. It alerted the driver to stop and a second later he pulled over. "Come," she ordered again. "You are in big trouble."

Off the bus, past a hamburger joint in the charcoal gray of the late afternoon, into a red van that waited, its engine humming to keep its passengers warm. The woman, "Sirje" by her nametag, sat in the front seat and started to fill out the paperwork, our ID cards in hand, us wedged in the back with the gypsies. There must have been four or five of us in there altogether, me male, the rest female. Maybe they weren't gypsies at all, maybe they were Navajos or Setos, but they had dark hair and long dark coats and seemed as if they had been sitting there for a long time. In fact, they said nothing, warming the seat like fluffy, feathery hens. It seemed like they sat in the Falck van every day. And we were now gypsies too.

"Please, we're really, really, really sorry, we just didn't know what bus we were on," Epp tried to soothe Sirje, and Epp was good at getting away with things. It had been said that she was *süüdimatu* – guiltless. When she cancelled an important interview, she would say, "I apologize a thousand times," and by the time she was done apologizing the other person would actually be asking forgiveness from her.

"Be quiet," Sirje snapped from the front seat.

"But we meant to punch our tickets."

"I said be quiet! I know you. You do this all the time."

"What? Why? Huh? What are you talking about?" Epp pleaded with her, and I recognized the strain in her voice, that deep, familiar, bottomless, vaginal sound, the throb of a woman pearshaped and ripe with estrogen. "We didn't know where the bus was going. That's why we didn't punch the ticket. I swear —"

"Don't lie to me!" Sirje snarled. "It says here you were born in Tallinn. So how could a Tallinn girl not know what bus she was on?"

"But I wasn't born in Tallinn!"

"That's not what your passport says."

"I was born in Viljandi! My mother and father were just registered —"

"Viljandi?" Sirje sneered. "You actually expect me to believe that? You really are a liar."

"No! It's not true." The throb in Epp's voice expanded, deep and gutteral, then the groaning glacier just gave way, crashing into the ocean. My pregnant wife was sobbing now, soaking everything. I could almost taste the salt from her tears. And then Salvatore snapped into focus, his twitching moustache, the spark from his pipe, the fedora hat, in the shadows in black and white, erect, angry, like a lightning strike, like a fist. "Be a man, Giustino!" He always said that when he lectured me. But what do men do, Salvatore? What do husbands do?

"We're leaving," I said in Estonian, my hand on the van door. I said it in a low voice, a calm voice, one that tried to conceal my smoldering anger, that squalid fury I had always managed to suppress.

"Not until you sign these documents," Sirje handed the clipboard back with yellow papers fluttering. And the gypsy women looked on, oblivious. Just another day in the van. Epp kept sobbing and saying, "I wasn't born in Tallinn, I was born in Viljandi," to herself, but Sirje didn't listen because she was cold.

I scanned the documents in the dim light of the van. It was warm now, the heat blowing from the vents, the sweat on my forehead, my underarms. Then I spoke to Sirje, but this time in English. "I'm sorry," I told her, again calm, "this is all written in Estonian. I can't understand."

"You know what you done," Sirje answered me, this time in her harsh, Esto pidgin English.

"No, I'm sorry, I don't." And Epp was still crying. "I don't know exactly what I have been charged with, so I refuse to sign."

"If you don't sign, you go to court."

"But how can I sign something I don't understand?" I asked.

"You didn't punch your ticket!"

"But I don't understand what the charge is. What law did I break? I was going to punch them, I just wasn't sure of the bus —"

"Just sign it, Justin," Epp whispered to me. "Just sign it and let's get out of this van. It's so hot." Her voice was weaker now, distant. I kept thinking of her falling in the church at our wedding blessing, fainting in the heat. "I feel dizzy," she moaned.

"Stop trying to get out of this with your fake tears," Sirje yelled to her. "I'm not letting you off this time. You're a repeat offender. I have caught you many times before and you lie me every time!"

"I'm so, so hot," Epp cried. "Please let me out, I'm pregnant."

Sirje just looked through her and at me, waiting for me to sign. If I signed, we could go free, pay the fine online, no questions asked, painless extortion.

I looked at the paperwork again, at all the zeroes where the penalty was denoted and at the court date if we chose to challenge it. And I was angry, because who was Sirje, anyway? Who was this little cold woman with the yellow hair who worked for the Danish security firm? And then I remembered how I had gotten caught outside Copenhagen the same way, in Rødovre, by a guard who didn't look too different from Sirje, one whose medallion also showed the fearsome falcon, except the Dane was polite to me, pleasant and fat-cheeked. When I told the Danish Falck guard I didn't understand what rule I had broken, she explained everything in English, and she didn't even fine me, she just let me go with a warning. Next time. Nothing. *Ikke én ting!*

So what was the difference? Was it Scandinavian egalitarianism? The succor of social democracy? Did being Danish warrant empathy? Did being an Estonian give you the equal right to be unkind, to chew up your fellow citizens, to make them your favorite food, to make pregnant women cry? Was that why Sirje was so cold? The low wages? The lack of sunlight? The shredded safety net? The vile history? Sirje had the right to fine us, and it really was all my fault, but in this way, in the back of a hot security van, telling Epp she didn't even know where she was born?

You really are a liar.

"I still don't understand what the charge is," I said and handed the clipboard back to Sirje.

---

* Nothing. (In Danish)

"Fine," she snapped and took it from me, her eyes down, maybe somewhere down in the dark pit of her mechanical soul a little ashamed. "That just means you'll have to go to court."

"Good," I said and shrugged. "I would rather go to court than have anything more to do with you."

Anger, heat, sweat, tears, and then calm, the cool Estonian air, black currant sky, and, finally, sweet caffeine, the nectar of life. We arrived to Järve Keskus, again by bus, except this time our tickets were punched. Nobody checked them.

"It was my fault," I said at a little cafe where they sold instant coffee and ice cream. "I'm sorry."

Epp smoothed out the week's *Eesti Ekspress** and took a sip of her drink. Her head rested on her arm, her elbow jutting out on the table. It was still only November, but Christmas music was playing from unseen speakers, hidden among the twinkling electric lights. "Jingle bells, jingle bells..."

"I'm not mad at you," she said and took a sip of her coffee, her puffy eyes fixed on the news. "I'm mad at that bitch."

"So, what do you want to do?" I said. "Tell the judge?"

"We're not going to court, we're not paying them anything," she said and turned the page. "We were holding our tickets, the bus just had started to move, and we weren't sure if it was the right bus. She had no right to treat us like that."

I said nothing.

---

* An Estonian weekly newspaper.

"On Monday, we are going to write a long letter to her bosses."

"Ok."

"You know what, let's write two letters! I will write in Estonian, and you, you will write in English, and you will tell them that you are a journalist, an American journalist. Make that the first thing you say in your letter. Tell them you write for *The Baltic Times*. And we will write down everything that happened, everything she said to us."

"And then what?"

Epp turned another page. "We'll see what they do," she said. "Actually," she pulled a small notebook from her bag and smiled for the first time in hours. "Let's start right now, while the memories are fresh."

So we took turns writing. We spent the next hour writing and editing each others accounts of our encounter with Sirje, and by the time we left Järve Keskus, we were in a good mood.

On Monday, the letters were sent and we waited for an answer, another opportunity to fight, except one never came, and Falck never came looking for its ticket money. By that time, though, we were so wrapped up in family life that I forgot all about Sirje. I let her go into the November dark, buried her in my memory like a sleazy one-night stand, and was done with her.

I always punched my ticket after that, though, even if I was on the wrong bus.

TOOMPEA
IS UNDER
ATTACK

*It was the time of the year when night was
preferable to day.*

For weeks, the sky had been milk of magnesia. It began where the
rooftops and treetops ended, depthless light gray, a soupy abyss
that hovered about but never left. The autumn sleets and rains
had left everything below covered in a filmy coat of brown filth;
the cobblestones, trucks, traffic signs, and roadside litter, all of it
encased in grime. People looked dirtier too. The sky had sucked
all the color out of their faces, the hard northern waters left
their hair unruly, the absence of sunlight drew out the darkness
beneath their eyes. Nobody looked good in November.

I spent my 24th birthday in the company of Edward
Burkhardt. We sat around a long table in a conference room
in the SAS Radisson hotel, a sterile space, white and beige,
passionless and carpeted, sexless with venetian blinds, the
milky gray light streaming through. My short life as a writer had
been confined to such spaces, to offices and conference rooms,

to the potpourri of vinyl and polyester. I sipped from a plastic water bottle with an image of a glacier on it and listened.

Burkhardt was there to address suspicions he was going to sell his majority stake in Estonian Railways to a Russian company. The rumors had been circulating in the newspapers all week, moving the government to officially "express concern" about the possibility of such a deal. And, with an untrustworthy foreign name like Edward Burkhardt, it was easy for Estonians to believe that the man before us was up to no good. He was your typical American, just out to make money, without regard for Estonian sovereignty. But Burkhardt denied it. In front of us, he swore the rumors were false.

The American railroad man sat at the head of the table, gray and spectacled, a patrician of transport. Besides this venture, he held investments in railways from Poland to California. I didn't know how long Burkhardt had been in Tallinn, but it had evidently been long enough for the country's climate to work its magic on him. His face had assumed the pallor of the Estonian sky, his disobedient gray hair stuck up in the back like a middle-aged Dennis the Menace. Edward did not look good.

The others in the room were Estonian journalists, pasty by nature, dressed in blue and white shirts, open at the collars, others in woolen sweaters. The reporters reclined in their chairs, laconic in their questioning, always sipping at their bottles of glacial water, idling away the day. My fellow scribes seemed seasoned, bored. In contrast, I felt green and anxious as we went around the table asking questions, because I knew that I would also have to ask the railroad man a question. It was my job. But what question to ask?

"But, Mr. Burkhardt, there is one thing that I just don't understand."

"I'm sorry," Burkhardt said. He cocked his head in the direction of my inflectionless accent, as if surprised to be met by another American in such a place.

"Who do you work for?" he asked. "What is your name?"

"My name is Justin. I write for *The Baltic Times*."

"Ah right, *The Baltic Times*." He said and cleared his throat and coughed. "So then, Jason, what is your question?"

"Well, if the rumors aren't true that you will sell your stake to the Russians then, um, who is responsible for spreading the rumors?"

I suddenly felt the eyes of every Estonian journalist in the room on me. Was it because I had asked such an obvious question? Or was it a question that nobody dared to ask?

Burkhardt cleared his throat again. "Well, I'll tell you who I think have been spreading the rumors," he said. "It's Edgar Savisaar and his Centre Party."

"But if the rumors are not true, then why would they do that?" I said.

Burkhardt stared at me, and then offered up a bitter smile. "Well, maybe you should go ask them that question."

The press conference ended shortly after. Later in the office, I tried to contact the Centre Party's spokesperson by phone and e-mail to see if she would address what Burkhardt had said. "There are rumors that you are spreading rumors," I wrote. But I never did get a response, and so the rumors lingered. In my article, Burkhardt accused the Centre Party of starting them, but it still remained an unanswered accusation.

Everything was wispy and opaque. It danced around me in the darkness as I headed home that night, the shadowy name of Savisaar on my lips. Who was this strange man who could spin rumors into newspaper articles? And what did he have to do with the Russians?

♦ ♦ ♦

Edgar Savisaar. It wasn't the first time I had heard the name. I had heard about Savisaar mostly from listening to Pets, Epp's brother-in-law. He was about ten years older than me, dark haired, dark eyed, a cigarette always hanging from his lips, like some kind of road weary Estonian rock star.

For months he had been at sea on a fishing boat in the North Atlantic out of Spain. *Mucho trabajo*[*], he said. They worked the crew cutting fish night and day, over stormy and calm seas, and when he finally got back to Tallinn that November, Pets took a cab from the port all 185 kilometers down to his home in Tartu, his bags filled with frozen fish for his family.

All through the autumn gloom, Pets had been upgrading his apartment with the money he earned at sea. The family had a new big screen TV, a new couch, new curtains, new carpets; he even bought his mother a new wood-heated stove. To support his family, Pets had to leave Estonia, but that didn't mean that Estonia wasn't close to his heart. He was usually quiet at first but after he got some coffee or beer in him, he would talk. That's how he was on his birthday, which happened to fall a few days before mine.

---

[*] A lot of work. (In Spanish)

"Ugh. Savisaar." He held a crumpled, day-old copy of *Posti-mees* in one hand, a cup of black coffee in the other. Pets always drank his coffee black. The mug was black, too. It read *Skorpion Oct 23 – Nov. 21* in gold lettering on the front.

Eva and little Simona sat across the room watching a Christina Aguilera video on the new big screen TV. Epp was in the corner typing an e-mail on the family's new computer. In the kitchen, Pets' mother was frying up more cutlets on her new stove.

"What about Savisaar?" I looked at the paper and could make out the politician's face on the front page, clumpy gray hair, head like a moraine, vast and expanding, 1950s schoolboy glasses, bushy eyebrows, dumpling cheeks, puckered amused lips, all rolled up in a gray-flannel suit. He was not what most would call handsome, and even though he had a reputation as a ladies man.

He had been a figure in the Estonian political game since Pets was just a fresh-faced high school kid, a leader of the Popular Front during the Singing Revolution. Despite this stellar trajectory, Savisaar's fortunes had since fallen, his activities mostly compromised. In the mid-nineties he was caught surreptitiously recording conversations with other Estonian politicians, and he had been forced out of political life, vowing to never again reenter, but he enjoyed the spotlight too much to stay on the sidelines. These days, he called himself the mayor of Tallinn.

"You really want to know what I think about Edgar?" Pets sipped from his black mug. "He's a good Russian boy."

"But Savisaar's not Russian. He's an Estonian. Like you."

"That's debatable," Pets looked up from the newspaper. Then he lay the paper down, picked up a fork, and jabbed it into the mountain of potatoes on his plate. Pets loved potatoes. I had hoisted three cutlets and six potatoes onto my plate as the birthday platters went around. Pets, I had counted, had put 15 potatoes on his plate, a volcano-like heap of starch that he had topped with exactly one cutlet. It reminded me of an Estonian proverb I had once heard: It's not a meal if there aren't any potatoes.

"Savisaar's mother was Russian," he said, as he chewed one of the potatoes. "And you know that Päts' mother was a Russian too, right?"

"No, I didn't." The insinuation was clear. Estonia's pre-war leader, the man who had given into all Soviet demands in 1940, had a corruptible blood line. Apparently, so did Savisaar.

"Well, now you know," Pets smiled and chewed, rocking his legs under the table. Pets was a little edgy. Only with a smoke in his mouth did he ever seem to be truly calm. "It's not like I dislike Russians, you know. They're just a little different. Like this guy I was on the boat with in Spain. He's from Maardu, a little east from Tallinn. He's been living in this country his whole life and he can't speak a word of Estonian, so I had to speak Russian to him."

"Do you even know Russian?"

"Ha! I didn't before I went to sea!" he let out a high-pitched chuckle. "I wasn't in the Soviet army so I never really learned it – I mean I had some lessons in school, but I had to learn Russian to talk to him because we worked together and he didn't speak any other language."

"But why didn't you try to teach him Estonian?"

"What?" Pets was startled by the absurdity of the idea. "No, no, that's just not how it works. Understand something: Russians live in a totally different world than us. They expect everyone to speak Russian to them, even on a Spanish ship in Canadian waters. And their media tells them totally different things, weird things. One time, my friend from Maardu woke me up in my bunk on the ship. 'Have you heard that *Postimees* is bankrupt?' he said. I said, 'Shut up, there is no fucking way that *Postimees* is bankrupt.' He said, 'It's true, I just read it on the Internet.' Now," Pets tapped at the newspaper with his hand, "I guess *Postimees* hasn't gone bankrupt yet, huh?"

"Nope," I said, looking down at the paper.

"Another time he woke me up in my bunk, he said, 'Pyets, Pyets' – that's how he said my name – 'Have you heard? They are going to devalue the Estonian kroon tomorrow. Call your wife! Tell her to exchange all your savings for euros tonight!' I said, 'Shut up, there is no fucking way they are going to devalue the kroon.' He said, 'It's true, it's true. My girlfriend just sent me a text message.' I said, 'It's not true. If it was true, I would have heard about it. This guy always thought there were all these conspiracies behind things. He believed every rumor. Like I said, Russians are a little different."

"But what does this have to do with Savisaar?"

"Ha! Savisaar? He's like their king. He gets all his money from Russia, and the Estonian Russians vote for him, which is why I have to vote for the conservatives in every election, so I can cancel out all the votes for Savisaar. My friend in Maardu could go on and on about what a great, wise man Savisaar is, and about how he defends the rights of both Estonians and Russians and how when he gets into power everything will be better and people will have higher salaries and it will be sunny in November. And he really believes it." Pets rolled his eyes, as if to say, that idiot.

"When do you guys go back?"

"I fly back to Spain at the beginning of January. Then it's back to work," he groaned and stretched out his arms. "They work us all the time, round the clock. *Mucho trabajo.*"

"It beats sitting around waiting for some guy to call, right?" I remembered how Pets had spent the previous winter waiting for one of his contacts to call him with an offer to go to sea. The apartment then was completely different, dark and dingy and musty, no new couch, no new curtains, no new big screen TV.

"Um, I don't think you understand what was really going on then," he said and leaned back a little, as if he took offense. "You see, this guy I was waiting to call me is a Russian," and the way he said it, I knew at once that Pets' business contact was up to something illegal. "He can get you whatever you want. I just wanted a place on a ship with a high salary. And, get this, this Russian offered me a position as navigator on the ship! He said that it paid more, and that he could get me all the necessary paperwork to prove that I knew how to navigate. But can you imagine if they hired me as a navigator and I got up there and I didn't even know what the fuck I was doing? I turned him down. 'I've got my sea papers,' I told him. 'I just want a well-paying job.' But this Russian can get you anything. Like, if you want a job at a university, he can get you a diploma that says you have a PhD. And it will all check out."

254

"Do you know anything about him?"

"I've heard he's from Narva or Kohtla-Järve," Pets said. "Either way, a real *tibla*." He chuckled.

"A *tibla*?"

Pets looked at me and straightened his back, a touch of alarm in his dark eyes. "Wait, you do know what a *tibla* is, don't you?"

"No."

"Oh, wow, well, a *tibla* is," Pets paused and scratched his chin. "It's kind of hard to explain. A *tibla* is a Russian, but not all Russians are *tiblas*. It's like," again he paused, his legs rocking under the table. "Like educated Russians aren't *tiblas*. Pushkin wasn't a *tibla*. Tolstoy, not a *tibla*. But this Russian guy who can get you a PhD diploma?"

"He's a real *tibla*," I said.

"Exactly. Do you want to know where the word comes from?"

I nodded.

"It's from the Russian, *ti blyat*. It means 'you bitch.'"

"You bitch? *Tibla*?"

"Yes!" Pets let out a high-pitched snicker. He was very amused, as if he were an older kid on the playground teaching a younger schoolmate some new dirty words. "Come on, you know the history of this country. When the Red Army came in in 1944," he shivered as if he had actually been there. "*Tibla*. *Ti blyat*. You bitch," he took another sip of his black coffee. "Probably the final words heard by many an Estonian."

"Right."

"Anyway, I've got to step outside for a sec," Pets set the black mug down and stood, his half eaten potatoes crumbling before him. "I really, really need a smoke."

◖ ◓ ◖

Edgar Savisaar, mayor of Tallinn, the king of the Estonian Russians, the man who controlled the rumors. No matter where you went in Estonia people wanted to talk about Savisaar, people wanted to talk about Russians. Even my fellow Language School students couldn't help but stick their fingers into the sharp-edged fan of the Russian question.

Manfred tended to side with the Russians when it came to some Estonian policies. "I don't know about these citizenship laws," he told me during one of our walks through the murky city. "I mean a third of the population is Russian."

"A quarter," I corrected him.

"Well, I read a third."

"It used to be."

"Well, what does it matter? It's a huge part of the local population. And they have to take some kind of language test just to get citizenship? And this law was made retroactively, after they arrived? Hmm," he raised a doubtful gray eyebrow, "no, this is just not right. This is revenge."

"So what," I played along. "What's wrong with revenge?"

Manfred winced. "Oh dear, listen to you, 'what's wrong with revenge'? Are you serious? Do you even know where I was born?"

"Berlin," I answered.

"No, no, I own an *apartment* in Berlin, Justin, I wasn't born there. I was born in Silesia."

"Silesia?" Now it was my turn to raise an eyebrow.

"It's a little province, now it is part of Poland but it used to be part of Germany. In fact, a newspaper wants me to go back and write some articles about it. My family had been living there for several centuries and would still be living there if it hadn't been for the fucking Nazis who had to go and just fuck everything up!" Manfred's voice grew tighter, he looked distressed. The man obviously wasn't a Nazi.

"Anyway, when the war ended, the Russians rounded us all up, put us on trains, and sent us to West Germany."

"That's terrible. Do you even remember that?"

"Of course I remember it! But it wasn't so bad, you know. I had no idea what was going on, so I thought it was fun. I was a little boy who got to ride in a big choo-choo train! But, getting back to my point, can you honestly blame a little boy like me for the Second World War?" He stared at me, hot and cold, a man who had easily won another argument almost without even trying.

"No."

"So you can't blame these Russians in Estonia for it either."

"I agree but I don't think the state will change its policies. The law's been on the books for so long."

"Ja, ja. Well, we'll see," Manfred strolled along, his hands in his pockets. "If this Savisaar character gets into power, a lot could change." He wrinkled his nose. "Not that that would be an entirely good thing."

"My wife's brother-in-law doesn't like Savisaar."

"Savisaar reminds me of our chancellor Schröder, you know," Manfred said. "Politics for him is like a game. And, like Schröder, he gets fatter each year."

We then stepped around groups of Estonian Russian teenagers in Tammsaare Park, gathered around the fatherly granite statue of the national writer Tammsaare, dressed in big black puffy winter jackets, smoking, the guys like oak trees, the girls slender, otherworldly babes. One of them had a little stereo, it was playing a dance song, and all the Russian dance songs sounded the same, with the electronic techno beat kicking up um-cha, um-cha, um-cha, um-cha, and the synthesized bursts of balalaika and the invisible chorus of erotic go-go girls moaning dah, dah, dah, dah and slurring through their strange *khzz*, and *oii*, and *rrra*, and *ossh* sounds.

"Their temperament is a little different," Manfred winked to me as we stepped through the crowd, and I wondered if he was comparing the Russians to the Germans or the Estonians when he said it, or both. "I think I understand some of the song lyrics, by the way. It's a song about candy."

Estonian Russians. Only they could groove to a sexy song about candy in Tallinn in November. Little did they know, but everyone in Estonia was talking about them. And their leader.

🌢 🌢 🌢

At last it was night. At night the gray went away and you could think, you could breathe, dream deep, pretend that on the other side of night was day, not this swirling gray milk that soaked everyone.

258

It was the night of my birthday, curled up in bed, stuffed with cake, warm and tired, watching a documentary on TV, a documentary of events from a year both Epp and I remembered but that now look aged and sepia-toned; ancient history.

It was May 15, 1990. The pro-Soviet Intermovement was attempting to storm the parliament building on Toompea. With their disco jackets and shaggy sideburns some of the protesters looked like the backing band from some lost Elvis Presley TV special. Except they were not funky or lively, they were angry and confused. These Estonian Russians were the parents and grandparents of those kids in the park, but they did not hold the Russian flag in their hands, instead they held red Soviet flags, and began banging at the iron gate and demanding the resignation of the Supreme Council, a council that happened to be led by a man named Edgar Savisaar.

He was thinner then, his hair was dark and thick, but he still had those 1950s schoolboy glasses, his puckered lips looked more concerned, less amused. In the documentary, Savisaar got on the radio and called all Estonians to Toompea to protect their nascent national government from a possible Intermovement putsch. "Toompea is under attack," he said, urgency in his voice, as if the crowds were just outside of his office door. "I repeat, Toompea is under attack."

"I heard him that day on the radio and I wanted to go so badly," Epp said beside me, that wistful Singing Revolution nostalgia in her eyes. "But my parents wouldn't let me. They said it was too dangerous and too far."

On our television, other Estonians finally arrived and forced the Intermovement crowds out, surrounding them in the space between the parliament building and the Aleksander Nevski Orthodox Church. They chanted: "Out! Out! Out!" And Intermovement exited! Then Savisaar and Marju Lauristin and other Popular Front leaders emerged on the balcony and thanked the crowds. And everything was non-violent. Not a drop of blood spilled.

"Back then Savisaar was the Estonian Gandhi. Now he's king of the Estonian Russians. What happened?" I asked Epp in bed.

"Maybe they vote for him now because at least they know who he is," she answered. "Plus you know that his mother was Russian, right?"

"Yeah."

"And no one knows who his real father was either. He was born while his mother was in jail. It was during collectivization in 1949. The rumor is that Savisaar's parents were arrested because they sold their horse before the collective farm could take it. The father got 25 years in Siberia, the mother got five years in Estonian jail. And his mother's name was Maria," she clasped her hands together. "Can you imagine, a woman named Maria giving birth in jail?"

"Jesus."

"But his legal father was in Siberia during the time when he could have been conceived, so there are all these rumors as to who his real father is. Some think he was KGB, others think the father was another prisoner. But nobody really knows."

Rumors, rumors. Our gaze returned to the TV set where it was now August 1991. In the wake of the putsch in Moscow, the Estonian authorities affirmed the independence of their country. Chairman Edgar Savisaar became Prime Minister Edgar Savisaar. The little boy born in a prison was suddenly leader of the nation. He would later write about this period in his 2005 memoir *Peaminister**. But that was yet to come. In the documentary, there were still Soviet tanks all over Tallinn. Tanks by the airport. Tanks by the railroad station. The Soviet army was an animal that could strangle Estonia if that animal wasn't so dazed at its center.

But there were tanks in the streets that day and it was scary. That's what it would look like if the Russian Army came back again, I thought, with tanks rolling through the forests and farmlands, past the airport down into the center of the city past it new sparkling casinos and shiny nordic shopping centers and hotels.

I could imagine the Russians rolling in, too, dressed in their puffy military jackets, smoking, AK-47s, berets, all of them with little handheld stereos playing that rhythm, that Moscow beat, *um cha, um cha, um cha, um cha.*

What would happen next? I wondered. Maybe the Estonian Russian kids in the park would rush to greet their liberators. Perhaps the Estonian yuppies would grab their laptops and make for the ferries to Helsinki and Stockholm. There would certainly be fire in the streets, panic, smoke, terror, disco all around, madness, chaos. And where would Edgar Savisaar be, the mayor of Tallinn, the one man who saved Estonia before and could save it again? Would he get on the radio and call his countrymen to arms?

---

* Prime minister. (In Estonian)

Toompea is under attack! I repeat. Toompea is under attack!
I opened one eye. Then the other. We had both dozed off and left the TV on. The documentary was long over. Now they were playing late night music videos. Some Russian dance group. Glistening cleavage and glittering stars. Sports cars and furry boots. High heels and bare-chested male dancers. I got out of bed, walked across the room, and turned the set off. Then I shut off the lights and went back to sleep.

OLD TOWN MAESTROS

I hadn't realized how Estonianized I had become until my parents arrived from New York.

Up until the end of that month, I had still imagined myself deeply foreign, an adventurous expat journalist. It was under my jeans, my green coat, something that couldn't be scrubbed free. I felt as if I carried my foreignness around with me at all times, into the bathtub, into the stores, into the office.

Only when they came and, especially, after they had left, did I understand the big changes that had taken place during my months in Estonia. These were changes that could not be measured in numbers of new Estonian words memorized, or the mastery of the Tallinn public transportation system, or knowledge of who was who in local politics. It was much more subtle than that. It was in the first sentence my mother uttered to me after the taxi driver left us at their hotel.

"Man, that guy had the worst BO," she said and gripped the sleeve of my coat as I helped with the luggage.

"Yeah he did," my father looked over at us and laughed.

"Oh my God, did you smell it?" she tugged at my sleeve again. "And did you notice how he didn't say a word to us?"

"Yeah, that was weird," my father said. "Taxi drivers usually want to chat. What's up with that?"

"Don't know," I said and worked my lips into a smile. The truth was that I could barely remember what the driver looked like, let alone what he smelled like. But I decided to play along. "Welcome to Estonia," I said.

My father was as tall as me, Mediterranean complexion, dark hair on top going gray on the sides, gray turtleneck, black leather jacket, face like a comedian. Mother wore a camel-tan coat, blonde hair to her shoulders, blue eyes peeking out from under her hat. She used to be a model in Manhattan in the sixties, looking fabulous beside a refreshing bottle of Pepsi Cola.

Here before me were two classic New Yorkers, and it was good to see the two of them, because I loved them, not just because they were my parents, but because I remembered the people who they used to be. Here, in Tallinn, I felt as if they had now become my own children, that I was responsible for their welfare. I wanted my children to enjoy themselves too, to fall in love with the Hansa city where I fell in love. And I only wanted them to notice the good things, not the taxi driver's body odor.

They had been blessed with fairytale weather. The weeks of gray had finally cracked on the morning of their arrival, allowing beams of sunlight to once again touch Tallinn's damp exteriors, reflecting the intermittent flurries that blanketed the city grime and left everything sugar white. My mother told me of how her fellow passengers on the connecting flight from Helsinki began to applaud when they flew above the clouds.

"Really? People on a Finnair flight were clapping?" I asked. It didn't sound right. I figured there must have been a lot of foreigners on the plane.

"Oh yeah. The woman next to me said that she hadn't seen sunlight for three and a half weeks," my mother said, pulling on my sleeve again. "Could you imagine?"

My parents stayed at the Old Town Maestro, a European-style boutique hotel in the southern part of the Old Town, downwind of Freedom Square, across from two British-owned pubs, both of which flew the Union Jack and advertised televised soccer matches. Their hotel was only a brisk, five-minute walk from our Khruschevka apartment on Kentmanni Street, but somewhere in those five minutes one reality vanished and another began.

To start with, one rode an elegant, old-fashioned elevator to their hotel room, situated alone on the top floor. It was a luxury suite, a good deal for tourists visiting in November, and included a large bathroom with skylights, a jacuzzi, and a private sauna. From its windows, one could look out towards the pale blue Gulf of Finland and watch the snowflakes settle on the red-tiled roofs of Old Town. It was a money view. "It is so beautiful here," my mother said looking out, her hand on my elbow. "I'm glad we came."

Besides the luxury bathroom, my parents' suite included a fluffy pillowed, king-sized bed and two television sets. "Wait, I don't get it," I said when I first saw them. "How the heck do you watch two televisions at the same time?"

"Are you kidding me? It's great," my father said picking up the remote control. "Mom can watch CNN on one and I can watch the football game on the other."

"Are you serious?"

"Is there something wrong with having two TVs?" my mother raised an eyebrow and once again gripped my arm. This time I pulled it away. It was just a reflex, an instinct, but she picked up on it. "Um, did I do something wrong?" she asked.

"No," I said and felt a little ashamed for pulling my arm away. "Not at all."

"Okay," she said and walked away, frowning a bit.

Half an hour into their visit and there was already weirdness between us. And why did it bother me that she touched my arm so much anyway? Once was sweet, twice was endearing, but three, four, five, six times? Maybe I just wasn't used to it, or at least, I wasn't used to it anymore. I thought back to Pets' birthday party from the week before, and I realized that I had never hugged my sister-in-law Eva once, nor shook Pets' hand. It was entirely possible that I had never touched either of them, ever. Maybe that's what was going on. As I watched my father stand there flipping through the TV channels and my mother unpack her luggage, I understood. These two were completely unprepared for Estonian life. And if my father's kid-like good-naturedness and mother's touchy-feely emotionality could irk me after half an hour, what would happen when they met Epp's family, a bunch of real Estonians?

⬧ ⬧ ⬧

They lined up outside the Old Town beer hall like the Estonian welcoming committee, the whole Saluveer clan. The lights from the crooked cobblestone street cast orange shadows in the dark. My parents went down the line, snow crunching underfoot, leaning in and shaking hands, like foreign dignitaries: the Duke and Duchess of Long Island, New York.

Epp's relatives were there to greet them. Representing Viljandi was Epp's brother Priit. On behalf of the city of Tallinn stood Uncle Tiit and Aunt Reeli and their daughter Ave-Liis. Mayor Savisaar unfortunately had another engagement.

A Tartu contingent was led by Eva, Pets, and Simona. Cousin Helina, who had been at our wedding blessing, was the only one on hand to represent Elva, where she lived. And the little town of Karksi-Nuia sent the largest delegation of all: Helina's cousin Maarja, also at our wedding, their mother Randi, as well as Epp's father Andres, his wife Tiiu, and Epp's little brother Aap. There would be fourteen Estonians and three Americans dining together, plus our little unborn child, whatever nationality he or she was.

"Hi, how are you? Nice to meet you! How are you doing?" I saw my father reach in and shake hands, up and down, a big grin on his jet-lagged face. He made eye contact with everyone and smiled. His teeth reflected the light from the snow. A few times, I saw him wink. The man was a salesman to the bone.

"Hi! Te-re! So good to see you!" My mother's eyes lit up as she wrapped her arms around Priit, Tiit and Reeli and Ave-Liis, Eva, Pets, and Simona, Helina, Maarja, Aap, and Tiiu. When she finally got to Andres, at the end of the line, she maneuvered her hatted head in between his shoulder and leather cap, and planted a big wet kiss on his fuzzy cheek.

"Oh my God! Your mother kissed my father!" Epp whispered in my ear. "I don't ever kiss my father!"

"You have a lovely daughter," my mother cooed, looking up into Andres' light blue eyes. "It's so nice to finally meet you."

"Tere," Andres answered. It was a plain "Tere," the kind of "Tere" you say to an acquaintance in the street. He stood there in place in the shadows, wrapped up stiff in a thick navy blue winter jacket, a touch of frost on his gray moustache, like Father Christmas. And after my mother kissed him, his cheeks were big red apples of embarrassment. Jolly indeed.

I shook Andres' hand and also said "Tere." I managed a short, tight wave to Aap and Tiiu in the darkness. Then we all went inside.

6 6 6

I had chosen the beer hall for the grand family get together because it seemed so generically European. It had bratwursts and schnitzels and big foaming pitchers of beer; long, dark, wooden tables and waitresses done up in old-fashioned aprons ready to take your order. I thought it would remind my father of his good old days in the army when he was stationed in Germany, or my mother of those nights in Zurich during our trip when I was 15. I had to go easy on my parents. They had just arrived. They weren't ready for blood sausages and meat jelly just yet.

With that many people and those many plates, it was hard to move your elbows let alone have a conversation. At first, my parents were seated across from their counterparts, Andres and Tiiu, the grandparents to be. We were at the other end of the table with cousins Helina and Maarja and Epp's brother Priit. From afar, I saw my mother and father try small talk with Andres and Tiiu at the other end of the table, but eventually they wound up moving in our direction.

"Justin," my mother slid beside me and squeezed my arm, a bit of an alarmed look dancing in her blue eyes, "most of these people can't speak any English!"

"I know," I said.

"I mean I was trying to talk to Andres, but I don't think he understood what I was saying. Or maybe he did. I couldn't tell."

"Don't worry about it. He doesn't say much to me either."

"And when I kissed him, it was like I dumped a bucket of ice water on him or something. Did you see his face? Did you see?"

"But, Ma, people usually don't do that here. I warned you, remember?"

"Don't do what?"

"Jump up and kiss each other."

"Well, why the heck not? Why don't they kiss each other? What's wrong with kissing? What's wrong with them? That's just weird!"

I was stumped. "Look," I said. "The guy's had a rough life. His first wife died and his house burned down. Cut him some slack."

"Justin!" she seized my arm. "If my husband died and my house burned down do you think I'd ever shut up about it?"

I didn't respond, but the answer was no, she wouldn't. For every word my father-in-law held back, my mother would gladly say five, 10, 15 words. She would tell anyone who would listen until they all begged her to please be quiet. Then she would talk some more.

"Maybe it's just an Italian thing," she sighed to herself. "You know how we like to talk."

"But Andres isn't Italian, Ma," I said looking down the table past the packs of elbows and dinner plates at Epp's father, who sat in silence. "He's an Estonian."

Two completely different families twisted into one clash of cultures and all this, our work, our will, our fault. Bratwurst and beer were neutral choices. If Andres was at home, he might be digging into a heaping plate of *sült* and vinegar. My mother might be standing over the kitchen sink, straining out the pasta. But it was not to be. Not tonight.

"Did you ever think when we first met in Helsinki last year that we would be here, like this?" Epp whispered to me.

"No," I offered my wife a bemused smile. "I can't say that I did."

"We were just two careless travelers back then," she said, and "back then," even if it was a year, now seemed like a really, really long time ago. "Do you remember how we were planning to go to Brazil?"

"And India," I said.

"And Chile?"

"Yeah."

"Do you realize what we've done? Did you see your parents trying so hard to talk my father and Tiiu before? I bet they never ever thought in a million years that they would wind up here, in a beer hall in Tallinn trying to talk to a bunch of Estonians."

"But that's just how it is," I said. "I wonder if they think I planned it this way."

That first night was the night that my parents met Reeli. My mother had gripped Epp's arm and asked her who was the British woman who was talking to my father at the end of the table. When she learned that the woman wasn't British, and that she just taught English at a school in Tallinn, my mother scooted in Reeli's direction, and she clung to her new English-speaking lifesaver for the rest of her beer hall encounter with the Saluveers.

When I think about it, Epp's aunt Reeli was the most appropriate person for them to deal with there. She was tall and lean, with short, curly reddish hair, wearing small silver hoop earrings, and a pleasant and ruddy face that had retained a doll-like quality deep into middle age, as if toy babies had been modeled on her. Reeli liked to smoke, she liked to make jokes, and her words were always delivered flat, with irony, so you couldn't tell if she was serious or not. When she was really amused, she would cackle loudly so that everyone could hear. Because of this, she reminded me a bit of a witch, but there was nothing malevolent about her, because Reeli was a good Estonian witch.

"You have a nice son," Reeli told my mother in the beer hall. She spoke with a proper British accent, light on the 'r's, while

271

still maintaining the machine-like cadence of an Estonian, pop, pop, pop, pop. "When I first heard that Epp was dating some American guy, I thought she was being foolish, and that it would never last, but once I met him," she gestured at me with her head, "I could see that he really loves her."

Reeli looked me in the eyes when she said it and ever so slightly winked. I managed to work my lips into a smile again. Was Reeli telling the truth? Did she really mean what she said? I remembered how she had squeezed me on the day of our wedding and said, "Take care of our baby." That may have been the last time an Estonian other than my wife had hugged me.

"Thank you," my mother answered Reeli, her cheeks hot pink from the beer and the compliment. Now it was her time to blush.

Reeli said she was pleased to have some new English-speaking specimens to work with. She invited all three of us – my parents and me – to her school to talk to her students. It would be good for her students to meet real Americans, she said, to break some of the stereotypes her countrymen had about our countrymen. We all agreed to go. Reeli said it would be fun.

At the end of the night, most of the Saluveers disappeared quietly into the night, bellies full of bratwurst, bodies aching from the funny Americans' embrace. My parents followed us back to the apartment on Kentmanni Street, too, pulling a lone suitcase behind them. It was still snowing as they finally stepped by the security perimeter of the American Embassy, and looked up to see its flag, our flag, red, white, and blue, tossed about in the night wind, a flag that was 6,600 kilometers from the one that hung outside my parents' front door.

I didn't want them to notice the poor condition of our place, even if we would soon leave it, especially when compared with their luxury suite, but they didn't say anything about the old Soviet building or the crumbling tiles in the room. Maybe they were just too tired in the end to be bothered by anything. It had no doubt for these two been one really long, surreal day, one that just had to end in bed at the Old Town Maestro with their feet poking out of the covers and the glimmer of CNN's logo on one of the TV screens to comfort them. Then they could finally sink into a jet-lagged slumber under a starry northern sky and rest.

They rolled the suitcase into the middle of our room and we opened its contents, gold, frankincense, myrrh! Actually, it was baby clothes. Big sealed plastic bags filled with baby clothes lugged from New York, most of them white and yellow, gender-neutral colors, for we didn't know our baby's gender yet, little onesies and pajamas and caps and socks. There was even a red pair of pajamas I thought I had seen before.

"This," my mother held up the small but significant item of clothing, "used to be Justin's."

"Wow, thank you so much!" Epp said as the new possessions were tugged from the suitcase, her eyes wide, and her tongue hung on the words "so much" because Eva had already given us one bag of hand-me-downs from when Simona was a baby and now there was all this. But Epp had already been to America,

273

and in America, she knew, there was always more stuff. She also understood that my parents had brought us all of these things not just to help us but to show us that they cared, as if they didn't know that just coming all the way to Tallinn from New York was enough.

Eventually, their post-dinner coffee highs wearing down, they were forced to admit that it was time to retire to the Old Town Maestro.

"I'll walk you home," I said. "It's only five minutes away."

"Don't worry, son," my father put his hand on my shoulder. "We'll just order a taxi."

"A taxi? But your place is right around the corner. I wouldn't order a taxi. You could be back in your room watching CNN by the time a taxi shows up and picks you up and gets you over there!" A Tallinn taxi driver might also pick up on the fact that they weren't from out of town and rip them off, but I didn't say it.

"Listen, Justin," my father sighed. He already looked like he was a little sick of me and my weird questions, his eyes were puffy and bloodshot. "I have been awake since, I don't even know, sometime yesterday. Your mother has too. We got here and then we went to the restaurant and then we came back here and we are exhausted. So we are not walking home, even if home is next door, do you understand? We are taking a taxi."

LIFE ON
THE MARGINS

We took a taxi to Reeli's school – and we wound up taking taxis most places during my parents' visit.

It pulled up to the big building's white steps, where we were met by Reeli, the good Estonian witch, who hugged us and led us into a bright auditorium with giant windows. In the front were three chairs: one for my father, one for my mother, and one for me, the very important people, the guests of honor, the Americans.

"They are all so excited," Reeli said as she led us to our seats. "These kids just don't get to meet real Americans every day and ask them questions."

For months, I had been teaching Estonians the English language in relative anonymity, trying to get them to talk for 100 kroons an hour. But now, with my parents around, we were suddenly quasi-celebrities. The kids wanted to hear me talk, and, most of all, they wanted to hear my parents talk. The little hands went up from around the room at the first opportunity and the Estonian kids didn't pull their punches.

Reeli called on one in the back, a teenage boy with a bowl of potato brown hair and big saucers of glasses. "Did you support the war in Iraq?" the inquisitive youth asked.

A collective gasp in the room. We looked at each other. "No, I did not," my mother finally answered, and I saw her bite her tongue in the side of her cheek in order to navigate through this minefield of school auditorium diplomacy. "I did think that the Iraqi people would welcome US troops more than they did, especially after all those years under Saddam. But, well, you can see how things are on the news."

Then a little girl with golden pigtails and a purple dress in the center asked: "How come your president sounds so dumb when he talks?"

"Young lady!" The girl was scolded by one of the teachers, but the scolding was overruled by the peal of nervous laughter that bounced off the walls and then rained down from the ceiling. When it subsided, my father smiled. "You know," he said. "I ask myself that same question every day."

More laughter, more questions. In the front row, another boy asked the very important Americans, "Can you speak any other languages?"

First there was silence, so the very important people had time to think. Then the answers came. My mother told of how she had spoken Italian with her grandparents but sadly lost the language. My father recollected a few German phrases from his army years but admitted that he really only spoke English. Then it was my turn.

"I learned Latin and Spanish in school," I said and looked out into the youthful crowd. "I know some Danish and Swedish, too. And, ha, oh yeah, I almost forgot, *ma oskan eesti keelt**!"

The words just slipped from my mouth, without me even thinking about what they meant or in which way to order the sentence or whether or not it was grammatically correct. It surprised me how quickly it had happened, my outburst of Estonian. It was if someone had pinched me and I had responded with an, "ouch." When they heard those four words, the students in the auditorium applauded en masse and then some even cheered. The high ceiling reflected the loud sound downward on us. It was jarring, cacophonous. My mother and father looked at each other.

"Well, this is kind of different, huh?" my mother said.

"Different? Uh, hello," my father mumbled to her, half proud, half freaked out. "In case you haven't noticed, our son speaks Estonian."

My parents' visit was a door into the world of the foreigner in Estonia. It was an opening of the eyes, a cleansing of the ears, a whetting of the palate. For even though I had lived as a foreigner in Estonia for nearly ten months, married an Estonian woman, conceived a baby that would be born in an Estonian hospital, I had somehow managed to do so few of the things foreigners in Estonia like to do.

---

* I know the Estonian language. (In Estonian)

277

Now, I did it all. Every night we ate at a new restaurant in the Old Town, restaurants I had passed myriad times but never stepped inside. In the evenings my father and I might go out for a beer at bars I had often walked by on my way to some appointment, glancing at the tourists in their reverie within. And I had always seen the tourists as just that, as different from me. My Estonia consisted of the trams and buses, offices and conference rooms, corner groceries and home improvement stores. With my parents around, I was finally able to look out a window and view the entire Old Town in all its UNESCO World Heritage Site glory. It really was beautiful, so how come I had not seen it that way before?

And being good foreigners, we went on a tour of the Old Town. Epp and I arranged it. My student Mats lived there and his art historian father Jüri had agreed to show us around. We were now among the elite, as Jüri had given the same tour to the Swedish royal couple, the prime ministers of India, Portugal, and Ukraine, and since I was such a good English tutor to Mats, and because Jüri loved history, he said he didn't mind giving a private tour to a group consisting of my parents and my Language School classmates and their wives.

Jüri. He was a man of history, a person who Epp said I always had to address in the plural 'Teie', the Estonian equivalent of the Italian 'Lei'. I rarely used 'Teie', not even with Epp's grandparents or her father. Strangers were sometimes 'Teie', but you were considered a patronizing oddball if you continued to refer to a person in the plural after making personal contact. Usually with new acquaintances you started with the plural 'Teie' and then went to 'Sina', the familiar "you." Not with Jüri. He was 100 percent old school, an individual who would forever remain in the plural.

Jüri was just a handful of years older than my parents, but he seemed much older, as if the whole saga of Tallinn was written on his skin. He was born in 1942, a year after his grandfather was deported and two years before his father fell on the Eastern Front in German uniform. "Under Soviet terminology, I was both the son of an enemy of the nation and a grandson of the enemy of the nation," he had told me when I had interviewed him for an article. And he was quite scholarly about it, as if it was a well-known fact, no bitterness in his voice. It had been on a dark November afternoon when we met. He sat in his library enveloped by walls of aged books, huge brown and black musty volumes that looked as if they might disintegrate upon touch. "I collect old things," he said. "History is my true love."

But loving history hadn't always been easy for Jüri. He had wanted to major in history when he left to attend the University of Tartu, but had eventually opted for art history instead. "This was the time when Khrushchev was in power, so they didn't teach real history in school, true history."

"But how did you find out about true history if they didn't teach it? How did you know what was true?" I asked.

"I heard the history," he said, his skinny legs crossed, head resting on one hand, a crane-like figure bent in thought. "I listened to the people who could tell me the truth."

On the day of the tour, Jüri met us on the Town Hall Square. He stood there: tall, rail thin in a black coat, fur hat, black leather gloves, looking like a veteran of 1918 risen from the grave and armed with knowledge, his bayonet of memory sharpened and fixed. His white moustache caught the snow flakes, and from under his hat I could see the long gold-white locks of his antiquarian haircut peeking out.

"Greetings! Tere! My name is Jüri and I live here," he announced. "I like living in the Old Town because it makes my days longer," he said, and with that began to walk, his black boots crumpling the snow.

"Justin, this guy is great!" my father leaned into whisper in my ear. "A real character."

"As you can see, we don't need any transportation to get around, and I am always filled with inspiration here because there aren't as many stresses as there are out there in the rest of the city. But life here is in development, every day houses are reconstructed, every two months new shops and restaurants are opening, we can see lights in houses that have been dark for years. Our official tourism slogan is 'positively transforming,' but this transformation has not been fast enough for me. In smaller towns, this so-called transformation is almost non-existent. But here, in the Old Town, you can see it on every street."

And you could. The place was crooked and charming, especially in the snow, with the lights warming the orange and pink and red pastels of the city, making it look like we had been set down inside a gigantic gingerbread cake. By some virtue, this place had escaped the destruction that had ruined so many other cities in Europe's long list of wars. Now its central square already hosted a small shanty town of peddler's cottages, the Christmas Fair, the *jõululaat*, a maze of hand-knit sweaters and wooden toys, marzipan cookies and boiling vats of sweet red

Christmas *glögi*, some with alcohol and some without, tourists all around.

My mother peeled a poster for the Christmas Fair from the side of one of the wooden booths. It had a cartoon of Tallinn's skyline with a jolly gnome winking over it in the sky. "Come here, look at this Justin, isn't it neat?" she said and squeezed my arm.

"Uh, yeah." I had probably walked by the Christmas Fair posters numerous times but never paid them much attention. When I looked at that grinning gnome though I could see it was quite festive.

"I think I'll have it framed and give it to Epp as a present," she rolled it up and slid it into her bag. "But don't tell her. Let it be a secret!"

Throughout the morning, Jüri indulged us in the city's architecture, in its mythology, introducing us to the trees where Peter the Great passed out drunk after wild nights of debauchery; the spot where the architect of St. Olaf's Church tumbled to his death in the 12th century, after which both a snake and a toad reportedly came crawling out of his mouth. And as we walked I watched my parents' faces, lit up like children, and felt again that they were now my children, and I had to make sure they had a good time.

Still, though Old Town was inspiring, all was not right with the place according to Jüri. "Here in Old Town, we have casinos, strip bars, cheap shops, Russian souvenirs, amber from Kaliningrad, Finnish tourists who are only interested in beer and vodka," he sighed as we followed him through the snowy streets. "This level of bad taste makes me very unhappy. I do hope we can in the future develop a higher level of tourism, cultural tourism, tourism with good taste! It is very important for us to do that."

At the end of our excursion, my father asked if he could have his photo taken with Jüri and me. We stood beside one another in front of a medieval house, and my mother took the picture. In his black leather jacket, a scarf tossed around his neck, next to me and Jüri, the man of history, the soul of Old Town, my father looked alive, happy and relaxed. And after it was taken, I wondered why I had never thought of having my photo taken with an Estonian legend like Jüri before.

Most tourists never left the Old Town. They stayed and played, sucked in by its marzipan charm. But my parents did get the opportunity to get off the ride, to step out of the medieval amusement park, if only for a few days. Sometimes I wonder if they should have just stayed there, titillated by the Christmas lights, bread and circus, costumes and roasted nuts, cookies and mulled wine.

The taxi let us off in front of the house on Valgevase Street and we climbed the two sets of stairs in the back to access the loft apartment on the third floor. They also liked it, and could see why we took it. Their money had helped to finance the apartment, but we agreed to pay it all back. As for the Kalamaja District itself, its puffy cats feeding at the dumpsters, the rickety old buildings, some half eaten by fire, the crooked roofs covered in green moss like Mayan ruins, my parents were mostly quiet, a little intimidated too perhaps, but my mother also mouthed the words "up and coming neighborhood" and "all gone in five years" when she saw the wrecks because she said she had that special innate real estate agent's sense of the future.

My father was less forward thinking. "God, the Russians really ruined this place," he sighed as we walked down the streets. There was still snow on the ground, but the weather had turned again, reversed, the light retreating, the gray clouds setting in, covering the rooftops and trees with that corrosive moist smog that just ate into your soul.

"It wasn't the Russians," I said, wishing Kalamaja looked better than it did. "It was the Soviets."

"That's what I mean."

"Come on! There are places like this in New York, too. Not near where you guys live, but in the city. There's got to be."

"Son, if there's one thing the world is full of, it's shitholes," he said to me. "But in New York? Houses like these? Half burnt like that, infested with cats? And people still living in them? Nah."

I thought he was lying a bit to himself about New York, when he said it, but I knew I was guilty of lying to myself a little about Kalamaja, too. But the truth has a way of leaking out, doesn't it? Of showing up uninvited, unwelcome, when one least expects it. Once my mother finally understood how "up and coming" Estonian real estate really was, she was curious if we could have gotten an apartment for the same price in the lovely Old Town, so Epp found a listing in our price range and we all decided to go.

It faced a courtyard in a gloomy building in the shadow of St. Nicholas' Church, not too far from my parents' hotel. We met the owner at the gate, a little middle-aged woman with curly hair. She looked kind and innocent and grandmotherly, like a librarian. Once we ascended the stairs to the little place, though, my parents were thrust into what one might call a pit of despair. It was cave dark, electric wires stapled haphazardly to the rotting wooden beams, a poorly done Euroremont job of cement floors covered in tattered carpets and bubbly vinyl colored to look like tiles, a single room that stunk of filth and mildew and vodka and hopelessness, like some kind of 19th century tenement apartment in the Italian ghetto on New York's Lower East Side.

I was ashamed, ready to split immediately, but my mother just had to ask, "And where is the bathroom?" And the little librarian-looking lady ushered us down a dark tunnel of a hallway to a back room that stunk of piss and was covered in cobwebs, where even I would think twice about shitting, if I had the choice. And all this was a minute away from the fragrant girls selling roasted nuts and *glögi* on Town Hall Square. Who knew? The tenant admitted it needed "a little work," but, of course, noted its central location within the Old Town, and who didn't want to live in the Old Town, right? We lied and said it had potential and thanked her and told her we would think about it and get back to her.

Outside my mother and father couldn't walk away from the building quickly enough. "Oh my God, did you see that? Did you smell that?" my father laughed nervously. "And the bathroom was down the hall. It wasn't even in the apartment!"

"Never in my career as a real estate agent have I seen something so foul! Never!" my mother cried. "I've got goosebumps on my skin. It is without a doubt, absolutely, positively, the worst apartment I have ever seen. In my entire life. Hands down. I am serious!"

It was a nasty apartment, but I knew firsthand that there were more of them, that Estonia was crowded with them. Blame it on the Russians, or the Soviets, or vodka, but it was probably going to take more than five years to wash this country clean. I only wished I could wash my parents' minds clean of what they had just seen.

During the tour in the Old Town, my father had been introduced to Manfred, and the two struck up a fast new friendship, one forged on a love of beer, of watches, of sports cars, all the things that make Germans and Germanophiles giddy. The old German had invited everyone from our Language School class and my parents back to his apartment in Kadriorg for drinks. We arrived there by cab at nightfall. It was a bit of a coincidence that the old German was living abroad on a street named "Weizenberg," but not really when you considered that men with German names had at one time formed the city elite.

And Manfred's apartment was upper crust. When I entered the immense flat, saw its high ceilings, sturdy walls, dark wooden furniture, oil paintings, the snow drifting down beyond its large, elegant windows, I realized that Manfred too had his own Estonia, one that was neither found in the medieval arcade of the Old Town or among the slum cats of

285

Kalamaja. And in Manfred's Estonia, his girlfriend Astrid stood in the kitchen frying up sausages and asking him questions in German.

Who was this young woman who had taken up with a much older man? The Astrid I discovered that night was an academic, the kind of woman who waited patiently to hear a person's argument, then shattered it with a tide of new questions. She was well suited for a life with an argumentative German, I thought, but when I looked at her, I could see that she couldn't be much older than me, which would make Manfred about three and a half decades older than her. That scoundrel! But he just had to have what he wanted, didn't he, the apartment in Kadriorg, the summer house in Salmistu, the attractive, intelligent young life mate? Once again I envied him. If only I too could seize life by its balls and tell it to do what I wanted, shake free of useless teaching lessons and dull articles and win every argument and get a jeep and drive it down the beach!

Astrid had caught my father's eye too. "Wait, how old is your girlfriend?" he asked Manfred, a little confused.

"Astrid?" he replied "She is, wait, how old are you darling?"

"I'm 28," she answered, now with a glass of wine in her hand, lounging next to Manfred at the long dining room table.

"She's 28," Manfred said and wrapped an arm around her.

"God bless you, Manfred," my father said and smiled and shook his head. "God bless you."

My father said he wanted to meet Manfred again, so I rang the old German up the following afternoon to arrange a get together at the beer hall.

"MANN!" Manfred had shouted his family name into the phone, like he had picked it up while he was doing pushups. When he heard my voice, then he again adopted his friendly, diplomatic tone with his "Ah, Justin," and "Ja, *ja*. Ja, *ja*." Why were Germans always shouting their names out anyway? Why didn't they just start with the friendly Ja, jas? Or try something entirely different. When my father answered the phone, he only said, "Hello." When Epp picked up the receiver, she let out a soft, "Epp kuuleb." But call up a German and what do you get? "MANN!"

"Man, I bet you nothing has changed in Germany since I was there," my father said, sitting at the bar the next evening waiting for Manfred to show up, half a beer already in him. "People used to do that back then too. I used to call them up. 'Schmidt!' 'Richter!' I was friends with a lot of Germans. They used to take me to the underground clubs, the clubs the other guys on base couldn't get into. The DJs would be these guys in black turtle-necks in a booth. "Und zat vaz Jumping Jack Flash by zie Rolling Stones." He laughed softly to himself and took a deep gulp of his amber-colored beer. "God, Estonia, Estonia," he looked around at the barmaids. "By the way, have I ever mentioned to you that I went to high school with an Estonian girl," his eyes were set straight in front of him. "But you know, her father, Karl was his name I think," he leaned in closer. "Yeah, Karl Linnas. Well, he turned out to be a Nazi." He whispered the last word as if it was so vulgar that no proper person should say it aloud.

"Really?" I said and recoiled a bit in my seat at the sound of the awful word.

"Yeah, they deported him to the Soviet Union and he died in jail. It was in all the papers." He gave me a 'that's life' look and took another gulp of his beer. "Well, how about that Old Town apartment we saw today, huh? I have never seen anything like it."

"There are a lot of them like that out there," I said and frowned. "Not everyone in Estonia has two TVs, a jacuzzi, and a private sauna, you know."

"Hey, what's wrong with jacuzzis and private saunas?" he snorted.

"Nothing's wrong with it."

"You and Epp certainly enjoyed using our jacuzzi and sauna the other night."

"Well, we don't have a jacuzzi or private sauna, if you haven't noticed."

"Justin, understand something. You chose to live on the margins. You chose this life for yourself. I didn't raise you to live in a little apartment in the former Soviet Union."

"Soon to be the European Union."

"Either way, you chose it. Can you imagine if you had never gone to Helsinki, never met Epp, where would you be now?"

"The same thing would have happened, just another way."

"What? Married at 23 and living in Estonia? No way!"

"Ok, maybe not exactly this way, but something similar."

"I don't think so. You'd probably be living in New York and having fun like everyone else your age."

"Sometimes you just know things about yourself."

"Okay, okay," he lifted his mug again and patted me on the back. "Well, Epp does have ambition. I think she's good for you. But have you given any thought to what you are doing to do after the baby comes? I saw that little Valgevase apartment. It's tiny. You can't exactly raise a kid there."

"I know," I sighed.

"And what about your job? Epp is going to go on maternity leave. How can you support a family doing what you do, English lessons, writing articles for *The Baltic News*?"

"*The Baltic Times*."

"Don't forget, you were in one of the best journalism programs in the country, maybe even the world! You should be bringing in six figures, easily. Easily."

I rubbed my forehead and said nothing.

"Look, I am not trying to lecture you here, Justin. You are just going to be a father and you need to think about things. That's all I am saying. Like this little cat, Miisu. Do you expect that Miisu will be moving into Valgevase too with the baby?" he cocked a disapproving eyebrow.

"No."

"So where is the cat going to go? Back to the street?"

"We haven't decided yet."

"Well, maybe you should think about that too. I know that you have a lot on your mind, but you've got to step up to the plate. And you have to think about the future. Do you really want to spend the rest of your life here, in this country?"

For the next few moments, there was only silence between my father and me. We sat on the bar stools, shadows of each other, the barmaids fluttering by with platters of steaming

289

schnitzels in their hands. I sipped my beer, looked up at the clock, and waited in desperation to see Manfred's good-natured face come bobbing through the door, cap on his head, hungry for a debate about ways of resolving the Palestinian issue or the local real estate market or the latest Porsche model. Anything other than my father's questions.

THANKSGIVING
AT BONAPARTE

*We had Thanksgiving dinner at Bonaparte,
down in the cellar.*

It was a French restaurant with all the fixings of elegance. It had arched brick ceilings, candelabras, wine, Edith Piaf, white linen tablecloths, baked snails, portraits of the diminutive 19th century French military leader, shadows flickering on the walls.

Had my parents not been around I might have forgotten it was Thanksgiving altogether. It would have been your average night in Tallinn, schnitzels and potatoes. They were here though and so we had to celebrate Thanksgiving. It was mandatory. I wondered why it wasn't that important to me. What kind of American was I? Could I just as easily forget about Halloween and the Fourth of July? Christmas? Easter? My own birthday? What had happened to me?

"Justin, what's happened to you?" my father asked, refilling my wine glass.

"What do you mean?"

"You talk differently now, have you noticed? You have like this weird accent," he squinted at me. "You're putting spaces between all the words. It's hard to explain."

"Maybe it's because I've been talking to foreigners all the time," I said. "I have to speak slowly so that they understand."

Both of my parents watched my mouth as I spoke, and then turned their heads towards one another and nodded as if to confirm the diagnosis.

"You know, I could tell something had changed in your voice just from our phone conversations," my mother said. "It's strange. It's not the way you say the words, it's more in the cadence, the rhythm of your words. It kind of sounds like, pop, pop, pop, pop. Like that. Very weird, just weird."

"Maybe Justin has an Estonian accent," Epp joked.

Nobody laughed.

"Scallop and tuna fish carpaccio?" the waiter arrived, dinner in hand.

"Right here!" my father smiled to the waiter and watched the plate sizzle as it was laid in front of him. Another delicious Old Town dinner. He was very happy.

"Smoked trout fillet-beetroot tartare?"

"That's for me!" my mother gestured before her. "Oh wow," she looked down at her fish. "Thank you. Ai-tah."

"Palun, palun," the waiter nodded and then left to bring another tray. I had ordered the Estonian beef carpaccio, Epp the chanterelle soup.

"Epp, are you sure you just want soup?" my mother asked.

"Oh, we've been out every night this week," my wife blushed a little in the candlelight. "I'm stuffed."

"But it's Thanksgiving."

"Soup is enough for me."

"God, I can't believe I am eating French food on Thanksgiving," my mother said, one elbow propped on the table, her head in her hands. "And here on the other side of the Earth, so far away from my family."

"What are you talking about?" I tossed a hand in the air. "We're your family too. We're right here!"

"Yeah, I know," my mother said. "It's just that I don't think I've missed a big family Thanksgiving ever." She paused to reflect. "No, I've been at every single one. Don't you miss everybody? Think about it. Your brother, grandma, your aunts and uncles, all your cousins, they are all celebrating this important day without you on the other side of the world, so far away. Don't you feel like you should be there with them?"

"Let's see if they show up for Thanksgiving when their wives are eight months pregnant and they live in another country."

"But they wouldn't wind up living in another country, Justin," my mother toyed with her food. "They're not like you."

It was a sad song, a tragic song, but I wasn't having any of it. Maybe there was coldness in my heart now. Maybe Estonia had worked its gray, icy magic on me, made me numb, but if it had, I couldn't feel it anymore. Besides, the idea of them all over there across the Atlantic piling up the turkey and mashed potatoes and pumpkin pie on their plates and sitting around watching football didn't move me one bit. I didn't even follow football anymore. It bored me. For so many years I tried fitting in, but no one believed it. It was only now that I had somehow wound up with an Estonian accent that I was being taken seriously, still a weirdo, but one who should be regarded with a bit more care.

Sitting there, eating my Thanksgiving beef carpaccio, drinking my wine, reflecting on my mother's sorrow, it was apparent to me, how ugly I had become. I had become the ugliest of Americans, the one who left America and didn't feel particularly bad about it; the one who had taken a foreigner for a bride and actually bothered himself with learning her obscure language; the American who ate French food on Thanksgiving. I had betrayed my nation's sense of universal superiority.

When the waiter brought the bill, my father took it in hand. I reached for it and pulled on the small black leather wallet in which it was enclosed.

"Get out of here!" my father pulled the bill away, laughing, tugging his reading glasses from his front pocket and fixing them on his nose.

"You've paid every night this week," I said. "Let me pay. Please?"

"You save your money."

"Come on."

"Tell you what, Justin, when you move back to New York, you can get a well-paying job to support your family and then you can buy us a nice dinner. How's that sound?"

"When you move back to New York." For him, my meeting with Epp may have been a bizarre chance, but the relocation to New York was destined. Epp and I had discussed moving to New York, sure, but there always the understanding between her and me that we could leave there too. We could live anywhere. We needed options, or at least I did. Nothing put fear in me like the question, "So are you planning to stay for good?" "For good" to me sounded like a life sentence. Judging by my partner's track record, she had similar reservations.

My father went over every line of the bill, counting silently to himself. I looked at the wrinkles around his eyes and thought he deserved a better son than me, a normal son, one without the ugliness, one who didn't ask stupid questions and could appreciate the luxury of having three TVs, one who wasn't some bitter lemon expat shithead. But we were similar in some ways. The old man did have adventure in his heart. He liked being back in Europe. He liked Tallinn. That morning, I had taught him how to navigate the icy sidewalks so he didn't slip, making short, flat steps, stiff backed, leaning a little from side to side. "Just imagine you're a penguin," I had said, his arm locked in mine. "You'll get the hang of it."

"Why are the sidewalks so icy?" he had asked. "Don't people slip and get hurt and sue?"

I knew why he asked it. In America such lawsuits were common. There were even "personal injury lawyers" who advertised on TV, saying things like, "Have you slipped on an icy sidewalk recently and hurt yourself? Then you may be eligible to damages of up to a million dollars!"

But an Estonian? File a lawsuit? For slipping on the ice? I had never heard of such a thing. "Not here," I had told him. "In Estonia, everything bad that happens to you is your own fault."

In the restaurant cellar my father sighed loudly. Then he went over the bill once more and then leaned over. "This is kind of a big check," he said. "How much are you supposed to tip in Estonia again? Ten percent? 15 percent?"

THANKSGIVING AT BONAPARTE

"Um, you're not supposed to tip."

"What?"

"Dad, please don't tell me you've tipped at every restaurant we've been to this week."

"Of course, I left tips at all the restaurants! You have to tip. So, tell me, how much should I leave this guy?"

"You shouldn't leave him anything."

"Are you serious? They don't tip in Estonia? That's terrible!"

"No it's not. I kind of like it."

"You would."

"Oh come on! You don't have to do any math, you just pay and go. He has a salary, like everyone else. It's great."*

"Well, I don't care what the guy's salary is. He was good to us, so I am going to leave a tip. No matter where I go, I always leave the waiter a little something. So how much should I leave him, 10 percent?"

"Sure," I said. "Go ahead."

"Terrific." My father pushed the glasses back on his nose and counted out exactly 10 percent of the bill. Then he slid the Estonian kroons into the bill wallet, and set it aside. And there we were, the four of us, or five, sitting around a table in the cellar of a French restaurant called Bonaparte, on Thanksgiving, waiting for the waiter to return to collect his tip.

---

* Nowadays, tipping in Estonian restaurants is more common, but in 2003 it was not especially widespread.

ONE LEG HERE,
ONE LEG THERE

*The sound of late-night laughter in the streets,
the expecting couple indoors.*

It was warm in our little apartment, cocoon-like and comforting, and yet melancholic as I followed the sounds of youth as they passed under our window, longing to join them, if but for one night, if but for one drink. The day was long over, and in Estonia in December the days had a bad habit of ending before they ever began.

Inside, in bed, another test of international relations was underway. An elephant stood in the corner of our apartment, or rather a snake. The dilemma: to cut or not to cut? To circumcise the child, should it be male, like most American boys, or to keep him whole, like most Estonian *poisid*?

"I don't even think most Estonian doctors know how to do it," said Epp. "Hypothetically, if we did it, we'd have to find someone with experience. But how many people know how to do that here?"

I looked up at the ceiling and said a silent prayer for a girl, because if it was a girl, there would be no reason to go looking for an "expert," maybe knocking on the doors of the Tallinn Synagogue to ask for a *mohel* because we didn't feel like submitting our child's manhood to the shaky scalpel of an inexperienced doctor.

"Is it really so important to you that we do it?" Epp had said earlier that day in the office, the homepage of the Estonian Jewish community open on her computer. "I mean, we're not even Jewish." I had also scanned the webpage, seen the bearded face of Rabbi Shmuel Kot smiling back in his dapper black hat.

Was it really important to me? I couldn't say. I had never considered it a question before. Circumcision was just something that I thought happened to most American newborns. It was something that was very normal in my country, but it was very abnormal in hers.

"I don't know if I could allow my son to be cut like that," she said that night. "And right after he's born? He's just starting to discover the world and some doctor cuts the skin off his dick? It's so cruel!"

It was a contentious issue, so I read about it more online. Circumcision had passionate advocates and equally passionate opponents and, like all people who believed passionately in things, they hated each other. One side argued that the procedure keeps the genitals cleaner and prolongs male sexual enjoyment, which I thought of as a plus. Who wanted their kid to grow up to be a lousy lay?

The other side argued that the pain of having one's foreskin sawed off left permanent emotional scars. Did it really? Was every circumcised man I knew – my father, my brother, my cousins and friends, myself – emotionally scarred from the operation? Well, maybe. Whether it was drinking or womanizing or self-loathing or gambling, most of us American men had at least one personal problem. Was circumcision the reason?

Faced with the big decision of to cut or not to cut, I did what I did in most situations: I decided not to do anything. There would be no big argument from me, pro or con. I would not choose a side. Instead, we would wait and see. If it was a boy, we would have to make a decision. But until the moment came where we were knocking on that synagogue door, hoping Rabbi Kot could recommend an experienced Estonian *mohel*, we were in the clear.

There was also the issue of what to call a male child. I had gone for weeks thinking that we would call the kid "Markko Märtin." At least, that is what we called it sometimes between ourselves. That's what we told my parents, they seemed to be cool with the name.

But a week after they left, Epp announced she had decided on a name for a baby boy. It was Uno. "It's kind of old fashioned and it's so funny! I mean only old guys in Estonia are called Uno," she said, laughing but at the same time dead serious.

"But what about Markko Märtin?" I asked.

"That was just a joke, Justin."

"So Markko is a joke and Uno is not a joke?"

"Oh, please! I am not going to name my son after some rally driver. Anyway, I called my sister and she said that she likes Uno too. Uno! I love it. And it sounds Italian. You said you wanted it to sound Italian, didn't you?"

"But Uno isn't a name. It's a number."

"It is a name in Estonia. Like Uno Loop."

"Uno who?"

"Uno Loop. He's an old singer. And Uno means 'one' in Italian and this will be our first child, so it's perfect! Trust me."

It was a done deal. Epp had found a name for her son and she wouldn't budge. I wasn't sold on Uno but knowing I couldn't convince Epp otherwise, I let the issue sit. Maybe she would eventually change her mind. Or maybe we would have a girl.

I kept thinking about Uno Loop, though. The name intrigued me. I filed through the CDs in a music shop one day searching for the mysterious singer who might be the namesake of our future son and at last I found it. Uno Loop. His 50 greatest songs. Judging from the album cover, Uno was a man from another era, collared shirt, acoustic guitar in hand, half Elvis Presley, half teddy bear. He was classically handsome with a strong nose, a strong brow, and the thickest, fattest, whitest pair of muttonchops I'd ever seen.

I turned the CD jewel case over to have a look at his songs. I had heard the ballad, "Mis värvi on armastus?" ("What color is love?") on the radio before, so I knew that the tender, deep voice that carried it must belong to this man. But there were others there; songs with titles like "To be your partner" and "Last kiss". The northern Elvis had also done a rendition of Antonio Carlos Jobim's "Desafinado."

When I told my mother, now safely back in New York, the name Uno over the phone, she hadn't exactly expressed approval. "Uno? Are you out of your mind?"

"But it sounds kind of Italian," I had said, offering a lukewarm endorsement of the moniker.

"Italian? It sounds Spanish to me. Maybe you want to call him Uno Latino Petrone? Are you hoping he might qualify for some kind of college scholarship for minorities?" she said. My father simply refused to talk about the possibility of having a grandson named Uno.

Uno Loop. I stared at the CD cover. This was the man that Epp wanted to name our kid after. He didn't seem like a bad guy, but still it was hard to imagine a little baby with those thick white sideburns.

It was the darkest time of the year. There were now fewer than seven hours of light per day, and we were headed towards the blackest day of them all, the winter solstice, a day comprised almost entirely of night. On that dark day, December 22, the sun was expected to rise at 9:17 am and be down by 3:21 pm. Out of 24 hours, only six would be light, should the clouds part and allow any light in.

The persistent darkness made people anxious and edgy, even angry. One or two days without sunlight was tolerable, but three days, four days, a week? It almost made you want to smack the city's pushy supermarket cashiers across the face when they had the nerve to ask you if you had any change, and they always asked because every transaction had to be nice and neat in Estonia, everything had to be in order. They really expected you to walk around with a bag of coins, just so you could hand over the 20 cents when the time came. This was probably why so many people didn't even use cash anymore, so the cashiers would stop bugging them. In the summer, I hadn't noticed it, but in December, it was profoundly agitating.

So it took more than stoic perseverance to get through the submarine-like atmospherics of Tallinn. People tried different ways to cope with the perils of light deprivation. An art installation across from Tammsaare Park, for instance, promised 'nordic light therapy': attendees were invited into a completely white room of fluorescent lighting to lounge about and read and improve their grumpy winter moods. I imagined I could live in that room. Nordic light therapy sounded fantastic.

But PÖFF was the city's main emotional crutch, and Coca Cola Plaza was its epicenter. PÖFF was short for the *Pimedate Ööde Filmifestival,* or Tallinn Dark Night's Festival: weeks of foreign and domestic films showing around the city, all to pass the time, all to get the people through the funk of the season, to hold us over until Christmas and the slow re-lengthening of the days.

Coca Cola Plaza was jammed with people, the sweat of the crowds, the ashy city ice of their boots melting below the fans in the entrance way, packs of roving teenagers in puffy jackets gulping down carbonated beverages. See you at the movies! We entered one of the large theaters, and Epp curled up in her seat, legs under her belly, to enjoy the film every self-respecting PÖFF attendee had to see: *Dogville*, directed by Lars von Trier.

302

In *Dogville*, Nicole Kidman's character Grace flees her mafia boss father to a remote mountain village in United States of America. She is first taken in by the kind locals, but eventually used and degraded. Betrayal, rape, sanctimonious moralizing, fire, retribution, revenge and murder without shame: that was *Dogville*, the human condition on celluloid, a 21st century saga shot on a soundstage in Sweden, all of it fallen from another northerner, Danish director Lars von Trier.

I had seen von Trier's *Dancing in the Dark* when I was in college. It was similar, with Icelandic singer Björk cast as Selma Ježková, a Czech immigrant in America who loves the movies, works in a factory, wears thick black glasses, and is going blind. Poor Selma. She was taken advantage of too, scapegoated, called a Communist, and hung out to dry. Selma's archetype was the naive selfless immigrant, the foreigner, the outsider who is unsure of the rules of the world around her and thus doomed.

Björk's Selma even looked like Epp a bit, with the broad cheekbones, the lilting singsong English, her naivety about the American world. Selma had a headscarf around her head in *Dancer in the Dark*, too, so did Grace in *Dogville*, the scarf of the pilgrim, the kind of colorful cloth Epp might use to hold back her hair while she washed the windows on a spring day.

I looked at my wife's face as we watched *Dogville*, the lights of the film reflected in the thick, dark-rimmed glasses she wore to the cinema, glasses her mother had given her. We had talked more about the possibility of moving to New York just that morning and my wife seemed strangely open to it, excited perhaps by the possibility to escape her life once again.

The fact that she had recently had a dispute with some of her colleagues in the Publishing House might have had something to do with it. She had come home one night and bundled herself up in the small kitchen, rested her head in her hands and sobbed. Officially, the office blowup of 2003 was about an expense report, but it really was just your typical scorched earth Estonian turf war. Did she really want to return there after she had the baby, to the Publishing House, that nest of ambition?

"I am up for anything," Epp had shrugged that morning, as if pulling up roots in Tallinn and heading across the Atlantic was no big deal. She said she could go anywhere. "As long as I can take care of this baby and write my books, I'll be totally fine," she had said. "Plus New York does sound kind of cool."

But what would happen to her if we moved to that giant city? Could she manage there? Or would she just wind up like the lead in a Lars von Trier film, an outsider, a foreigner, a pilgrim with a scarf on her head, scorned for her contrariness, despised for being different? I worried about it as I stuffed my face with popcorn in the theater. Could she really cope there?

Could I?

Late at night. Laughter in the streets again. Why did all of Tallinn's partygoers have to pass under our windows? Inside my wife was under the covers, flipping through a magazine, *Stiil*. Some punk actor named Juhan Ulfsak was on the cover, dressed up in fairy wings. I gave English lessons to Juhan's wife

Reet, a short, smart-mouthed fashion designer who would complain and complain during lessons in that very dry, ironic Estonian way about how the men in her country loved to drink. "An Estonian man is not a real man if he doesn't spend five out of seven nights at the pub!" she lamented. So maybe that explained Ulfsak's angel wings. He was probably tipsy during the photo shoot. And I wanted to join him. With the weather, the ongoing Valgevase renovation, the articles and English lessons and Danish movies, I was dying for a beer. Or two. Or five.

It was simple. I needed to get drunk. All the Lars von Trier films or light therapy rooms couldn't change it. I longed to be back in Copenhagen with my old friend Eamon, strolling along the back streets. Eamon had come up to visit me from Prague, and he enjoyed himself thoroughly, the man would just relieve himself where he saw fit, right into the canals. Eamon would have pissed on the royal palace if the mood had struck him. "We are Americans in Europe!" he would exclaim in the foggy night after watering some city monument. "We can do whatever we want!"

In Tallinn, the pressure of coming winter squeezed me and squeezed me, not to mention impending fatherhood. It was all just weeks away. It would change everything, or already had. That old itch resurfaced; the itch to drink. I needed at least one night out, soon, or I was going to lose it and go running through the Christmas Fair on Town Hall Square naked at midnight screaming "fuck" at the top of my lungs.

So when Leena Saari called me later that week and told me she was in town and wanted to meet up for a drink, I gladly obliged her.

Leena Saari. The first time I heard the name, I thought it belonged to some Bollywood actress. I had imagined her to be one of those fluid singers with the broad sexy smiles, Persian green eyes, covered in jewels, the crimson bindi dot on the forehead. But Leena was a Finnish woman, a big Finnish woman from up in the forests near Turku on the West Coast. And I knew how big and Finnish Leena was. I had seen her naked.

Leena was our host mother for a weekend during the Finnish Foreign Correspondents' Programme I had attended the year prior, the same program where had met Epp. During the weekend I spent at her house, she introduced me and another correspondent, a British journalist named Natalie, to the intimacy of Finnish sauna culture. We had all sat in the hot room in Leena's house in summer, totally nude, a little drunk. I had done karaoke twice that night at a local pub where some Finnish gypsy woman in full regalia had caught Natalie talking to her husband and smashed a beer glass on the floor and threatened to slit Nat's throat. It was a very entertaining time. And I kept looking over at Leena in the sauna and the showers, just out of curiosity.

Getting naked with two foreign women on a Friday night was not exactly part of my repertoire at that point in my life. This level of intimacy was not part of my culture. I had expected Leena and Nat to sauna together, and me to sauna separately. Getting used to the mixed sauna took time, not out of shame, but because it wasn't every day you had a big, round, naked Finnish woman standing beside you asking for a whack with a bundle of dried birch branches. And when the branches hit her skin and the steam rose off her back, I noticed how Leena looked like some kind of ancient fertility idol, the folds of flesh hanging around her waist, the jungle patch of black shaggy hair between her legs. It was all there.

That was the last time I saw Leena Saari. Now I made my way through the Christmas Fair in Old Town for our second meeting. We agreed to meet at the beer hall off of Town Hall Square. I brought along a photo of Epp to show them my new wife. It was one of my favorites of her, thick curly hair pulled back, the mischevous smile on her lips, snapped on a train in London.

When I handed the photo to Leena, who was fully clothed, she peered at it through her glasses and said, approvingly, "Good work! She's very cute. Looks just like an Estonian girl."

Leena passed the photo around the table to her friends who made similar remarks. I didn't think Epp looked particularly Estonian, but, again, what did Estonians look like? A lot of them looked just like Finns. Leena's fellow drinkers that night could have been Epp's aunts. Päivi and Virpi were two middle-aged Finnish teachers with blonde hair who I imagined looked about the same as Leena did in the sauna. And Epp had no problems with me going out drinking with a bunch of middle-aged Finnish ladies. Her only concern was that I would not make it home. "Watch out, Finnish women are tough, they drink like men," she had warned me. "Actually, I think Finnish women are even tougher than the men."

Watching Leena, Päivi, and Virpi down beers and smoke cigarettes like cowboys, I decided Epp was right. Within half an hour, I already had two and a half beers in me and I was feeling good, refreshed, a little slow. I was now playing cards with some old Finnish dames at a beer hall and learning how to speak Finnish. The numbers were easy. One, *üks* in Estonian, translated to *üksi* in Finnish, two, or *kaks*, was *kaksi*. I sat around, liquored up, blurting out *üksi*! or *kaksi*! depending on what cards were in my hand.

"Hey, your Finnish is getting good," Leena said to me from across the table.

"I've been taking Estonian lessons," I announced, waiting to be patted on the back, anticipating the "some people have been living here 50 years" line that always made me feel so superior.

"Heh, of course you are!" she snorted. "You have to learn it. If you didn't, I'd have no respect for you."

"Do you understand it at all?"

"Jo," she affirmed. "I have been coming to Tallinn for a long time, since back in the bad old days, way back in the seventies. I used to take the ferry over. And this country has changed a lot. A lot! I used to stay at the Viru Hotel, which was completely bugged by KGB," she rolled her eyes, as if to say, those idiots. "I have friends here, too. Other English teachers. They all used to have to wait in line for simple things. Can you imagine? Wait in line for meat, bananas? But my good friend Toomas had a friend at the shop. He would just go around back early in the morning and trade for something. That Toomas! He always had plenty of bananas and he was so proud of it!" Leena's laugh was broad and deep, like a hammer pounding on rubber.

"Things have changed," I nodded. "There are plenty of bananas now. And everything is under construction here. Last year there was a hole behind our apartment building. Now there's a new building!"

"Yeah, sure, there's a lot of new money here, but there is also a huge gap between the rich and the poor. I feel it every time I get off the ferry. There's always some old lady holding a cup in her hand. For the rich, Estonia has changed a lot. But for poor people, even for teachers like my friend Toomas, things aren't so great, you know. There are a lot of havenots in Estonia, and I worry about them. You know I am still a social democrat at heart."

When she said it, the toughness drained from her face, and I could see her as I remembered, as the empathetic, community-minded single mother of a young son, living in the woods.

"I don't think the social democrats are going to get in power in Estonia any time soon, Leena. Everyone here loves Milton Friedman."

"That won't last!" she threw her hands in the air. "Too many people in Estonia are too poor. Give it a few years." The smoke curled around her face. "The havenots will get organized, and rise up, and take what is theirs," she banged her hands on the table. "It happened in Finland. It will happen here too."

Päivi and Virpi just looked at their friend with bemused smiles and smoked on. It seemed that Leena got into a revolutionary mood when she drank.

But was she right? Would it happen? Would all the poor of Tallinn, dwelling out there in the detritus, the crumbling apartments beyond the city's fairytale Old Town, eventually look in their hearts and see social democracy? Would they organize and rise up and take "what was theirs" from the greedy

Friedmanites? Theoretically it was possible, but I thought it would take a very long time, if it even happened at all. There were too many barriers to that kind of social movement: Estonians versus Russians, urbanites versus farmers, old versus young. The poorer classes were too divided to do anything about their living conditions. All any smart rightwing politician needed to do was invoke these divisions and a reconstituted left would collapse into infighting over who did what in the Second World War. Leena's "havenots" would in the meantime have to continue to stand in line at the supermarket, grateful for the new money being pumped into their liberal economy, content that they now only had to wait a few minutes to get their hands on some bananas.

The night rolled on, more beer, more cards. God, it felt great to be drunk, and the more I drank, the better Leena, Virpi, and Päivi looked. The Finnish ladies didn't pay much attention to me, though. It was like that old joke about Finns and Estonians. "Two guys meet in a sauna after not having seen one another for years. One guy says after an hour, 'How are things?' The other answers 'Did we come here to babble or did we come here to drink?'" The Finns were just there to drink. Eager to spark discussion, I tossed out some bait to break the silence.

"What do you ladies think about Swedes?"

Leena looked up slowly from her beer, as if I had tapped on her shoulder and asked her outside to fight. "You really want to know what us Finns think about the Swedes?"

"Yeah."

"Really? Are you sure?"

"Yes."

"Fine," she grunted, pulling her mobile phone from her pocket. "Here's a joke that's been going around in Finland." She showed me the phone's screen, the long lines of 'ä's and 'ö's. Finnish gibberish. "It says, 'Newsflash. Swedish authorities have just discovered that the weapon used to kill Anna Lindh is different from the one that killed Olaf Palme.'"

"Jo*, jo," Päivi and Virpi chuckled and sipped at their beers. They had received the gag text message too. It had been three months since Lindh's murder.

"But Olaf Palme was shot," I said. "Lindh was stabbed."

"I know," Leena said and slid the phone back in her pocket. "So, yeah, that's what we Finns think of Swedes."

"You know what my wife wants to call our kid if it's a boy?"

It was later now, we had moved to another bar, one down in a dimly lit cellar. The high from all those beers had worn off, my black nights anxiety with it, and now my brain was settling into a post-drunken state of enlightenment.

"What does Epp want him to be called?" Leena said, beer in hand. Even after six drinks, she still seemed entirely sober.

"Uno."

---

* Yes. (In Finnish)

"UUNO!" Leena cackled, drawing out the 'u' in the name. "Uuno's a fucking great name! Uuno Petrone. It sounds fantastic, why, it could even be Finnish. Like Uuno Turhapuro!* Right, girls?"

"Jo, jo," Päivi and Virpi agreed, nodding their heads, "jo, jo."

"Uuno!" Leena said it again. "Maybe I should have called my boy Uuno instead of Antti. Oh well, too late now."

"But we are talking about moving to New York," I said. "How's a guy with a name like 'Uno' or 'Uuno' going to get by in New York?"

"Well, Justin, how exactly is a girl with a name like 'Epp' going to get by in New York, huh?" Leena asked. "You think that it will be any easier for her over there than it has been for you in Estonia?"

Leena stared me down, a bull of a woman. Maybe one day she would go into politics, taking from the haves and delivering to the havenots, her social democratic heart beating red. But for now she was just a teacher on vacation in Tallinn having a beer.

"I am worried about her. But we can't really survive here in Tallinn. I mean, I make almost no money."

Leena's gaze softened. Again she was someone's mother. "You know, you've changed a lot since we first met. It was only a year and a half ago that we went out to the karaoke bar and you sang 'Somebody to Love.' I remember, you got up and dedicated the song to that old Finnish guitar player, what was his name?"

---

* A Finnish comedy character created by Spede Pasanen that gained popularity through a TV show and a number of films in the 1970s. In the English versions of these films, Turhapuro is called "Numbskull Abortivebrook."

"Jorma Kaukonen."

"Think about it! You were like a kid then and now here's a man sitting beside me. So, I'm going to give it to you straight. Even if you give your kid an American name and move to America, you will still be stuck in Europe."

"But..."

"Listen to me, I'm forty years old now and I know what I am talking about," she wagged a finger in my face. "I have seen it all before. You can go and live in New York, live like New Yorkers, pretend you really aren't outsiders, but it won't matter because you will always have one part of you in Europe, one part of you in America. This woman, this baby. One leg here, one leg there. That's how it is. That's your fate, Justin. It's been decided. No matter what you do, you will always be straddling the ocean."

For the first time all night, I felt like drinking my beer in silence, save a "jo" here and "jo, jo" there. An image rose to the top of my mind while I drank, though, me atop the globe, one leg on one side, one on the other, the deep Atlantic waters rushing below.

But how could one person like me straddle the ocean? Even in my imagination, my legs didn't seem that long. I could feel the strain in my thighs, the slide of my rubber soles against the rocky coasts of the different continents. I was slipping, trying to regain my perch. One strong wind though and it could all give way. If I wasn't careful, I could just fall into the Atlantic and disappear. And if I did, would that also be fate?

NO KEY

My back was against the door, my rear edged against the step, arms stretched out by my side, legs straight on the ground, toes pointing towards the street.

I kept moving my toes. You had to move them to keep the blood circulating. The wind picked up, and with it more snow. I turned my head away, but it was no use. The white powder just came at you, found its way into your eyes, up your nose, up your sleeves. It made you taste it, taste the salty mixture of ice water and snot.

I pulled my head up and banged it against the door. "Boof!" My head throbbed a bit and I let it rest there against the wood and breathed a little bit more, slow breaths, trying not to inhale any snow. I watched the puffs of moisture escape my mouth and rise toward the stars.

Winter had come in at daybreak like a shark, swimming over the city, snow falling in thick clumps until it was hard to open doors and the small details of the streets vanished under foot, smothered by the frost, frisky electricity discharged to all pedestrians. Tread lightly, tread carefully. When I had walked Eva and Simona to the train station earlier, Simski on my shoulders, I had to turn my back to the strong gusts of wind because I sensed the wind could knock me off balance, tossing us both to the ground. It was just so much stronger than me.

Epp's family was now gone, Eva and Simona on the train, Aap who knows where, the moving of our things into Valgevase was complete. The house itself wasn't completely finished though. While most new apartment owners had moved in, it still didn't have a working door bell. I thought about the woman who lived on the first floor, the one with the pleasant round face and the pretty eyes and the curly hair and the violin. I could hear her practicing every time I carried a moving box past her door.

"Boof!" I let my head fall again. I had tried knocking but it was late, maybe already the next day, and there were no lights in any of the windows. Epp was up there on the third floor, probably asleep, my key to the house resting atop some unopened box, a key I had stupidly forgotten to take. I had left the house's back door unlocked when I left, too, but some responsible tenant must have relocked it. To get in, I had tried throwing a few snowballs at our attic-level window and shouting, but there had been no response. I had a cellphone, but Epp didn't, and our landline wasn't installed yet, so I couldn't call her.

What would happen if I fell asleep out here in the streets, I wondered, drunk, in the middle of a blizzard? Would I freeze to death, rosy cheeked, like Hans Christian Andersen's "*The Little Match Girl*"? In that story, the little girl had lit all her matches, and her grandmother came to take her away to a better, warmer place. Would great grandfather Salvatore now descend to escort me to the big speakeasy in the sky? Probably not. Real men didn't get cold. And besides, I didn't have any matches.

Maybe I should just go back to the Old Town, I thought. Some of the pubs were probably still open. Maybe Steve was over there, with Tim and Ivan. Could I do it? Get up on two legs, head through the winds back to the Old Town? No. In this weather, every step cost you, and I was completely sapped of energy. All I could do was bang my head against the door and hope someone inside would hear me.

It was the winter solstice, the first big blizzard of the season. It had been the shortest day of the year. Why did it feel like one of its longest?

The days before were busy, busy, busy. The big move into Valgevase, sorting and packing, packing and sorting: an Estonian's paradise. The moving van was ordered, Eva and Simona and Aap were coming to help. I had even taken some bags all the way across town to the new apartment on foot to save us the taxi fare. In the middle of this circus we got rid of the cat.

We escorted Miisu to Sürgavere, the small village in south Estonia where Epp's grandparents lived. It was two days before we were supposed to move and Epp's grandfather Karl had met us at the frosty railroad stop in the woods, a little old man, cheerful as always, unfazed by the weather. The thing about Karl was that he was always so jolly. The Soviets had deported his father and forbade him from studying geography, but the retired veterinarian never said an unkind word about anybody in my presence. Even when his wife nagged him, Karl would just laugh it off. "Jah, jah. Jah, jah."

We had skidded along the icy back country roads to their home in the neighbor's old Lada. "It's colder down here," I had told Karl in the car, wrapping my arms around myself, shivering. "Jah, jah," Karl had answered with a droll smile. "You know, there's no such thing as bad weather in Estonia, Justin, only the wrong clothes!" And then he had chuckled and Epp had chuckled too. They had mocked me together, those Estonians.

After we arrived, we set the cat's carrying crate down in the corner of the main room next to the wood-heated furnace so that Miisu could get used to her new surroundings. She hid at first, but eventually came out, lured by a bowl of food, and the moment she stepped outside the crate, Välk, the big fat male cat in the house, came right over and pushed his pushy pink nose into the backside of the new pussy. *Ah, a female. How delightful!* Välk purred. The male cat was an absolute gangster. He had a flat scarred face, and was gray all over with a white fringe. "You know what 'Välk' means don't you?" Epp had whispered in my ear, enjoying the primitive sight. "It means 'lightning.'"

So Miisu's new boyfriend was named 'Lightning.' Terrific. We had decided to give our cat over to Epp's grandparents with the agreement that she would be neutered, so that none of her offspring would have to be euthanized the old-fashioned way. Grandma Laine had protested at first. "It's not right to do that to a cat. Let her enjoy herself, let her have fun and lead a natural life!" But we insisted. Miisu would have to be fixed.

317

And judging by the quick liking Välk had taken to her, our little kitten needed to be fixed as soon as possible!

The day after we left Miisu in Sürgavere, Epp and I bundled ourselves up and went across the street to the Tallinn Central Hospital, just as I had once imagined, dark shapes set against a white ground on a cold morning, heads to the wind like adventurers at the top of the world. In the 19th century, some of the Russian empire's most talented Arctic explorers had come from Estonia, people for whom cold seas and islands and Tallinn city streets were now named: Eduard Toll, Otto von Kotzebue, Friedrich von Bellingshausen, Ferdinand von Wrangel. Of the four Baltic German adventurers, Toll was the least lucky. He had vanished in the Arctic Sea in 1902. I had once seen a grainy photo of Toll, fur clad, shaggy beard, fire in the eyes; a man of the north. I imagined he had disappeared in such weather.

Back up the hospital stairs we went for another ultrasound, past the melted ice in the entrance, pausing to don the mandatory blue plastic slippers. Half an hour later I put in a quick call to my parents to tell them the gender of our baby. It was still early in the morning in New York and they didn't pick up, so I left a message on their answering machine.

In it, I said three words: "It's a girl!"

Naturally, I was happy. No reason to argue over names or hit up the Tallinn Synagogue for a *mohel* to perform a cosmetic circumcision. Still, I felt that I had lost something. For months, I had lived with two images in my mind, a son and a daughter. They were like twins, twin futures, but one of them had never existed. There had never been an Uno or a Markko. All this time, we had been waiting for a daughter.

"Boof! Boof!" I rocked my head against the door two times. The back of it ached. The alcohol was wearing off, but nobody came to help. The wind was still tossing snow all over. Maybe someone else would come home late, like one of the girls who shared the apartment across from ours. Or maybe that violin player would finally hear me. How could I be so stupid to forget the key? I lifted my right arm up slowly and brought my wrist to my mouth. Snow had found its way in between the cuff of my jacket and the glove. I blew into the crevice to melt the ice. The hair on my wrist was wet, the skin numb. "There's no such thing as bad weather, Justin," Karl's jolly words rang in my ears. How long had I been out here? 15 minutes? Half an hour?

When I set my arm down I felt the paper that Benny had signed crumple beneath my jacket. At least I still had it because, given the night's activities, I could have left it anywhere. But it was right here, safely tucked into the jacket's inner pocket, and we needed that document if we were going to get any money out of the parish.

Ah, yes. The money from the parish. It was hard to explain, even to Benny, but when I had called him up earlier in the week, he listened. Every Estonian was tied to a place, registered to a certain municipality. For years before she met me, Epp had lived in Viimsi, a parish on the outskirts of Tallinn. When she moved to Kentmanni Street, she didn't change the place where she was registered, and why should she have? She might have moved again.

Viimsi probably didn't mind the discrepancy. It was keen to keep her as an official resident because it meant that all

319

of her tax money went there, instead of whatever district (or country) in which she happened to be working at the time. And as a Viimsi resident, she was entitled to a certain amount of local financial support when she gave birth, money we were counting on to pay-off my parents' loan, in addition to the state mother's salary. But the law had been recently changed. Both parents now had to be registered in the parish to receive the money. And since I wasn't registered in Viimsi, they wouldn't be paying Epp any financial support!

"Oh, this is some real Estonian bullshit," Epp had said to me when she heard about the law. There was frustration in her voice, tension. "You know why they are doing it, don't you? They want all these young families where both of the parents are professionals to register out there, even if they don't live there. That way they can get even more tax money."

Viimsi still wanted Epp's tax money, but we would both have to be registered there for her to get any of it back. And we needed that money. We were broke, living on discount Lithuanian sausages and Latvian cheeses and Estonian vanilla puddings from Säästumarket, the budget shopper's last hope. I had eagerly taken on some copy editing work with an advertising company right before Christmas with the hope that the pay in the end would supply us with enough cash to get a baby carriage for our daughter. The only way for us to collect the municipal support was to have me registered into the parish too. But who could register me into this particular parish? Who did I know that lived in Viimsi and would be willing to sign a paper that said that I did too?

Then I remembered who. Benny.

$\bullet \quad \bullet \quad \bullet$

I was supposed to meet the affable Swedish businessman at Järve Keskus. I figured I would walk down to Pärnu Road, catch one of the trams and ride it all the way out past Lake Ülemiste. There we would meet at the cafe that served the instant coffee, share a few jokes, and he would sign the paper that said I lived in his garage. Maybe he'd give me a ride back into town, too. Then Epp and I would just have to file the rest of the paperwork before the end of the year, and we could collect the municipal payout for the little baby we produced for Estonia. I felt a little guilty because it seemed more and more likely that we would be leaving the country, but not guilty enough to let those 5000 kroons just slip away.

Everything would have gone according to plan if the blizzard hadn't hit Tallinn that morning. It took me half an hour more than I expected just to make it to Pärnu Road because I was held up pushing through the snow on the sidewalks. By then it was already dark, and the dark is what made the sight before me so hilarious when I saw it.

The city trams were lined up from the Old Town all the way through the intersection of Liivalaia and Pärnu Road, past the office of *The Baltic Times* and out towards Järve Keskus. It was like staring at a herd of dead elephants. Some of the abandoned trams were red, a few blue, a few green, and the lights were on in all of them, though there was, save for one or two stubborn travelers, nobody on board. It was a ghost train, stretching from the center of the city to the horizon.

321

Something happened to me when I saw the abandoned trams. There was rush of blood to my gums, I felt the sweat on my body. It was as if I was back in Mexico for a moment, hot tequila pulsing in my veins because, for once, in Estonia the trams didn't run on time. For once, everyone's plans had been dashed. For once, no one could get where they were expected to be. Appointments had to be cancelled, meetings postponed. For once, nothing was in order. Everyone was late. Late!

This is what GOD thinks of you and your watches and your schedules and all your calm punctual workaholic Germanic Nordic Baltic Finno-Ugric bullshit! I wanted to scream at the trams. This is what GOD thinks of your pushy cashiers and your obnoxious security guards! Your tickets aren't punched? Well, punch these tickets, you blonde, meat-jelly loving, tibla-hating, cross-country skiing automatons!

Chaos. I loved it, but was distracted by the scene. I took one step forward and that was enough to lose my balance. My boot scraped against the ice below and a moment later I was on my back in the snow in pain. My elbows had broken my fall. I moved my limbs slowly. Nothing broken, just throbbing. I rolled on my side and looked down again at the ghost train of trams. Then my phone rang. It was Benny.

"Justin, where are you? We were supposed to meet at 4.30 at the instant coffee place in Järve Keskus, remember?"

"Oh shit. Shit, shit, shit!"

"Shit. Calm down! What's the matter?" Benny laughed. "Where are you anyway? Are you outside? The connection is terrible."

"I can't get to Järve Keskus, Benny," I said and finally got off the ground, dusting the snow off my body. "None of the trams are running. But you should see them. They are all stuck here in the city center, nobody on board. It's just chaos, Benny. Chaos!"

"Can't you come out with your car?"

"I don't have a car."

"Oh, that's right."

"I could try to get a taxi, but I don't see any around."

"Forget about it. Tell you what. We have to pass through the city center on our way home. Let's meet at the Olümpia Hotel in about half an hour. There is a bar called Scotland Yard. We'll have a drink and get you all taken care of."

It took a good twenty minutes of pushing through the snow just to make it from Pärnu Road to the Olümpia Hotel. When I finally walked into the bar I felt like some kind of Himalayan beast. I dripped water. My face was ruddy and moist, my hair stuck out everywhere, the whiskers on my face were stiff from the frigid winds, and my elbows still ached. And there was Benny sitting at the bar already, warm and dry with a tie on, smoking a cigarette.

"*Jösses**! What happened to you?" he said, raising both of his gray eyebrows.

"In case you haven't noticed, there's a blizzard outside."

"What? This?" he gestured out the window. "This is nothing. I'm Swedish, remember? This is like a flurry for us," he grinned.

"Shut up."

---

* Jesus. (In Swedish)

"You know, it only took us ten minutes to get here. Ten minutes! The road was clear. All the cars and buses were broken down." He laughed softly to himself. "These Estonians can't handle it. They're amateurs!"

There was a woman standing by Benny's side, and a girl of about 12 beside her and if there was one word to describe both of them, it was Viking. The woman had thick blond hair, so light it was almost white. It hung down to her shoulders. Her face was round, but I recognized it as the face of an Estonian, the eyes, the lips, that impartial stare, as if to say, 'Nothing surprises me so don't even bother trying.' The daughter was like a miniature version, hair pulled back in a ponytail.

"Justin, this is Mari, my girlfriend," Benny introduced me to the woman. "And this is her daughter Kristi," he gestured to the girl beside her. "Hey Kristi, remember that guy who called the house last week who you said was speaking really bad Estonian? This is him."

"Tere," I said, a little embarassed, and looked down at the girl.

She nodded back but didn't say a word.

"So," Benny flicked the ash from his cigarette into a tray. "I understand you have some paperwork for me."

"I do." I reached inside my jacket pocket and pulled out the papers, slightly dampened by sweat. "You know, you don't have to do it if you don't feel comfortable," I said, handing him the documents. "It's your decision."

"Be quiet, of course I am going to help you," Benny said and put on a pair of reading glasses. "Shit, plenty of people helped me along the way. It's the least I could do." He read over the text on the page, and then signed his name on the line that said I lived in his house. "There you are, registered to my house now," he handed it back to me. "Welcome to the family!"

"Thank you so much!" I felt like hugging him, but knew I couldn't. The trams may have been out of order, but I was still in Estonia and Benny was still a Swede.

Benny smiled. "Now that that's done, care to share a drink with us? It's on me."

The Scotland Yard bartender poured me a tall glass of amber-colored beer and I swallowed half of it in one gulp.

"You drink like an Estonian," Mari said with that expression-less look on her face. There was humor behind that stare though. Estonian humor.

"This weather is getting to me," I yawned and rubbed my weather-worn face. "It makes me thirsty. Very, very thirsty."

Mari watched my lips and her pale blue eyes a grew little wider. "Now you can understand why so many people in our country drink so much," she nodded. "And the winter is the hardest season."

"And to think it's only just begun!" Benny sipped his beer. "Not everyone can withstand a Nordic winter, and this is your second winter here, right?"

I nodded.

"Well, congratulations! You are now an honorary Swede. Or Estonian. Shit, whatever. You know what I mean."

"Man, I'm not sure if I can do another year of this, Benny," I said and rubbed my face again. "Maybe Epp and I should move south, you know. She dreams of going to India, I would like to go to Brazil, and I have a potential job offer in Chile."

"Shit," Benny laughed. "Maybe I'll come with you!" He thought I was kidding. But was I? I still had the contacts of that language school in Santiago, the one I had corresponded with in the spring before we learned the baby was coming. And on a day like this one, the darkest day of the year, the thought of moving there, as soon as possible, was very, very tempting.

We sat there drinking and talking for awhile, a few fleshy figures illuminated inside Scotland Yard's black windows, enjoying warmth that could only be appreciated from outside. Benny, Mari, and Kristi then put on their coats to go home and I made my way over to a bar called Woodstock.

🜄 🜄 🜄

Back against the door, the wind howling all around. The Kalamaja District was about to swallow me. The street was like a Christmas card. The yellow light from the lamps. The red and green houses. It looked so innocent, and yet behind those winds was murder. In the distance I could see the cats by the dumpster, furry and comfortable in the snow. How could it be that they had no clothes and could manage and I had on thick gloves and a hat and scarf and was still freezing? And how come I had forgotten my bloody key!

From under one of the street lamps a shape emerged. Another human being, a man, and he was coming my way! Maybe he was also a new resident, I thought. Maybe he had a key. As he got closer, though, I could see it was just an old drunk, bent over a bit, white scruffy beard, face like rotten meat. The kind of man you would see digging near the rubbish bins for empty bottles by the local *taarapunkt*. I had been in the small bottle depository once already. It was foul and humid and stunk of alcohol and body odor, the word "malaria" slipped in and out of my mind. The old drunk passed me, pausing just for a moment to see if there was an empty bottle in one of my hands. He frowned a bit when he saw that there wasn't and went on his way.

Even a few hours after I walked into Woodstock to meet Steve, it was hard to remember exactly in what order events had taken place. Steve was playing pool, I remembered that. The veteran expat was just about to break when he looked up from his pool cue and said:

"Jesus, Justin, what the hell happened to you?"

"In case you didn't notice, Steve, there's a blizzard outside."

"I know, but you look like the abominable snowman."

He reviewed his shot again and made it. The crack of the pool balls. Jerry Garcia's guitar runs played like confetti in the air: "One More Saturday Night."

There he was, San Francisco Steve, the man with the witty oneliners. Steve had recently cut off his long black ponytail to try to look like a professional journalist, but he wasn't fooling anyone, because almost everyone in Tallinn knew Steve to be but one thing: a party animal.

There were others in Woodstock with him that night. Some guy I had never seen before was standing beside Steve, holding a pool cue, and Ivan was there too.

"Justin, this is Tim, from *The Baltic Times*' Riga office," Steve introduced me to the man I had never seen before.

I shook the Tim's hand and looked into his face. He was shorter than me, maybe a few years older, freckles, curly red hair, button-up white shirt, your average Britisher. With a face like that he could be a fisherman or a vicar or a grocer. Not a politician though. Tim looked too decent.

"So you're Justins, eh?" he said. Tim had been living in Latvia so long, he just put a letter 's' at the end of any male's name, no matter what country he actually happened to be in.

"Nice to meet you, Tims," I responded.

"I've come up to Tallinn to spend the weekend before I head home to London for Christmas," Tim said. His voice was soft and slow, like a BBC news anchor's. "What about you? Heading home for the holidays?"

"Home?" I answered. "You mean New York?"

"Yeah."

"Not this year," I said, feeling a little guilty.

"Care to play?" Tim held out the pool cue.

"Nah," I declined. "I'm not so good at pool."

"Well, it is a tricky game. Kind of philosophical, I think," Tim said.

"Pool is philosophical?"

"Well, it does take a bit of luck. Like, you can try to hit a shot ten times and still not get the ball where you want it to be. But you can also hit it blindfolded in one shot and sink it. Some might call that an accident. Others might call it fate."

Ivan stood there with a pool cue listening, waiting his turn. Even with a beer in his hand, he looked sharp, serious.

This was a man who spoke fluent Russian, fluent English, and fluent Estonian. If he had been a native Estonian speaker with the connections that came with it – the family ties, the membership in University of Tartu student corporations – he might be a high-ranking editor for one of the country's dailies. Instead he wrote news for *The Baltic Times*. It was a dull job, and maybe that's why on all those day's in the office, Ivan had seemed so bored. That night in Woodstock, though, Ivan was in a better mood. When he heard Tim talking about pool, he raised his glass.

"This toast is to fate!" Ivan held his beer aloft and smirked, poking fun at Tim's philosophizing.

"To fate?" I was a little confused.

"Well, why not, we've already toasted art and love tonight," Tim chuckled and asked then in mock seriousness: "But does fate really exist, Ivans? Or would we just like it to exist because it makes life more convenient?"

"Listen, Tims, did we come here to talk philosophical bullshit or did we come here to drink and play pool?" Steve knocked a ball into a corner pocket. "It's your turn, by the way."

"To fate," Ivan said again and downed his beer. I raised my glass and did the same. I had known Ivan for almost a year, sat next to him everyday, and yet I still couldn't find it within myself to reach out and tell him that I was going to be a father. I had told Benny, but Benny was a foreigner. Ivan was a homegrown citizen of Estonia and that meant there was a gulf between us, a big cloud of mist, protecting one's emotions from reaching anybody else. I wasn't sure if such clouds just manifested themselves in this land or if the cloud had sprung from Ivan's particularly dry, journalistic soul, but it was there, I could sense it, and it kept me from communicating openly to him. Ivan never talked about himself and I never talked about myself. That's just how it was. But tonight could be different. Tonight the trams weren't running on time. Tonight, Estonia was in chaos. Tonight, I had San Francisco Steve and Tim the British philosopher and alcohol on my side.

Still, it took two more beers to get it out of me. We were trudging through the streets to another club when I finally summoned the courage to reveal my deepest secret to these men. "Guys, I have something to tell you. I am going to be a father!"

And to my amazement, Ivan was the first one to step up and press his hand into mine. "Mazel tov!" he cheered and looked up into my eyes. "When is the baby due? July? August?"

"In two weeks."

"Two weeks? Why the hell didn't you tell us sooner?" he stammered. "You mean you've known for months and you didn't tell any of us? I know Heli in the office is going to be upset. She loves babies. She's got her own little boy, you know."

"She does? But then, how come she never said so?"

"You didn't ask."

"But nobody talks in the office."

"You don't talk in the office," Ivan shrugged.

It was true. I usually just hid in the corner behind my computer screen, avoiding eye contact with all the others. I hadn't reached out to anybody, so why should I have expected them to reach out to me? Maybe I had been the one with the cloud around me, the cold one, the most alienated, detached, atomized Estonian in the land. Unable to reach beyond myself, I had projected my alienation onto others. Maybe Estonia hadn't made me feel this way? Maybe I just felt this way.

But maybe I could put it behind me. Because on that day, the coldest, shortest, blackest day of the year, I felt suddenly very alive, vibrating with emotion. I was still a bit shaky from telling them about the pregnancy, partially because I was preparing myself for the American response, the whispered voices, the cool congratulations belying a barely repressed thought that I was fuckup because I was too young and because I didn't have enough money. I braced myself for a "you should get a vasectomy" comment from my colleagues, but one never came.

"My sincerest congratulations, Justins," said Tim. "I know a guy in Riga who was just a terrible person before he became a father. He drank, slept around. He was like a walking STD. Now he's got a little girl, he's settled down, happy, a big ball of fluff."

"What are you trying to tell me, Tims?" I squinted at the Brit through the falling snow. "Do I look like a walking STD?"

"Oh, please, lighten up, mate," he tapped my chest with his glove. "I'm trying to say that if that jerk can do it, so can you. Christ, I need to buy you another beer."

🔥 🔥 🔥

Tim took an acute interest in my pending fatherhood that night. It seized up in his deeply philosophical British mind, like a stallion in a Jane Austen novel. He started by asking me the usual questions about the duedate and baby gender. Slowly, he worked his way towards the more sensitive topics. "So how are your parents dealing with the fact that you're having a baby over here?" he asked after several more beers.

"They are ok, I guess," I said. "My mom's really excited. She said she already bought a DVD for the baby. *Finding Nemo.*"

"*Finding Nemo*?" Tim coughed. "Are you serious?" he wiped the foam from his mouth. "Look, don't take this the wrong way, mate, but I don't think your baby girl is going to 'get' *Finding Nemo*. That's a really complex movie. Very deep. Very philosophical. Not for newborns."

"Only you would think *Finding Nemo* was philosophical, Tim," Steve said.

"But you didn't answer my question, Justins," Tim said, ignoring Steve. "How do they feel about you being here?"

"They see it as temporary," I said. "I think they see it as some kind of bizarre twist of events. Something that could have been avoided somehow if life had played out a different way."

"Well, fate is fate," Tim mused. "But what if this is what you want? They have got to at least accept that. You know, my mum's the only one who understands why I am in Riga. All my friends in London are always asking me, 'When are you coming home?' 'What are you doing wasting your life over there?' They just think it's inevitable that I stay put in London. In their minds, London is the center of all things. But my mum understands me. She knows what I am doing over here."

"I wish somebody understood me," I sighed.

"Don't even worry about that, mate," Tim said.

"I have guilty dreams, too," I admitted. "Dreams where I've done something really bad except I don't even know what it is."

"Are you kidding me? You are going to be a father soon! That's fantastic! When the baby comes you'll be so tired, you won't even have guilty dreams."

"Well, we are thinking of leaving Estonia."

"What?" Tim perked up. "But, but you're one of the best freelancers we've worked with in years. You can't go!"

"Yeah, Justin," Ivan looked up from his beer. "Why do you want to leave us? You were just starting to get the hang of things."

"But I can't support a family here," I shook my head.

"So where are you going to go?" Tim asked.

"Well, we've played with the idea of getting jobs as English teachers. I've been in touch with a school in Chile for a while. They could hire me from next September."

"Chile?" Tim said. "That's really far away."

"But at least it's warmer! This weather is killing me. And it's not like that many people will miss me. I don't think I even have one Estonian friend!"

"Hey man, I've been living here for six years and I have only got one or two and we're not even that close," Steve said. "It takes a long time to become an Estonian's friend. They're not exactly the easiest people to get to know."

"Well, I think we're pretty set on leaving. Epp says she wants to go to India but I don't know what kind of job I could get there. But Chile could work out."

"What about your folks in New York?" Tim raised an eyebrow.

"I haven't told them our plans yet. We are considering going to New York too. It's not exactly a boring place and that's where I'm from."

"I don't even think about going back home anymore," Steve said. "I mean, can you imagine, having to interview other Americans? In English? I've never done that in my life!"

"But we need more money," I said. "How am I going to support a wife and kid here in Tallinn? Doing copy editing work? Writing articles about branding campaigns until I'm old and gray?"

"I'm a little disappointed in you, Justins," Tim clicked his tongue and looked away. "Money isn't everything. There are people on earth who have plenty of it and they're miserable."

"So what?"

"So, what you have to do is ask yourself what you really want in life. Not what your parents want or what job will give you the most money. The question is what do you really want? Once you have that all figured out, and I am still trying to figure it out myself, all you have to do is go out and get it."

"Dude, did you read that in some bullshit self empowerment book or something? I don't even have enough money to buy a stroller for my kid!"

"I'm just trying to help you out, dude."

"Well, Tims, you might be the friendliest English person I have ever met." I snorted. "Actually, man, it's nice you even care."

"Maybe you two should get a room," Steve elbowed Tim towards me.

"That reminds me of a toast, Steves," Tim elbowed Steve back. "I believe it was Kierkegaard who said–"

"Oh please, shut up about Kierkegaard," Steve rolled his eyes.

Just then, my phone rang. It was my father-in-law, Andres.

"Tere," I answered.

"Tere," he said through the staticky connection. I could imagine him down there in Karksi on the Latvian border, at the end of that dirt road that led to his house in the woods, snowed in.

"Can I speak to Aap?" Andres asked.

"I think he's back at the apartment, with Epp," I told him in Estonian.

"You mean you are not in the apartment?"

"No," I covered the mouth of the phone but it was too late. Between my slurred speech and the loud eighties pop music in the background it was pretty obvious that I was in a bar.

"But do you know where he could have gone?" Andres grumbled. "He said something about trying to come home and I don't want him to travel in this weather. The roads are too dangerous. I tried to call him, but his phone is turned off."

"I am sorry, but I just don't know where he is," I told him.

"So," he grunted. "You don't know." Then he hung up.

"Who was that?" Tim asked with concern in his eyes.

"My father-in-law."

"How do you two get along?" Tim asked.

"I don't know," I said. "That was the longest conversation we've ever had," I sighed. "Shit," I rubbed my beer weary face. "What time is it anyway?"

"It's 1 am." Steve replied.

"Are you serious? I told my wife I would be back before midnight. I have to go."

"I think it's time we got out of this place, too," Steve yawned.

"Well, what else is open?" Tim asked.

"Let's go back to Hell Hunt," Steve suggested. "It's close to my apartment. We'll hit Hell Hunt and then we can crash."

I left them at the door and took off toward home, back into the deserted streets, the vast emptiness, not a soul in sight.

I raised my head up once more and let it fall against the door. "Boof!" I heard it echo in the building's foyer. Someone had to come. How could they not hear me? I let my head stay there against the wood again and breathed out and watched the snow coming down in sheets. Valgevase. It was such a pretty street. I could stare at it all night, let the cold into my veins, into my heart.

But suddenly the door behind me gave way. It opened and I looked up and saw her.

It was the violin player!

"*Issand jumal**!" she looked down at me, her big pleasant cheeks flush. "I kept hearing this noise so I got up, but I had no idea there was somebody out here."

"I forgot my key," I managed to say, rolling off the ground, dusting off the snow. "Thank you so much."

"Um, it's fine," the violin player looked a little distressed. We had met in the corridor before but she probably did not recognize me and thought I was some drunk trying to pull a fast one on her. But she had to let me in now. The door was open.

---

* Oh my God. (In Estonian)

When I made it to the third floor, I paused to undo the frozen laces of my boots. Then I knocked gently at our apartment door. A minute later it opened.

Epp was there in her nightgown, hair pulled pack, squinting into the light. "Hey," she smiled to me. "I'm sorry. I just realized your key was here on the box."

I stared at her and said nothing.

"Why are you just standing there like that?" Epp raised an eyebrow and moved closer to me. When she did her vision must have come into focus because when she saw my man-from-the-North-Pole ruddy face, the frost on my hair, her expression changed. There was horror in her eyes.

"*Issand,*" she whispered and put her warm hand on my snow-covered arm. "What the hell happened to you?"

LITTLE
ALIENS

President Arnold Rüütel declared the Christmas Peace at noon on Christmas Eve.

It's a 350-year-old tradition in Estonia, one that began in the seventeenth century by the order of Queen Christina of Sweden. And, Soviet legacy aside, Rüütel was the right man for the job. With his perfectly groomed white hair combed back and a grandfatherly twinkle in his eye, he called on his citizens to celebrate the holiday peacefully, quietly. We obliged him. There were plenty of unpacked boxes in our new Kalamaja apartment, but they would stay closed for the rest of the day. Instead we lounged around making gingerbreads and heating *glögi* on the stove, brewing up the sweet drink with raisins and nuts, drinking it straight from the ladle.

Estonian Christmas cards celebrated such scenes with words like *Häid Jõule* ("Merry Christmas") or *Häid Pühi* ("Happy Holidays"). But the real word of the season was *mõnus*. In English, it translated as snug, cozy, comfortable, enjoyable, sweet, but no foreign word could really do *mõnus* justice. The closest concept to which I could compare it was a word I had learned in Denmark, *hygge*, a term that brought to mind the same things, gingerbread, mulled wine, a roaring fire and sympathetic company. But even *hygge* wasn't exactly *mõnus*. *Mõnus* was just something that could only be experienced. And even though we were surrounded by unopened boxes, living out of a tiny refrigerator in a tiny apartment with a fold-out bed, our Christmas Eve, the last one we would celebrate as a couple, was especially *mõnus*.

On Christmas Day we walked around our new home in Kalamaja, peeking through gates at rambling old homes set back from the road in the snow, the smoke curling up from the chimneys. A few more houses were under renovation, a sign of the money slowly making its way to the district. The gangs of wild cats were out, too, begging for a scrap of anything that wasn't frozen. Some people left them open cans of sprats and sardines, which they licked clean and then returned to their hiding places to last the winter. Kalamaja. Something felt right about the place, run down as it was. When we walked, we talked about our future. Where would the coming year see us? Would we stay in Tallinn or would our adventures continue elsewhere?

"Man, I have no clue what we're going to do," I said to Epp strolling along.

"Remember when we got together last year, we dreamed of going to India, Brazil," she said. "Whatever happened to our dreams?"

"Chile and New York are the most realistic options," I said.

"Did you hear back from that school in Santiago?"

I nodded. "They seem interested, but we would have to start in September. But can you imagine us? Living in Santiago with a kid?"

"I could see it. You could go to work. I could sit and write by the Pacific Ocean with our little baby."

"Yeah, maybe that could work out. But New York sounds kind of cool too. Plus we won't have to worry about residence permits."

"My grandma would be really upset if we move away," Epp said. "She'll afraid she will never see me again."

"My parents probably already feel like I've deserted them."

"We could always just hit the road, you know," Epp said. "India, Brazil, and never stamp out Australia, remember?" she tittered. There was nervous energy in her laugh. Sadness, too. "I've seen these Hippie couples living on the road with little kids. They seemed content, lived cheaply, doing odd jobs."

"Do you really want to live like that?" I raised an eyebrow. "Out of a bag? On the road? With our daughter?"

"I don't know. What do you want?"

"I have to think about it more," I sighed and put my arm around her.

"Let's just see where the water carries us," she said. "We just have to trust the water."

"But what if it doesn't take us anywhere?"

"Then we'll pick something," she shrugged. "It shouldn't be so agonizing. It's just life, right?"

But it was agonizing; the torment of family, the anguish of friendships. If we stayed in Estonia, we would have to answer to my family, Epp constructed as the evil Eastern Bloc witch who seduced Justin, a modern day Esto Yoko Ono who broke up the band. If we left it would be the same way, instead I would be the greedy foreign man who plucked another Estonian maiden away from the motherland. No matter where we went, someone would always criticize our decisions because we had left the place they intended for us to stay for good. This was our destiny in life, the deep pain we had created because we hadn't married someone from next door.

The situation made me angry, but I didn't know whom to blame. I couldn't fathom why I felt inside that everyone hated me so much and yet I knew with dead certainty that I had disappointed them: you, the one who had to be different and come here; you, the one who decided to be different and move away; you, the one who decided to steal our granddaughter; you, the one who decided to ruin Thanksgiving and Christmas. For the Estonians, I would never be Estonian enough, even if I learned their crazy language, ignored my feelings, and made myself useful with home improvement projects. For the Americans, my wife would never be American enough. She would always have that weird three-letter name, that strange unrecognizable accent. "Estonia? Where's that?" Some New Yorkers probably thought Estonia was a district in Queens, right next to Astoria. In Estonia, I was the weirdo who didn't know the inner mechanics of a wood furnace. In America, Epp would be an oddball with a handkerchief on her head washing windows with old rags, or pinning laundry to a line so that it could dry in the sun instead of using a clothes dryer.

I had never intended this. I had never set out to ruin Thanksgiving or Christmas. I am sure that Epp had never planned to abandon her grandparents. Yet it had happened all the same. Supposedly I had chosen this emotional anguish, but I didn't remember thinking so far ahead on those warm summer days in Helsinki when I first met Epp.

Still, when my mother called us on Christmas night, and they passed the phone around at the big family celebration on the other side of the earth, the party we could not attend, no one seemed to judge us. Instead, they said they missed us. "I can't wait to hear how long the baby is and how much she weighs!" Uncle Frank said with cheeks full of mashed potatoes. The voices were big, warm and familiar. It was the tonic of the Italian-American family, the hell of judgment, the heaven of acceptance, and that middle-ground purgatory of being merely tolerated. That night I was accepted and it was heavenly. I could feel them pulling on my limbs, their big meaty embrace around my shoulders, tugging me through the telephone line. They wanted me back.

And they had questions for me, questions that buzzed across the world. "Aren't you ecstatic?" They asked. "Aren't you thrilled?" "Aren't you ready to be a father?" I wanted to tell them that, "I'd be ready to be a father if I actually believed the kid was going to come out!" But some part of me still didn't believe it. I had never experienced a birth before and so my intuition was blank, my imagination a series of Hollywood clips, the climax of a romantic comedy starring Hugh Grant and Julianne Moore. "Push, push, puuusssh!" Then the happy scream and the tears of joy and the roll of the credits and some old, goodtimey rock'n'roll song to sweeten the catharsis. No. Even with a week or two to go, the birth seemed eons away. There was a haze around the whole thing.

The image that protrudes most in my memory is of the Olümpia Hotel. It pokes out of the murkiness, a towering superconductor of metal and glass. On that night, two days before New Year's Eve, the hotel was alive with tourists, every window lit up in the dark, a complex of lights against the blue night that made it look like the Titanic giving way to the cold northern seas.

Around this image swirled a storm, the last of 2003's Big Weather. When the avalanche of frozen hail pellets fell on the spectral hotel, I looked up and took note, mouth agape. What the hell is that noise? It was startling and cacophonous, heavy and violent and it went on and on. Something was shifting up there in the skies above the Olümpia. The hail storm was merely a sign.

At that moment, Epp sat comfortably in her room at the maternity ward, delivered an hour earlier by ambulance to the hospital. The vehicle had zoomed through the dark streets of Tallinn, the lights of the buildings streaking through its dark glass, its stoic crew dressed in red jumpsuits, listening without any discernable enjoyment to George Michael croon over punchy synthesizers on the radio: *"Last Christmas, I gave you my heart, the very next day, you gave it away..."*

We registered downstairs and then were taken up by elevator to the maternity ward, where we set up camp in room 6. The corridors were dark and the night staff were already on duty. New lives seemed to materialize every hour. All night long we heard the sounds of screaming babies and groaning women. We sat there waiting for the proper contractions to start and trying to prepare ourselves for what would come next.

I passed the Olümpia Hotel while I was on my way to the 24-hour apothecary. I arrived at the building on the edge of the Old Town shivering, partly because I had left my gloves in the hospital and partly because I was getting more and more manic by the second. There was now raw energy in me, a prickling sensation, like I had drunk a thousand black coffees. Maybe it had been the hail that put the fear of God into me or the little sound of the child's heartbeat in the delivery room, clipping along at a healthy rate. Whatever it was, the powerful tides in my blood were moving towards some new, more awesome direction.

I wanted to tell everybody about the hot feelings inside me. It eclipsed anything else I had ever experienced. The energy bubbled up, I could have wrapped my arms around Tammsaare's statue in the park and kissed the stony head of the dead writer who was Epp's distant cousin, and she always reminded me of the fact when we passed it, she was just so proud. Soon Tammsaare would be getting a new little cousin!

But the truth was that I didn't think anyone else in Tallinn really cared. In Estonia's capital, if two strangers met on a side street on a sunny morning, they wouldn't even bother to make eye contact, let alone wish a fellow pedestrian a good day. The fact that I was an imminent father-to-be was not enough to disturb the bored-looking business type in line at the apothecary from the sanctuary of text messaging on his mobile phone, nor to bother the glazed-over cashier with the curly hair who sold me the diapers and *nõmmeliivatee*, a special Estonian tea that was supposed to speed the delivery. She must have known why I bought those items, but the seller was so very eager to see me out the door so she could close up for 15 minutes and take a quick inventory that she didn't say a word to me. If only there was another American around, I thought. Someone I could talk to.

And yet when a small group of American kids passed me on the street, recognizable by their huge backpacks and road-worn clothes, out-of-place loud voices and broad "We're Americans in Europe, we can do anything!" grins, I didn't say a word to them. Not a word. Nothing. I tried to, I tried to mouth the words, to call out, but it was as if I had suddenly lost my voice. Something was choking me. I just couldn't talk to strangers. It was simply not done. Not here. Not in December. I watched the Americans and feigned the bored look of the Tallinner instead. There was an insurmountable wall of glass between us. Maybe it's because we were now just too different, I thought. They were New Year's revelers out for kicks in a foreign city and I was about to become a father. Maybe my presence would make them think twice about those late night hostel hookups, the promise of a different future, the allure of the foreign woman, all those things that had once propelled me forward.

"I used to be a traveller, too," I thought, hanging in the shadows. Then I turned and headed back to the hospital, pausing only at a supermarket to procure some cabbage. As I walked below the Olümpia Hotel a second time it occurred to me that I had become a man. There was simply no other word for a person like me who walked through the streets of Tallinn late at night with a bag full of diapers and tea and cabbage - because cabbage leaves were supposed to soothe the swollen boobs of the breast-feeding mother when the milk came in. At least, that's what the old Estonian wives said. And who was I to argue with the wisdom of the old Estonian wives?

In the delivery room, my ear had become timed to the baby's tiny heartbeat. I had listened to the steady pop for any indication of change, and had rushed down the hall several times when there was an alteration in rhythm. Once the heartbeat stopped completely, and I panicked and sprinted to summon the nurse who adjusted the position of the baby in a second and the heartbeat resumed, as if nothing had happened.

Not that it was easy for me to even communicate with the nurses. I used a mix of beginner's Estonian, English, and body language. One time that night I went looking for a garbage can, asking around for the word Epp had told me, '*Prügikast*? *Prügikast*!' but the nurses took me as a Russian and started speaking to me in that language, the soupy swamp of Slavic sounds. "*Net*!" I had told them in the corridor. "*Net po Russkie*!" and then repeated "*Prügikast*? Garbage?" holding out the crumpled paper towel.

One of them, who I took to be an Estonian Russian from her warm smile and flamboyant poofs of orangey hair, finally understood what I meant. "Ah, a *prügikast*," she grinned. My 'u' had just not been deep enough for their very sensitive Estonian ears. "Ah, you wanted a *prügikast*," the nurses laughed at me. "We have never heard of a '*prugikast*' before." Then the Estonian Russian nurse pulled me aside and whispered in my ear, "Hey, you're Estonian's pretty good. Some people have been living here for 50 years and they can't even say a word."

During the night I had called my parents from the payphone in the hall. "Keep us posted," they said. "Do your best." "Epp needs you." My father had a Cuban cigar he had procured from his trip to Tallinn that he intended to smoke upon being informed of the birth of his first grandchild. My mother had acquired a balloon that she said she would tie around the mailbox so everyone who drove past their house would see: "It's a Girl." They said they would send me a digital photo of the balloon after the baby was born. I promised to e-mail them photos of their first grandchild as soon as I could, as they wouldn't be there to hold her in person. In New York, they would all be waiting in the hospital corridor, anxiously awaiting the news, jockeying to be the first to get their pictures taken with the newborn child. So I was actually relieved I didn't have to contend with a pack of relatives that morning. Epp was too. "I wouldn't want anybody but you here," she told me from the hospital bed. I wondered what would happen if we went to New York. Would she really be able to blend in? And how could either of us manage in Chile, a country where we didn't even speak the language properly? These were questions that would have to be answered later, after the baby came. For now, I could only concentrate on the next few hours.

On the way back to room number 6 around noon my cell phone rang. I had forgotten to turn it off, so picked it up and heard a familiar German accent.

"Justin, it's me, Manfred. Are you and Epp busy tomorrow night? Astrid and I would love to have you over. We are going to have a little New Year's Eve party. Everyone is coming. Manuel, Joris, Simeon..."

"I don't think we can make it," I told him. I could hear the deep groans of another woman in labor echo down the hallway.

"Oh, come on! Wouldn't you and Epp like one last night out before the baby arrives? I know she's pregnant, but one little glass of good champagne can't hurt. And I have the very best. Something to remember when you are in the hospital!"

"But Manfred, we are at the hospital right now."

"What?" he shrieked. "You mean she's giving birth today?"

"We've been here since last night. Her water is leaking, so they said we should stay until the delivery, but no big pains yet."

"Ja, ja, well, the first one always takes time," he said. Then he paused a second to clear his throat and collect his thoughts. "Dearest Justin," he said now, as if reading a speech, and I remembered that he had spent most of his life as a diplomat. "Please know that we are with you and Epp today. Astrid and I are keeping our fingers crossed, waiting for the good news. And you've got to give it your best. I know you can do it." His pace increased, the words coming more rapidly from his lips.

"But Epp needs you. You need to be there for her!" I could feel his energy through the phone line, too. It was almost as if the old German was as excited as I was.

"Thanks Manfred. But, listen, I need to get back to—"

"And this is a wonderful day!" he went on with his speech, the tone of his voice rising. I imagined he was now pointing his finger in the air. "The sun is shining. The sky is blue. Nothing can go wrong!"

"Thanks Manfred, but Epp is wait—."

"Those who are born on the 30th of December are extremely lucky in life, Justin," He cut me off again. "Like I am."

"Wait," I was a little confused. "Is today your birthday?"

"IT IS INDEED!" Manfred's voice boomed into the phone. "But now you must go," his voice was suddenly hushed, as if he was in the hospital with me. "Go back to Epp! Go!"

"Wait. Manfred? *Manfred*?" I wanted to thank him for the New Year's invitation, but he had already hung up.

The contractions started shortly after I returned to the delivery room. When the midwife arrived, young and thin, blonde and pretty with a laid-back countenance, dressed in jeans and a black t-shirt, a tribal tattoo poking out from one sleeve, I sensed a trembling in the cosmos, an exchange, not just of dialog but of movements.

"I'm two weeks early," Epp informed her between deep breaths.

"The moon is growing," the midwife said with the deep certainty of a priest. "We always get a lot of deliveries during the growing moon."

Epp seemed to accept the midwife's reasoning. It resounded in her moon-loving soul.

Do this, stand over there. The midwife softly called out orders in Estonian and I followed them as best as I understood. But I was a mere accessory. Mostly the rhythm flowed between Epp and the midwife. The two of them went back and forth through the afternoon as the orange sun began to dip below the white landscape, finally vanishing into darkness, the bright hospital room lights bearing witness to the gory spectacle of delivery.

When the child arrived she was terrified and screaming. The midwife examined her little slime-covered body in the light. Epp comforted the howling babe for some time, stroking her until she calmed. It seemed so natural how she did it, as if she had always known how to care for a crying newborn. Then the midwife wiped the tiny gnome clean, clothed her and tied a pink bonnet around her round head, the dark clumps of gooey hair sticking out at its edges. She presented the bundle to me.

"This is your daughter," the midwife said to me, calm as ever, the faintest sparkle in her pretty eyes. "Maybe you want to take her for a little walk while we get this place cleaned up?"

At this moment, all the pain and passion and lust of my life, all the decisions and fates, shot through space like an arrow, all to this one end.

"Here, take her," the midwife said again.

I took the small human in my hands, trying to negotiate her body weight, to put the hands in the right places. Spine along the forearm, hand under the neck. When I held her, she calmed. I could see her face, the fuzzy eyebrows and the tiny nose. The skin on her hands was peeling because she had been swimming in Epp for a long time. She knew how to trust the water.

♦ ♦ ♦

In the corridor of the maternity ward it was once again evening. I found a seat at the end of the hall and slowly maneuvered into it, so as to not lose the gentle balance the child had found in my arms. I looked down into the baby's very big blue eyes. There was no fear there, no anxiousness, or love, or jealousy. Instead I saw inquisitiveness, a very deep interest in the new world around her, a world she hadn't seen before.

A man seated near me held a small newborn in his arms too. He was about the same age as me with a shock of dark hair and dark stubble on his chin. He looked over to me and said something in Russian in a deep voice.

I cradled the child in my hands and shook my head to him, to let him know I didn't understand.

"Boy or girl?" he said in English.

"A girl," I said. "Marta Maria."

"Pretty name," he smiled. "This is my daughter Nino."

"Nino?"

"It's a Georgian name," he whispered something to the child and rocked her in his arms. I watched him do it, and tried to rock Marta the same way.

"Is it your first?" he looked at me.

I nodded.

"They are like little aliens," he swayed the bundle in his arms. "From another planet."

Marta squirmed in my arms and then she opened her tiny toothless mouth wide and yawned. I studied her tiny features more as my body got used to supporting her small weight. Her face was red from the birth, and she was so completely overwhelmed by the night's events to do anything else but stare.

Sitting there, holding our little baby in the corridor, I was sure of it: I had always wanted this. No matter where we lived a year from that day or two years or ten, what mattered was that I had found my home.

On the way to the fabled Estonian-Latvian border with Epp's niece Simona on my shoulders.

Kassari chapel on Hiiumaa, where we found a name for our child.

Whimsical Hiiumaa, where the roofs are made of thatched straw.

Cycling across Hiiumaa and making friends.

Nothing. Not a sound. No cars. No radios. No construction. Only the lapping of the waves and, in the distance, the gentle cry of a sheep. This is Hiiumaa's island idyll.

The island of Hiiumaa was a long way from my home in New York. Even Tallinn seemed distant.

An old sailor in Kuressaare told me that Saaremaa pirates traveled everywhere, "to the Mediterranean and the Black Sea, even Africa."

Kuressaare Castle on Saaremaa. "I stooped down and strained to squeeze the building – if a castle could be called such a mundane word – into one postcard-ready photo."

With Epp in the Vigeland Sculpture Park in Oslo. But where is our dear friend Sigrid?

Miisu and me in our Kentmanni Street apartment. We rescued the nervous and neurotic urban kitten from the building's stairwell.

Epp's very blonde cousin Karin and me. The Estonians said I was *tõmmu*, dark, an adjective they used to describe a smoked sausage or chocolate candy.

Kalamaja used to be a working-class district, and its street names are a testament to this history. This house is on Tööstuse, or "Industrial" Street.

Two of Tallinn's many alley cats. The one on the left is probably called Miisu, and the one on the right is most likely named Nurr.

Even though there are a lot of ruined buildings in Kalamaja, the condition of the district improves day by day. There is hope that it will one day look as good as it did before the Second World War.

"Never mind that," Epp would say, pointing to an abandoned building or a heap of trash in Kalamaja. "All of it will be gone in five years."

Kalamaja! For the first time on our real estate hunt, I could close my eyes and envision myself pushing our little baby in a carriage down the street.

During our real estate search, I learned to appreciate the comical sight of old Soviet cars and worn chairs, which existed together in a shabby sort of harmony.

Stalin-era architecture in Tallinn. Many of these houses were built by German POWs, and people tend to think they did a good job.

My mother, Epp and me in front of our house in Kalamaja.

"What kinds of people lived here in these magnificent buildings?" I wondered, strolling through the streets of Old Town. What was it like to live in a UNESCO World Heritage site?

Stenbock House, seat of the Estonian government and, in 2003, home to Prime Minister Juhan Parts and his cat, also named Miisu.

Being shown around Tallinn's Old Town by Vana Toomas, I mean art historian Jüri Kuuskemaa.

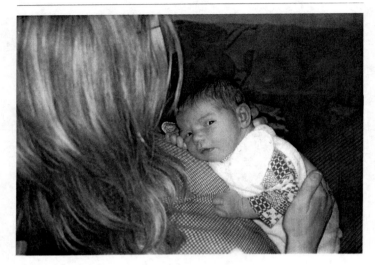

Our little alien, a few days after her arrival.

Three generations: Epp's father Andres, my daughter Marta and me.

CPSIA information can be obtained at www.ICGtesting.com
Printed in the USA
LVOW06s1513111115

462082LV00019B/657/P